The Rise of Neoliberal
Philosophy

The Rise of Neoliberal Philosophy

Human Capital, Profitable Knowledge, and the Love of Wisdom

Brandon Absher

LEXINGTON BOOKS
Lanham • Boulder • New York • London

Published by Lexington Books
An imprint of The Rowman & Littlefield Publishing Group, Inc.
4501 Forbes Boulevard, Suite 200, Lanham, Maryland 20706
www.rowman.com

86-90 Paul Street, London EC2A 4NE, United Kingdom

Copyright © 2021 by The Rowman & Littlefield Publishing Group, Inc.

All rights reserved. No part of this book may be reproduced in any form or by any electronic or mechanical means, including information storage and retrieval systems, without written permission from the publisher, except by a reviewer who may quote passages in a review.

British Library Cataloguing in Publication Information Available

Library of Congress Cataloging-in-Publication Data

Names: Absher, Brandon, author.
Title: The rise of neoliberal philosophy : human capital, profitable knowledge, and the love of wisdom / Brandon Absher.
Description: Lanham, Maryland : Lexington Books, 2021. | Includes bibliographical references and index. | Summary: "Brandon Absher demonstrates that the neoliberalization of higher education has led to a paradigm shift in contemporary philosophy in the United States. Neoliberal philosophy aims to produce human capital and profitable Knowledge"— Provided by publisher.
Identifiers: LCCN 2021020612 (print) | LCCN 2021020613 (ebook) | ISBN 9781793615985 (cloth) | ISBN 9781793615992 (ebook) | ISBN 9781793616005 (pbk)
Subjects: LCSH: Neoliberalism—United States. | Human capital—United States. | Education, Higher—Aims and objectives—United States. | Education, Higher—Economic aspects—United States.
Classification: LCC HB95 .A24 2021 (print) | LCC HB95 (ebook) | DDC 302.01—dc23
LC record available at https://lccn.loc.gov/2021020612
LC ebook record available at https://lccn.loc.gov/2021020613

Contents

Acknowledgments	vii
Introduction	1
Chapter 1: Philosophy in the Neoliberal University	19
Chapter 2: The Performativity of Neoliberal Philosophy	37
Chapter 3: The One-Dimensionality of Neoliberal Philosophy	65
Chapter 4: Diversity and Neoliberal Philosophy	97
Chapter 5: Toward a New Paradigm	129
Conclusion	149
Bibliography	161
Index	175
About the Author	185

Acknowledgments

For all his many failings, and they were legion and despicable, Heidegger said a few things that, to my ears, nonetheless ring true. Among them, I might list, most of all, that *thinking* is always a matter of *thanking*. Connected to this, I would offer what I might like to consider a thought of my own: that thinking only truly thrives in a gift economy—it is essentially gratuitous, the granting of an unearned favor. We each owe to one another, and fortunately usually give, this most necessary of gifts. And through this, of course, we also each incur a secondary debt. Sometimes, as I figure it, I think on layaway; I pay a little here and there as I can. Accounting in this domain becomes quite tricky. Many of my debts will almost certainly remain unpaid. Despite the inevitable insufficiency, not to say insolvency, of the gesture, I must thank many people, whose time, ideas, and encouragement made this book possible.

First and foremost, I cannot imagine this project without my partner, my wife, Rachel Walsh. Her voice and ideas are present on every page. Were it not for her, the power and depth of her engagement, her incisive will to find the nugget of truth and express it clearly, fully, I would not have been capable of this work. I think fondly of our walks in the summer, my mind carried away with the book, our dog, Bartleby, dragging us along—all the while, her sustaining the dialogue that prevented my wanderings and wonderings becoming a pandemic-induced solipsistic hallucination.

To Joseph Trullinger, I owe more than I can say. There are few people to whom anyone can turn in both travail and triumph. And with decades of friendship now behind us, I am grateful to say that Joseph is one of those few in my case. Unrelenting sincerity, indefatigable dedication to the life of the mind, not to mention the spirit—few are possessed of such virtues. In large part, we have grown up together, learned together, and, to the extent that I may speak on his behalf, dedicated ourselves to philosophy as a way of life together. The courage of his idealism stands as a sharp rebuke of those who passively accept the comforts of a broken world or lack the passion to love it in its brokenness.

My friends and comrades in the Radical Philosophy Association remind me regularly why I do philosophy. Their commitment to justice and engagement as scholar-activists is an example I can only hope to emulate. There are many people to thank here; most especially, Tanya Loughead, Harry van der Linden, Richard Schmitt, José Mendoza, and Sarah Vitale. They have provided me with support and inspiration in ways that go far beyond our professional lives as academics. There are others to whom I have looked for advice and who offered me important encouragement since I was a graduate student; Anatole Anton, Richard Jones, Anne Pomeroy, and Richard Peterson deserve special mention. Whatever I do well, I have only learned by watching.

My Academic Happy Hour team made life in Buffalo possible, even sometimes when I feared that it would not be. You are all dear to me, but I must mention particularly Derek Seidman, Melissa Mosko, Christopher Culp, Şerife Tekin, and Devonya Havis. I hope that I bring as much intellectual excitement and laughter to your lives as you have brought to mine. Similar thanks must go to the "Lexington School." Few academics punch above their weight with such regularity and skill. Your collective example routinely reminds me that I have been lucky to have wonderful, generous colleagues from the moment I entered graduate school. Likewise, I must thank all my colleagues at D'Youville College. John Abbarno and Eli Finnegan, in particular, have stood out as examples of integrity and dedication to the craft of teaching.

To all my activist friends who have played such an important part in shaping who I am and how I view the world, I owe you beyond measure. I can only hope that I have added anything to your lives and to the struggle for justice and liberation in which we are engaged collectively. I cannot help but mention my mentors and allies in the Buffalo Anti-Racism Coalition. Most especially, my thanks go to Luana Dejesus, Ivy Yapelli, and Eve Shippens. I remain in awe of your commitment and have difficulty sometimes believing what we have been able to accomplish together.

My unending gratitude is due, as ever, to my family and in particular my parents, Delbretta and David Absher, and my grandparents, Henrietta and Delbert Anderson. Life does not come with an instruction manual, and I have pieced mine together as best I could. Luckily, I have always had someone there to offer tools and guidance.

Finally, thanks go to Jana Hodges-Kluck, Bryndee Ryan, and everyone at Lexington Books whose labor made this book possible.

To any whom I continue to owe, I beg your grace and forbearance. May the gift that I give stand good for this debt of gratitude that I know I can never fully repay.

Introduction

In this book, I argue that the neoliberal "reform" of the university has resulted in a paradigm shift in philosophy in the United States, leading to the emergence of what I call "Neoliberal Philosophy." Neoliberal Philosophy, I contend, is performative, in the sense that it seeks to attract investment by demonstrating that it can produce optimal return. Recalling Herbert Marcuse's critique of postwar U.S. culture, I further argue that Neoliberal Philosophy is one-dimensional inasmuch as philosophers in the neoliberal paradigm internalize and reproduce the values of the prevailing social order in their work, reorienting philosophical desire toward the production of attractive commodities. To state it simply, the aim of philosophy in what I call the "Neoliberal University" has become the production of human capital and profitable knowledge. This orientation, I show, reproduces systems of exploitation and oppression through appeals to merit. In contrast to Neoliberal Philosophy, in this work I call for an alternative philosophical paradigm based on values of creative self-discovery and collective liberatory praxis. This new philosophical paradigm rejects the "realism" prescribed by neoliberalism, instead looking toward possibilities and horizons that promise a world beyond the prevailing social order.

With respect to the university, neoliberalism has been most dramatically apparent in the defunding of public institutions of higher education and the corresponding treatment of both knowledge and education as private consumer goods. It is further evident in the insinuation of market logics and corresponding forms of subjectivity into educational practice and research, creating what Sheila Slaughter and Gary Rhoades have termed the "academic capitalist knowledge/learning regime."[1] To demonstrate the effects of this change on philosophy, I follow the method developed by John McCumber in his *The Philosophy Scare: The Politics of Reason in the Early Cold War*.[2] According to McCumber, a paradigm shift occurred in American philosophy in the mid-twentieth century that resulted in the emergence of what he calls "Cold War Philosophy." This change, he argues, was the result of pressures placed on philosophy by McCarthyism. Similarly, I describe the shift to Neoliberal Philosophy in the decades following the Cold War due to the pressures arising from the neoliberal restructuring of higher education in the United States.

FROM COLD WAR PHILOSOPHY TO NEOLIBERAL PHILOSOPHY

According to McCumber, the rise of Cold War Philosophy in the U.S. was quite sudden and amounted to something akin to a "scientific revolution," as conceived by Thomas Kuhn. Kuhn himself imagines such a revolution in terms of a change of worldview, a gestalt switch, or "shift of vision" in which new phenomena or aspects of phenomena become visible or salient. He uses the analogy of inverting lenses to provide a sense of what occurs during a revolutionary change of paradigm.[3] It seems clear that something like a Kuhnian paradigm shift took place in philosophy at the mid-century in the U.S., establishing Cold War Philosophy. Indeed, the revolution is nicely described by Richard Rorty in his account of the condition of the discipline in the early 1980s. In Rorty's narrative, the revolution was aided by the emigration of such towering figures as Rudolph Carnap, Alfred Tarski, and Hans Reichenbach, who fled the Nazis to join philosophy departments in the United States. As Rorty recollects,

> By 1960, a new set of philosophical paradigms was in place. A new sort of graduate education in philosophy was entrenched—one in which Dewey and Whitehead, heroes of the previous generation, were no longer read, in which the history of philosophy was decisively downgraded, and in which the study of logic assumed an importance previously given to the study of languages.[4]

The form of philosophy that emerged was assiduous in its avoidance of ethics, politics, and metaphysics and devout in its commitment to logic and natural science as the standard-bearers of knowledge. Itself a relatively new phenomenon in the U.S., graduate education in philosophy would now consist in learning to apply the new tools of logical analysis with little regard for the "mighty dead" of the now obsolete philosophical canon.

Supporting Rorty's recollection of this revolution, Joel Katzav and Krist Vaesen document rapid changes in the types of articles published in top philosophy journals in the 1940s and thereafter. *The Philosophical Review* and *Mind*, which they analyze, were among the most highly regarded English-language philosophy journals at the time and remain so today. As Katzav and Vaesen present the matter, these journals were robustly pluralistic in the early decades of the twentieth century, with work from various specializations and across the available methodological spectrum of the period.[5]

However, this methodological pluralism came to an abrupt halt with changes in editorship (Gilbert Ryle taking the helm at *Mind*, for instance) and the journals in question subsequently published very little that was not readily identifiable as what came to be called "analytic philosophy."[6] Katzav and Vaesen refer to this phenomenon as "journal capture," a change in editors and editorial policy served to install a particular philosophical method in the position of power by promoting it while silencing others. Through such tactics, among others, analytic philosophy emerged into dominance in the period after World War II.

McCumber, as I have already indicated, argues that the triumph of analytic philosophy was in large part a result of Cold War "red hunting." It is further important to note, however, the confluence of the hegemony of Cold War Philosophy with the so-called golden age of the American university system, which corresponded to the post-war economic boom and the integration of higher education into the military-industrial complex. John R. Thelin, a historian of higher education, notes the massive growth of the U.S. academy during the period, with enrollments increasing exponentially from 1.5 million students in 1939–1940 to over 7.9 million in 1970. For Thelin, this growth was in large part a result of the role that higher education and scientific research played in World War II and the belief that it might have a significant part to play in the post-war economy.[7] Slaughter and Rhoades refer to the broad configuration of higher education that came into existence as a result of the boom as the "public good knowledge/learning regime."[8] Surely, the ascendance of Cold War Philosophy was bound up with these developments. As a result of these and other myriad and overdetermined causal histories, it is clear that in the 1950s a new paradigm of philosophy corresponding to new institutional and social imperatives had consolidated itself across the U.S. academy and was busy eliminating or marginalizing rivals.

While there were, of course, important differences among practitioners, Cold War Philosophy was primarily oriented toward a critique or "elimination" of metaphysics through the application of logical or linguistic analysis and the deployment of one or another epistemological or semantic theory.[9] Philosophy in this paradigm generally relegated normative questions of ethics and politics to the purportedly noncognitive shadowlands of emotion and poetry. Further, such philosophy often sought an ideal of clarity and imagined itself as especially rigorous in comparison to alternatives—an ideal later criticized by Ludwig Wittgenstein in his *Philosophical Investigations* as guided by a "*preconception* of crystalline purity."[10] One might take Carnap's famed essay "The Elimination of Metaphysics Through Logical Analysis of Language" as an exemplary expression of this perspective. In his mocking criticisms of Martin Heidegger, Carnap systematically compares Heidegger's statements about "the Nothing" to statements about rain, providing formal logical notation for each statement.[11] Through this procedure, Carnap sought to show that Heidegger's ideas were not only false, but literally meaningless—at best expressing an "feeling toward life."[12] One can find a number of similar performances throughout the works of the philosophers who would go on to become central to Cold War Philosophy. Reichenbach, for example, opens his manifesto, *The Rise of Scientific Philosophy*, with a scornful denunciation of G.W.F. Hegel in which he submits a passage from the latter's *Lectures on the Philosophy of History* to a similar analysis. In explanation, he writes, "Analysis of error begins with analysis of language."[13] Such operations were central to the ethos and discursive practice of early analytic philosophy, even beyond the school(s) of logical positivism and logical empiricism to which Carnap and Reichenbach belonged.

While remnants of these deployments of logical analysis no doubt survive in contemporary philosophy in the U.S. academy, there have been enormous shifts since the period of the Cold War. Indeed, the anti-metaphysical thrust and epistemological strictures of the period have largely disappeared. To see this, let us recall another famed essay, Donald Davidson's "Knowing One's Own Mind." Davidson's short essay is, I think, fairly considered a classic in contemporary Anglophone philosophy. In this work, Davidson presents a thought experiment involving a character he dubs "The Swampman," basically imagining the creation of a physical replica of himself lacking all the causal history and relations characteristic of the original.[14] Focusing less on Davidson's argument, conclusion, or even the legitimacy of his method, it is noteworthy that such a thought experiment might be well received within and even exemplary for the contemporary practice of philosophy in the United States. It strikes me as a far cry from the approaches that characterized discussion of the mind in the post-war period, when one or another form of behaviorism was clearly the order of the day. Consideration of the essay, then, points toward a number of developments characteristic of what I am calling Neoliberal Philosophy: rehabilitation of metaphysics and philosophy of mind, development (and subsequent critique) of methods focused on thought experiments, abandonment of phenomenalism and positivism, and so on.

To see what has emerged as the dominant form of philosophy in recent decades, it is helpful to take a look at the questions posed to philosophers by David Bourget and David J. Chalmers in a recent survey, as reported in their essay "What Do Philosophers Believe?"[15] Setting aside the survey results, the questions reveal a great deal about the debates and positions that are taken at present to be of perennial or contemporary significance by mainstream philosophers in the United States, as well as the philosophers and approaches that are now central. Among others, Bourget and Chalmers list questions about the conceivability of "zombies," physicalism and the mind, the metaphysics of personal identity, the nature of perceptual experience, and debates regarding internalism versus externalism with respect to mental content, epistemic justification, and moral motivation.[16] One may judge how far what is now dubbed analytic philosophy has come from its traditional roots by comparing these questions to the problems identified by Bertrand Russell in 1912 as the central issues of the discipline in his *Problems of Philosophy*.[17] Likewise, one might meditate on the wide range of metaphysical questions that now proliferate in defiance of the kind of austerity advocated by, for example, W.V.O. Quine, that proponent of "clearing" ontological "slums," in his *From a Logical Point of View*.[18]

The dominant approach to philosophy in the United States today may share the title "analytic" with its progenitor and appear to espouse much the same methodological creed, then, but it has changed in some very important ways. While, for example, Bourget and Chalmers give normative ethics and political philosophy relatively short shrift in their survey, even a casual observer of the contemporary philosophical scene would have to note the resurgence of interest in normative ethics and political philosophy. Certainly, it is true that top journals in the field continue to focus their publishing on so-called core areas.[19] Yet, to a much greater degree than previously, political philosophy and normative ethics have a hearing. Thus, in contrast to the allergic rejection of metaphysics and mind, apolitical posture, and denigration of ethics that characterized logical positivism, ordinary language philosophy, and the array of related projects and approaches that ruled Anglophone philosophy at mid-century, contemporary philosophy in the United States is more than open to metaphysical speculation, reflections on the nature of consciousness, political theorizing, and normative prescription. Why and how have these changes taken place?

In the final chapter of his *A History of Philosophy in America, 1720–2000*, historian Bruce Kuklick reflects, as many have, on the relative isolation of philosophers within the U.S. academy and their absence from public debate in the final years of the twentieth century. He explains these phenomena in terms of the religiosity of the broader culture and the secularism and abstraction of the dominant strands of the discipline.[20] Turning his attention to the issue of the "end of philosophy," a theme he identifies particularly with the work of Rorty, Kuklick expresses what seems an optimistic view: Philosophy is not at its end and something recognizable as philosophy will continue on into the future in the United States. He writes,

> It might be true that certain research programs have reached a dead end. But such a result is not much different from what happened, for example, to American theology, post-Darwinian idealism, or logical positivism. The "end" of these projects did not mean the end of philosophy, nor did it mean that what followed was severed from what had gone before.[21]

Taking the long view characteristic of a historian, Kuklick views philosophy in the United States at the millennium as at once continuous with its past and as punctuated by fissures and discontinuity, marking the obsolescence and demise of significant "research programs" as well as the birth and ascendance of new ones. Perhaps it is true, Kuklick suggests, that a particular "research program" or group thereof had come to an end by the close of the millennium, but not philosophy itself.[22] Following Kuklick, my contention is that something new was born in the last decades of the twentieth century and, compared to alternatives, has thrived in the Neoliberal University.

To explain and conceptualize this transformation from Cold War Philosophy to Neoliberal Philosophy, an important first step is to recall what anyone with even the most limited experience of academia already knows from personal experience: individual faculty and departments generally act strategically with regard to the political pressures exerted upon them.[23] When it comes to philosophers and philosophy departments during the period of the Cold War, McCumber argues that this strategic action largely took the form of what he calls "stealth."[24] That is, philosophers and philosophy departments advanced programs of research that, while ensuring the autonomy and relative independence of the individual or department, concealed the true content of philosophical writing from the public at large. McCumber presents naturalism as an example. In contrast to the avowed atheism of existentialism and Marxism, Cold War Philosophy put forward a theory of naturalism as scientific reductionism. In this way, individuals and departments were able to avoid public scrutiny and direct conflict with religious conservatives while nonetheless pursuing a robustly atheistic philosophical agenda. The thesis of reductionism and the debates surrounding it were basically indecipherable to non-experts and seemed largely divorced from issues pertaining to conventional religious belief, thus protected from the ire of religious conservatives who formed a significant popular base for McCarthyist attacks on the academy.

Similarly, I suggest that Neoliberal Philosophy has emerged as a paradigm through strategic responses to the pressures exerted upon the discipline. While there are certainly social realities that still necessitate, or at least strongly incentivize, stealth on the part of philosophers and philosophy departments, the much more significant contemporary strategy within the Neoliberal University has been for philosophy to market itself to the public. Rather than conceal its true content, philosophers now seek to advertise philosophy to "stakeholders" as a good investment. In general, I argue, the marketing of philosophy suggests that it offers human capital enhancements, what I call "technologies of optimization," to students and that it produces applicable knowledge, in the sense that philosophical research can contribute directly to private profit. The marketing of philosophy shapes the practice, so that philosophical pedagogies, methods, and ideas that more easily fulfill the demands of the "knowledge economy" are privileged over others.

THE CHAPTERS TO FOLLOW

The burden of the chapters to come is to provide an account of these changes and an accompanying critique of Neoliberal Philosophy. Chapter 1 provides a broad overview and theorization of the Neoliberal University. I conceive neoliberalism as simultaneously a social movement, a retrenchment of class power, and an "art of governance." Within higher education, neoliberalism reorganizes and governs academic life through (1) defunding and effectively privatizing universities and colleges, (2) reorienting curricula toward job training, (3) instrumentalizing and commodifying knowledge, and (4) centralizing and bureaucratizing academic administration. In general, the Neoliberal University is imagined as serving the economic interests of all involved by supplying the "human capital" necessary to compete in the twenty-first century knowledge economy.

In the second chapter, I utilize the work of Jean-François Lyotard to show how philosophy departments in the United States have reshaped their curricula and research agendas in accordance with the demands of the Neoliberal University. Famously, Lyotard argues that postmodernity is a cultural condition in which people are skeptical toward the "metanarratives" that once legitimated scientific practices and, indeed, cultural and social institutions more broadly.[25] In such a condition, science must operate without reference to an external discourse of legitimation (i.e., metaphysical philosophy). For this reason, according to Lyotard, along with its reliance on costly technology, scientific discourse is submitted to economic criteria of success. Postmodernity, therefore, results in a conflation of truth with what he calls "performativity"—that is, knowledge production comes to be governed by economic discourses. Following Lyotard's argument, I suggest that in a capitalist culture skeptical of metanarratives that might provide metaphysical or epistemological foundations, philosophy appears superfluous and must, like the sciences more broadly, demonstrate its capacity to contribute to economic ends. That is, philosophy, along with science, is subsumed by economic forms of evaluation and judgment.

At the same time, neoliberalism has redefined the nature of the economic ends of education so that they no longer correspond to the public good (formerly understood in the United States in terms of the geopolitics of the Cold War). Rather, now the return on social investment is conceptualized in terms of meeting the needs of the neoliberal knowledge economy, where the lives of workers are precarious and work itself has been fundamentally reorganized in accordance with automation and computerization. In order to survive in this environment, philosophy departments have strategically sought to demonstrate the value of philosophy as a commodity, to market themselves. The marketing campaign for philosophy has focused on showing that a philosophical education offers human capital in the form of critical thinking skills that are readily exploitable by employers in the new economy. The marketing of critical thinking skills redounds upon philosophical pedagogy, however, transforming philosophical education so that it increasingly conforms to the demand to train future knowledge workers. As I argue, however, the change of orientation brought about by this marketing campaign subjects critical thinking—the primary skill hawked by philosophers—to the logic of the market, so that it fails to interrogate the social system and values underlying its practice.

Chapter 3 draws on the work of Herbert Marcuse to argue that Neoliberal Philosophy is "one-dimensional" insofar as it adjusts and conforms philosophers and students alike to the status quo, such that they internalize the imperatives of the neoliberal knowledge economy. In his account of "one-dimensional society," Marcuse suggested that the central feat of modern, affluent societies was their ability to contain class conflict through the promise of improved quality of life and consumer choice.[26] The one-dimensionality of society has important implications, he argued, for consciousness itself. Writing in the late 1950s and early 1960s, Marcuse viewed the United States as inculcating a repressive and deeply conformist psychology, unable to think or desire beyond the bounds of the goods on offer within the prevailing social order. According to Marcuse's account, such one-dimensional consciousness identifies with the social totality and internalizes the needs and demands of society as its own. Similarly, I argue that philosophers have internalized the demands of the neoliberal knowledge economy.

Within the knowledge economy, knowledge production is distributed throughout society, appearing in a variety of sites of application and judged according to a range of incommensurable local criteria. The most important thing is that knowledge have "real world" impact, primarily in the form of direct applications to profit-making enterprises. Knowledge must show return on investment. Strategically marketing itself as producing such profitable knowledge, Neoliberal Philosophy evaluates philosophers and their works on the basis of quantifiable metrics said to measure performance. These metrics range from department rankings to impact factors, from citation tallies to outcomes assessment measures. "Good philosophy" is whatever meets these criteria which are internalized by individual philosophers and form the basis of their judgments in everything from hiring decisions to research projects. Neoliberal Philosophy is therefore integrated into the neoliberal knowledge economy and reproduces its social stratification, inequality, and alienation.

Concerned about employability, philosophers and students alike are adjusted to the prevailing social order through the internal work culture and implicit value system of Neoliberal Philosophy. Neoliberal Philosophy thus results in a form of one-dimensional thinking that excludes theoretical frameworks that call into question the legitimacy of the prevailing social order and its values—most especially profit itself.

The fourth chapter addresses the issue of diversity as it relates to Neoliberal Philosophy. Taking up the work of Jodi Melamed, I argue that neoliberalism generally promotes a form of individualized multiculturalism that overlooks and in fact obscures systemic identity-based oppression and its intrinsic connection to capitalism.[27] In this process, the social order is imagined as a natural meritocracy that promotes those who are deserving in a "colorblind" or otherwise neutral evaluation of character and abilities. While this neoliberal multiculturalism may allow a few women, people of color, or LGBTQ+ people into positions of prestige, status, and power, it nonetheless reproduces systems of oppression even as it conceals its own operation in supposedly neutral standards and metrics. Put otherwise, neoliberal multiculturalism invokes an ideal capitalism, a meritocracy, in which success or failure is unrelated to one's identity, by pathologizing those at the bottom as undeserving. Global capitalism can therefore claim diversity as an attribute even as it reinforces the brutal racialization of populations that exposes many to extreme deprivation, violence, and death. Rather than ending identity-based forms of oppression, then, neoliberal multiculturalism recalibrates them to the demands of the global knowledge economy while also obscuring their existence through the invocation of notions of cultural pathology.

Much as with the Neoliberal University more broadly, Neoliberal Philosophy markets itself as diverse and therefore as producing the cosmopolitan skills and dispositions that are necessary for work in the global knowledge economy. One learns these skills in the philosophy curriculum because it presents the student with "intellectual diversity," mostly in the form of "methodological pluralism." In fine, Neoliberal Philosophy sells diversity as a kind of human capital and cultural commodity. Nonetheless, in line with the broad trend of neoliberal multiculturalism, the discipline remains anything but diverse. Indeed, despite its purported methodological pluralism, the discipline is deeply segregated and committed to an essentialist and universalist vision of itself, according to which there is no philosophy properly so-called beyond its confines. Such a view, however, presupposes the reification of Neoliberal Philosophy, imagining that it constitutes the only way in which one can do (good) philosophy and its practitioners as the only (good) philosophers. It further dismisses the many explicit factors that render the discipline hostile for women, people of color, and LGBTQ+ persons. In any case, members of marginalized or subordinate identity groups may be allowed into Neoliberal Philosophy, but only insofar as they perform according to the supposedly neutral standards and metrics of evaluation characteristic of Neoliberal Philosophy. Works and authors who do not conform to these standards—to the degree that they are able to survive in the academy at all—are relegated to marginal status, excluded from scholarly engagement in mainstream conferences and journals, and lose prestige. Neoliberal Philosophy at once avows an official epistemology according to which social identity and systems of oppression are irrelevant to its practice and simultaneously carries out a "whitewashing" in which its reproduction of such systems is concealed, and their very existence erased.

Chapter 5 presents an alternative to Neoliberal Philosophy and calls for a paradigm shift. Neoliberal Philosophy performs; that is, it promises return on investment. Ultimately, its practitioners and their works are judged on the basis of their ability to produce graduates with readily exploitable skills and knowledge that facilitates more directly profitable enterprises. In contrast, an alternative philosophical paradigm would judge philosophers and their works according to their ability to engage students and publics in processes of creative self-discovery and collective liberatory praxis. Neoliberal Philosophy, by contrast, is one-dimensional in that it adjusts the individual to the neoliberal knowledge economy. My proposed alternative would promote multi-dimensional forms of thought, producing oppositional and revolutionary sensibilities oriented to values that are excluded or marginalized within the prevailing social order. Philosophy in this paradigm would promote radical love, leading to what Martin Luther King Jr. referred to as "creative maladjustment."[28] In contrast to the whitewashing of systems of oppression, exclusion, and exploitation characteristic of Neoliberal Philosophy, this new paradigm would elevate the voices and interests of those traditionally excluded from the discipline, consciously integrating knowers and knowledges formerly defined as unphilosophical into its canon. Overall, a new paradigm of philosophy would democratize and desegregate philosophy, embedding it in struggles for collective liberation.

To conclude, I discuss the concept of "realism" with particular reference to Mark Fisher's treatment of what he terms "capitalist realism." In everyday life, "realism" signifies an attitude in which expectations and practical projects are adjusted to what is considered possible within the situation. Realism is about adjusting one's expectations and desires to what is practically possible. Most often, realism in this sense is contrasted with "idealism" or "utopianism"—stubborn insistence on practical principles or values that are impossible to achieve in the "real world." It is this meaning of the term that Fisher draws on in his discussion of capitalist realism.[29] For Fisher, capitalist realism is a broad cultural condition in which the subjective sense of there being possibilities beyond capitalism has been foreclosed, the lived experience of Margaret

Thatcher's dictum that "there is no alternative." Organizations of society other than capitalism appear in such a situation as the delusions and fantasies of people beset with, to borrow a phrase from Vladimir Lenin, an "infantile disorder." According to Fisher, capitalist realism results in psychological attitudes he calls "reflexive impotence" and "depressive hedonia." In other words, in such a cultural condition, people largely recognize that things are bad, but feel that they themselves are powerless to change the situation. This sense of powerlessness is accompanied by widespread depression and immersion into the momentary pleasures associated with narcotics, in the broadest sense of the term. By contrast, social movement activists have long insisted that "another world is possible." The new paradigm of philosophy I propose is one that orients itself toward the achievement of this heralded possibility.

A BRIEF METHODOLOGICAL NOTE: PHILOSOPHY AS DISCURSIVE SOCIAL PRACTICE

I assume throughout this work that philosophy is a discursive social practice or interrelated nexus of such practices and that, as such, it is shaped by political, economic, and cultural forces that impinge upon it in a variety of ways.[30] Of course, to describe philosophy as a discursive social practice is not yet to differentiate it from other discursive practices, such as for example, legal discourse or political debate. Even so, such a way of thinking about philosophy does situate it in the world of practical social interaction and in the concrete historical and material circumstances within which such interaction takes place. Accepting that shifts in the funding, aims, and administration of higher education have resulted in changes to the practice of philosophy is already, at least in some measure, to take up this perspective and to step back from the idealist posture generally adopted by philosophers toward their own practice. Philosophy, from the viewpoint I take up here, can be considered neither as hovering above its time—no matter the extent to which it may seek to "comprehend it in thought"—nor as transcending its place—regardless of its pretensions to universality. Philosophy must therefore be understood as inheriting and giving expression to the finitude of reason, its formation in a historically given social world, and embeddedness in the concrete discursive social practices through which such a world is produced and reproduced.

Furthermore, like all aspects of human life, philosophy is shaped by power. And power, as Foucault has taught us, is productive. That is, power not only restricts or constrains, but also creates and sets into motion.[31] Philosophy is therefore, among other things, a manifestation of power-relations in which social actors are situated with respect to one another. Philosophy, as a discursive practice, is molded at any given moment by the interplay of contradictory social forces that relate people to one another and, to a great extent, determine their outlook on and conceptualization of the (social) world. Such forces are not exclusively repressive but can operate through the creation and satisfaction of desire, the inculcation of sensibility, and consensual alignment of judgment. In sum, the framework within which I analyze the current condition of philosophy in the United States conceives it as a discursive social practice bound by time and place and also as a locus of conflict where opposing social actors of various kinds and at various scales contend within a structured field of sedimented meanings.

Within this framework, I adopt a broadly anti-essentialist stance concerning the nature of philosophy. Borrowing from Wittgenstein, I treat philosophy here as a "family resemblance" concept.[32] This anti-essentialist stance has implications for the argument(s) to come. Essentialist claims about what philosophy is or should be, particularly those that would seek to conform aberrant practices to a pre-given model or definition, must be understood as "political" in nature. In other words, they are attempts to govern the practice or to justify its governance by appeal to criteria and values that are not recognized by all as having rational validity. One may refer to the practices and mechanisms through which such governance is exercised as "discipline policing." The policing of philosophy may come from outside or it may arise within the discipline itself or indeed through the establishment of the boundary between the inside and the outside. Policing that comes from the outside, what we might call "censorship," can only appear as arbitrary or misguided from the position of philosophers and must necessarily make appeal to claims that lack philosophical justification. By what right and with what legitimacy does one determine *from the outside* what philosophers, speaking as philosophers, may say? Such censoriousness would seem deeply pernicious since philosophy is a practice which, among other things, is concerned with determining the rational validity of normative claims in general. Anyone who would attempt to define or limit philosophy by appeal to valid normative claims would have to do so by invoking philosophical reasoning. Put differently, any attempt to determine the value of philosophy requires a philosophy of value.[33]

Internal policing, however, is not in a much better position. It attempts to impose a particular model or conception of philosophy as normative for the practice as a whole.[34] For example, philosophy might be defined as the pursuit of knowledge, to rely on a common formula. Knowledge, in this case, would be the teleological end in terms of which philosophy is defined and evaluated. But there is no internal consensus that knowledge is the end goal of philosophy, neither ancient nor (post-)modern skeptics, for example, are likely to agree to such a conception. What is more, those who say that philosophy is defined in terms of the pursuit of knowledge, must admit that there are no shared criteria for what constitutes knowledge and that, in fact, precisely this question is subject to debate within philosophy. For reasons such as this, the anti-essentialist stance takes it for granted that there are a variety of practices that philosophers might identify as (good) philosophy and that there is no list of criteria or substantive definition of philosophy that does or would enjoy anything near universal consensus among philosophers. Methodological pluralism, one might say, is not only a normative goal, then, but also an ontological condition of philosophy.

It is useful in this context to mention philosopher Kristie Dotson's diagnosis of professional philosophy in the United States as maintaining what she calls a "culture of legitimation," which she argues presents a barrier for diversity in philosophy. Broadly speaking, legitimation in her usage amounts to aligning one's own work or discourse with previously established norms or precedents. She identifies three central features of a culture of legitimation: (1) it evinces an interest or places value on practices or narratives of legitimation, (2) it assumes that there are shared justifying norms to which participants should appeal in such practices or narratives, and (3) it holds that the norms of justification are univocally relevant to all participants.[35] For Dotson, such a concern with legitimation is clearly on display in the, not infrequently issued, demand that philosophers, particularly women and people of color, demonstrate that their work is philosophical.[36] Such demands that philosophers defend the philosophical status of their work by appeal to common norms or narratives are, I claim, a form of discipline policing. That is, they seek to shape the practice to align with a pre-given model or exclusionary conception that is not shared by all through means other than rational persuasion. One may thus think of Neoliberal Philosophy, as I will describe it in what follows, as, among other things, a ruling paradigm established through forms of discipline policing that appeal to particular norms and narratives to which philosophers are supposed to align their practice. As Dotson makes clear, such policing may act to exclude individuals who identify as members of oppressed or subordinated identity groups even when this is not their stated or conscious purpose.

As I have already mentioned, in narrating the rise of Neoliberal Philosophy, I will largely follow McCumber's methodological approach. Following Kuhn and Foucault, McCumber treats Cold War Philosophy as a nexus of discursive social practices that integrates a variety of non-and extra-discursive elements into a relatively coherent institutional and practical form, what Foucault called an "apparatus" or "*dispotif*."[37] A significant feature of McCumber's approach is his view that certain philosophical positions and methodological approaches were better able to survive and achieve dominance within the context of the Cold War. One might think of this in terms of an analogy with natural selection: The hegemony of Cold War Philosophy was, according to McCumber, the result of selective pressures exerted by anti-communism, the associated investigations and purges, and the broader chilling effect these achieved. Again, such pressures should not be conceived exclusively or even primarily as restricting or constraining what philosophers could do or say. Rather, they must also be understood as productive; that is, as enjoining or inducing philosophers to say and do particular things and as shaping their very subjectivities, desires, and pleasures. Applying this approach within the context of the neoliberal restructuring of the university, my claim throughout this book is that the political pressures exerted by the Neoliberal University have similarly resulted in the consolidation of a new philosophical paradigm, Neoliberal Philosophy.

NOTES

1. Sheila Slaughter and Gary Rhoades, *Academic Capitalism and the New Economy: Markets, State, and Higher Education* (Baltimore: Johns Hopkins University Press, 2010).

2. John McCumber, *The Philosophy Scare: The Politics of Reason in the Early Cold War* (Chicago: Chicago University Press, 2016), and see *Time in the Ditch: American Philosophy and McCarthy Era* (Chicago: Northwestern University Press, 2001). See also Thomas Kuhn, *The Structure of Scientific Revolutions, Fiftieth Anniversary Edition* (Chicago: University of Chicago Press, 2012), and Michel Foucault, "Confessions of the Flesh," in *Power/Knowledge: Selected Interviews & Other Writings 1972–1977*, ed. Colin Gordon and trans. Colin Gordon, Leo Marshall, John Mepham, and Kate Soper (New York: Pantheon Books, 1980).

3. See, for example, *The Structure of Scientific Revolutions*, 120–122.

4. Richard Rorty, "Philosophy in America Today," in *The Consequences of Pragmatism* (Minneapolis, MN: University of Minnesota Press, 1982), 214–215.

5. For a longer discussion of pluralism, see chapter 4. The pluralism in question here is a weak form that I will call "methodological pluralism," which has to do with the presence of multiple competing paradigms and methodologies that are relatively tolerant of one another and compete on a more or less even playing field. For criticism of this form of pluralism, see Bonnie Mann, "Three White Men Walk into a Bar: Philosophy's Pluralism," *Radical Philosophy Review* 16, no. 3 (2013), 733–746.

6. Joel Katzav and Krist Vaesen, "On the Emergence of American Analytic Philosophy," *British Journal for the History of Philosophy* 25, no. 4 (July 2017): 772–798 and Joel Katzav and Krist Vaesen "Pluralism and Peer Review in Philosophy," *Philosophers' Imprint* 17, no. 9 (September 2017): 1–20. See also Michael Beaney, "What Is Analytic Philosophy," in *The Oxford Handbook of the History of Analytic Philosophy*, ed. Michael Beany (New York: Oxford University Press, 2013): 3–29. Beaney views analytic philosophy as an evolving tradition that developed out of its early origins in the works of Gottlob Frege, Bertrand Russell, G.E. Moore, and Wittgenstein. He considers several ways of defining the tradition and seems to settle most firmly on the thesis that analytic philosophy can be defined in terms of its canon,

its style of writing, and its methods. He writes, "Each analytic philosopher may have different aims, ambitions, backgrounds, concerns, motivations, presuppositions and projects, and they may use these tools to make different constructions, criticisms, evaluations, and syntheses; but there is a common repertoire of analytic techniques and a rich fund of instructive examples to draw upon; and it is these that form the methodological basis of analytic philosophy" (26).

7. John R. Thelin, *A History of American Higher Education, Second Edition* (Baltimore, MD: Johns Hopkins University Press, 2011), 261ff.

8. See *Academic Capitalism and the New Economy*, 28–29.

9. In *The Philosophy Scare*, McCumber characterizes Cold War Philosophy in the following terms: "Composed of heterogeneous elements that mainly had in common a mathematical veneer and their adaptability to Cold War political pressures, this 'new and improved' version of philosophy valorized concepts of scientific objectivity and practices of market freedom, while prudently downplaying the anti-theistic implications of modern thought" (1). Here, in line with the analysis I will present in chapter 3, I emphasize the anti-metaphysical ethos and reliance on logical and ordinary language analysis that characterized the period. McCumber's point, however, that Cold War Philosophy was composed of "heterogeneous elements" is absolutely important. The positivistic tendency in Cold War Philosophy may have been dominant and extremely influential, but it was never without critics.

10. See Ludwig Wittgenstein, *Philosophical Investigations, Revised Fourth Edition*, eds. P.M.S. Hacker and Joachim Schulte and trans. G.E.M. Anscombe, P.M.S. Hacker, and Joachim Schulte (Malden, MA: Blackwell Publishing, 2009), §108.

11. Rudolph Carnap, "Überwindung der Metaphysik durch logische Analyse der Sprache," *Erkenntnis* 2 (1931), 230.

12. Ibid., 238ff.

13. Hans Reichenbach, *The Rise of Scientific Philosophy* (Berkeley, CA: University of California Press, 1951), 3.

14. See Donald Davidson, "Knowing One's Own Mind," *Proceedings and Addresses of the American Philosophical Assocaition* 60, no. 3 (January 1987): 441–458.

15. David Bourget and David J. Chalmers, "What Do Philosophers Believe?" *Philosophical Studies: An International Journal for Philosophy in the Analytic Tradition* 170, no. 3 (2014): 465–500.

16. Ibid., 469–470.

17. See Bertrand Russell, *The Problems of Philosophy, Second Edition* (New York: Oxford University Press, 1998). Russell primarily considers and offers philosophical treatments of issues bequeathed to him by modern philosophy after Descartes.

18. W.V.O. Quine, *From a Logical Point of View* (New York: Harper & Row Publishers, 1961). Quine's chummy discussion of a debate between "McX" and "Wyman" combines with his unfortunate invocation of a metaphor dripping in racial eugenics to "offend the aesthetic tastes" of many of us who are perhaps less inclined toward "desert landscapes."

19. For more on the idea of "core areas" especially as this relates to power and segregation in the discipline, see chapter 4.

20. Bruce Kuklick, *A History of Philosophy in America, 1720–2000* (New York: Oxford University Press, 2001), 282–283.

21. Ibid., 285.

22. In "What Is Analytic Philosophy?" Beaney reacts against the idea that there has been a fundamental break in the tradition of analytic philosophy, arguing instead that it has ramified throughout all areas of philosophical concern. Yet he acknowledges that there has been a massive shift toward metaphysics and an increasing "diversification" of ideas, approaches, and so on. Cf. 5–6. Some, but certainly not all, of the changes in question were inaugurated by the dismantling of positivism carried out by, among others, Quine, Wittgenstein, and Kuhn and the critique of "semantic internalism" initiated by Hilary Putnam, Saul Kripke, and Ruth Barcan Marcus. For more on these specific developments and their metaphilosophical relevance, see Maria Baghramian and Andrew Jorgensen, "Quine, Kripke, and Putnam," in *The Oxford Handbook of the History of Analytic Philosophy*, ed. Michael Beany (New York: Oxford University Press, 2013): 594–620.

23. For an informative discussion of strategic action in the academy, see Justin Pack, *How the Neoliberalization of Academia Leads to Thoughtlessness: Arendt and the Modern University* (Lanham, MD: Lexington Books, 2018), 91–95.

24. *The Philosophy Scare*, 25ff.

25. See Jean-François Lyotard, *The Postmodern Condition*, trans. Geoff Bennington and Brian Massumi (Minneapolis: University of Minnesota Press, 1984).

26. See Herbert Marcuse, *One-Dimensional Man: Studies in the Ideology of Advanced Industrial Society* (Boston: Beacon Press, 1964).

27. See Jodi Melamed, *Represent and Destroy: Rationalizing Violence in the New Racial Capitalism* (Minneapolis, Minnesota University Press, 2011).

28. Martin Luther King Jr., "The Role of the Behavioral Scientist in the Civil Rights Movement," in *Journal of Social Issues: A Journal of the Society for the Psychological Study of Social Issues* 74, no. 2 (1968): 214–223.

29. See Mark Fisher, *Capitalist Realism: Is There No Alternative?* (Winchester, UK: O Books, 2009). As Fisher notes there is a resonance with aesthetic concept of "socialist realism" and the term "capitalist realism" was first coined as a kind of parody of socialist realism. In contrast, in his theorization, Fisher describes capitalist realism as a "pervasive *atmosphere*, conditioning not only the production of culture but also the regulation of work and education, and acting as a kind of invisible barrier constraining thought and action" (20). Emphasis in the original.

30. For a detailed account of the kind of metaphilosophical position I adopt here, see Dimitris Gakis, "Philosophy as Paradigms: An Account of a Contextual Metaphilosophical Perspective," *Philosophical Papers* 45, nos. 1 and 2 (March and July 2016): 209–239. As Gakis writes, "What a contextual metaphilosophical perspective stresses, no matter whether occupied with philosophy-in-general, with philosophical traditions or schools, or with the case of a specific philosopher, is that philosophy never ceases to be the product of human praxis and as such is spatially and temporally conditioned being situated in concrete historical, social, and cultural settings" (236).

31. See especially Michel Foucault, *History of Sexuality, Volume 1: An Introduction*, trans. Robert Hurley (New York: Vintage Books, 1990).

32. See *Philosophical Investigations*, §67.

33. For more, see chapter 5.

34. For an excellent account of what I am calling "discipline policing" that is broadly similar to my own, see Rebekah Spera and David M. Peña-Guzmán, "The Anatomy of a Philosophical Hoax: The Politics of Delegitimation in Contemporary Philosophy," *Metaphilosophy* 50, nos. 1–2 (2019): 156–174. Where I speak of internal discipline policing, Spera and Peña-Guzmán discuss "legitimation by force." Following Foucault, McCumber also discusses a "rough and ready" distinction between "strategies of force" and "forms of knowledge" in *The Philosophy Scare*. He writes, "A 'strategy of force' can be defined for present purposes as a practice, discursive or not, that affects other discourses in ways independent of its own rational validity—where 'rational validity' must itself be defined contextually" (8).

35. Kristie Dotson, "How Is This Paper Philosophy?" *Comparative Philosophy* 3, no. 1 (2012), 7.

36. Ibid., 9.

37. For an important discussion of Foucault's use of the term, see Giorgio Agamben, "What Is an Apparatus?" in *What Is an Apparatus and Other Essays*, trans. David Kishik and Stefan Pedatella (Stanford, CA: Stanford UP, 2009), 1–24.

Chapter 1

Philosophy in the Neoliberal University

I argued in the introduction that there have been significant changes in academic philosophy in recent decades, producing a paradigm shift. Following the work of McCumber, I theorize this change as produced by the external political pressures of the Neoliberal University that impinge upon and shape the practice of philosophy through the strategic responses of individuals and departments. In order to adequately conceptualize these changes, it is necessary first to understand the transformation of higher education in the United States wrought by neoliberal "reform." As I will show in subsequent chapters, the Neoliberal University places a new strategic demand on philosophy. Philosophy must market itself. This demand to market philosophy presupposes that the discipline is subject to economic discourse and that it should therefore orient itself to the dictates of the knowledge economy.

PHILOSOPHY IN CRISIS

To explain the emergence and character of Neoliberal Philosophy and the Neoliberal University in which it finds its home, it is useful to begin with a story that is characteristic of our neoliberal epoch. In November 2015, during the Republican primary debates preceding the 2016 election of Donald Trump to the presidency of the United States, then-presidential candidate and Florida Senator Marco Rubio claimed, "Welders make more money than philosophers. We need more welders and less [sic] philosophers."[1] Rubio's remarks generated an outpouring of online commentary, largely aimed at defending the value of a degree in philosophy and disputing Rubio's claim that welders make more money than people with philosophy degrees.[2] In part, no doubt, the response to Rubio was driven by the desire from many quarters to combat the perceived disregard of facts and evidence that had become a significant feature of the debates by that time.[3] For many academics, however, the comment stoked long-simmering anxieties about the "crisis of the humanities" and the crisis of higher education more generally.[4] For many academics, Rubio's comments, with their faux-populist valorization of manual labor and apparent antipathy toward philosophy, seemed yet another soundbite encapsulating a much broader anti-intellectual trend. His words signaled less a call for greater federal focus on training in the skilled trades than one more in a long series of grim reminders heralding looming existential threat. Tanya Loughead relates the mood characteristic of this crisis in the opening words of her 2015 work, *Critical University: Moving Higher Education Forward*: "Anxiety and foreboding mark the state of higher education today."[5]

For faculty members in the liberal arts and humanities the sense of alarm and the threat to which it responds is difficult not to take seriously. Consider, for example, that in just three years, from 2013 to 2016, colleges and universities in the United States cut 651 programs in foreign languages.[6] Or that the Republican governor of Alaska, Mike Dunleavy, proposed a one-year cut of $130 million in funding for the state's higher education system in 2019, amounting to roughly 40 percent of the system's total operating budget.[7] It is hard to imagine that liberal arts and humanities disciplines will fare well in Alaska in the coming years as layoffs and austerity sweep the state. It requires little effort to find similar stories of budget cuts, reduced faculty numbers, and shuttered universities all across the United States—indeed, the trend only appears to have worsened during the COVID-19 pandemic. It would seem that education in the liberal arts and humanities, however defined, is not as socially valued as it once was and that scholars in these disciplines are on the slow road to extinction. Referring to the situation as a "silent crisis," philosopher Martha Nussbaum has compared the changes afoot to cancer.[8] In response to this "cancer," there is an entire genre of books, articles, and opinion pieces dedicated to the defense of education in the liberal arts and humanities. And, clearly, this book can, to an extent, be included among them.

I recount the story of Rubio's comments, one episode among many, because it exemplifies the tenuous political and economic condition of philosophy in our contemporary moment. As is clear, the discipline, along with others across the liberal arts and humanities, is imperiled and called upon ever more frequently to justify its existence before skeptical decision-makers who, more often than not, frame it as an elitist and inefficient waste of the ever-diminishing pool of public or university funds. As the *New York Times* headline reads unequivocally, "In Tough Times, the Humanities Must Justify Their Worth."[9] The terms of the exercise are largely set in advance. Philosophy, among other disciplines, is to be judged by such economic criteria as whether it "generates revenue" for universities and colleges, whether it meets the "workforce needs" of the state or country, and whether graduates can find ready, gainful employment. Similar criteria are outlined in the infamous 2005 "Spellings Report" commissioned by then-President George W. Bush. The report highlighted the need to ensure the "accountability" of educational institutions in meeting the goals of global competitiveness, social mobility, and improving standard of living.[10] From the standpoint of the report, educational institutions and disciplines that cannot demonstrate their contribution to the achievement of these economic ends should be considered unworthy of investment. In this regard, in fact, public funding for philosophy—or for higher education more broadly—is taken to be in more or less the same situation as any other policy decision. As then-President Barack Obama emphasized in his 2013 State of the Union address, all policy decisions in the present order are to be guided by three questions: "How do we attract more jobs to our shores? How do we equip our people with the skills needed to do those jobs? And how do we make sure that hard work leads to a decent living?"[11] If philosophy cannot serve these ends, it would appear, it is not worth federal funding.

CONCEIVING NEOLIBERALISM

The invocation of economic measures to determine the value of philosophy corresponds to the broad social changes wrought by neoliberalism and the accompanying transformation of higher education, or what is also sometimes called its "corporatization" or "commercialization."[12] Much like corporatization and commercialization, neoliberalism is an unfortunately capacious term. In his classic treatment, *A Brief History of Neoliberalism*, Marxist geographer David Harvey distinguished two related meanings. In the first place, he argued, neoliberalism refers to a paradigm of economic thought and an accompanying political-economic project that seeks to use state power to establish competitive markets in goods of all kinds, advance individual liberty in the marketplace, and encourage entrepreneurship in as many domains as possible.[13] This agenda has been advanced internationally by a cadre of intellectuals, politicians, and billionaires for nearly a century. For this reason, sociologist Steven C. Ward describes neoliberalism as a transnational social movement.[14] Among other things, this movement has sought to implement policies of deregulation, privatization, and austerity measures globally. Such policies contribute to the second meaning identified by Harvey—namely, the reassertion of the political and economic power of bourgeois elites in the decades following the 1970s.[15] Along with deregulation and cuts to welfare initiatives and public goods, the world has witnessed the emergence of nearly unprecedented levels of economic inequality, ecological instability, hyper-surveillance, mass incarceration, and permanent warfare. Traditional organizational and legal bulwarks of working-class power have essentially collapsed, with socialist and labor parties and unions capitulating or falling apart entirely, while regulatory agencies of all kinds have been captured and dismantled. Understood as a project of securing bourgeois power and control over labor, neoliberalism is not, it should be said, primarily about removing or reducing the influence or role of the state in markets or in human life more generally. Rather, neoliberalism mobilizes the state to buttress elite power by privatizing and commodifying formerly public or common goods, enforcing market logics even in spheres where proper markets are (as yet) unworkable, imposing this economic order and its values as absolute, and punishing those who are recalcitrant or ineffective. Harvey therefore refers to what he calls the "neoliberal state."[16]

Accompanying such a Marxist analysis of neoliberalism, there is also the analysis originally advanced in Michel Foucault's *Birth of Biopolitics* lectures, and recently repurposed by political theorist Wendy Brown among others.[17] From this perspective, neoliberalism is viewed as a "governing rationality" or an "art of government" that shapes individuals according to its own logic. In her *Undoing the Demos*, Brown describes the triumph of neoliberalism as a "stealth revolution" in which economic values and forms of thinking have achieved dominance in all aspects of life. According to this analysis, neoliberalism refashions the social world according to market principles, conceiving human beings as *homo economicus* and fitting them to its mold. People are made to think of and relate to themselves primarily in market terms; as "entrepreneurs," "investors," and so on. Political scientist Sanford Schram explains, "Neoliberalism disseminates economic rationality to be the touchstone not just for the market but for civil society and the state as well."[18] In this sense, neoliberalism functions as a politics less through the direct use of force or capture of the state and more through the imposition of a form of rationality commanded by markets and cultivation of associated forms of subjectivity. Brown therefore compares the governing rationality of neoliberalism to Plato's homology between the *polis* and the soul; both must operate according to the requirements of economic rationality.[19] The criteria by which institutions of higher education and disciplines within them are judged as (un-)worthy of social "investment" represent but one extension of this "stealth revolution" in which economic rationality comes to dominate all arenas of social life.

Neoliberalism is a multifaceted phenomenon, then. It is a transnational social movement advancing a particular group of economic and political ideals. It is also a re-entrenchment of class power. Further, it is an art of government in which economic rationality proliferates throughout the social world, ordering institutions and people according to its own imperatives. It is important to emphasize as well that what I might like to call "actually existing neoliberalism" is always an unstable assemblage produced by the interaction of a wide range of agents operating across multiple scales, negotiating various local and personal histories and contexts. In what follows, I use "neoliberalism" to track all of these phenomena and refer to the transformation of U.S. higher education achieved through them, what is sometimes referred to as "education reform," as the "Neoliberal University."

THE NEOLIBERAL UNIVERSITY

In discussing the Neoliberal University, I thus refer to a mix of interrelated trends and processes produced by the neoliberal reordering of higher education in the United States: (1) defunding higher education and reframing it as a private consumer good, (2) reconceiving the purpose of higher education as training rather than education, (3) the instrumentalization and commodification of knowledge, and (4) the centralization and bureaucratization of administration.[20] Neoliberal Philosophy, I argue, is the dominant form taken by philosophy within the Neoliberal University.

Defunding and Privatizing Higher Education

The defunding and privatization of higher education has been central to neoliberalism, deeply impacting institutions across the United States. In general, education and other goods formerly considered public or promoting broad social welfare have been cut in order to shrink deficit spending, service debt, and "balance the budget." Beginning with the "Tax Revolt" of the 1970s, states have faced debilitating budgetary constraints. Aimed at "starving the beast," in the metaphor of their advocates, tax cuts and other interventions were intended to limit spending by tying it to outside indicators, requiring supermajority support in legislatures for budget increases, and shrinking revenue.[21] In consequence of these trends, legal scholar Jeremy Pilaar describes a shift from what he calls the "Investment Age" to what he calls the "Retrenchment Age."[22] Whereas, in the Investment Age, U.S. states increased tax revenues to pay for expanded and improved infrastructure, healthcare, and education, flattened tax revenues since the 1970s have led to declining outlays, evisceration of public benefits, and infrastructure falling into disrepair. As Pilaar documents, though their populations have largely continued to grow steadily, states' spending on public or common goods has not.[23] Since the onset of the Great Recession, budgetary constraints have only become more severe, and education has been a prime target. Indeed, according to the Center on Budget and Policy Priorities, U.S. states slashed overall funding for public two-and four-year colleges by $9 billion in the years between 2008 and 2017. On average, they spent 16 percent less per student in 2017 than they had in 2008.[24] These recent data, however, are only the extreme expression of developments that have been brewing for decades. As discussed by economists Robert A. Archibald and David H. Feldman, in 2011 "state effort" in higher education funding, meaning the dollars appropriated by states per $1000 USD of personal income, had decreased by 40 percent from its peak in the 1970s.[25] There are several factors influencing this decline in state funding of colleges and universities. Spending on healthcare and prisons, for example, has increased significantly. But Archibald and Feldman demonstrate clearly that tax laws enacted as part of the "Tax Revolt," particularly "tax expenditure limits" and "supermajority requirements," have played a major role in forcing states to cut education spending.[26]

As public funding has been cut for institutions of higher education, colleges and universities have become more heavily reliant on tuition as their main source of funding. Referring specifically to New York and California, Michael Fabricant and Stephen Briar explain that decreased funding from state governments has led universities in these states to increase tuition and rely heavily on private donations. As they write, "These dramatic reductions in base aid levels have forced public institutions to search for other sources of revenue. These public institutions have had to fill yawning budget gaps with private dollars including, but not limited to, increased tuition and private donations from the wealthy."[27] Hence, according to a 2017 College Board report, published in-state tuition at public four-year institutions has more than tripled since 1987.[28] The effect of such rising tuition costs is predictable. By the end of 2018, total student loan debt in the United States stood at an astonishing $1.47 trillion USD.[29]

Simultaneously, to make ends meet and fund an increasingly large administration, colleges and universities across the country have cut programs and come to rely increasingly on casualized academic labor. Noam Chomsky sees this trend as resulting in the rise of an academic "precariat." Much as major corporations rely on "flexible" labor divested of the job security, benefits, or expectation of loyalty characteristic of Fordist production, so, too, higher education in the United States has steadily come to rely on adjuncts and short-term appointments.[30] Indeed, the American Association of University Professors (AAUP) reports that part-time faculty comprised 40 percent of all instructional faculty in the United States in 2016.[31] Whereas tenured and tenure-track faculty were 45 percent of the total in 1975, by 2015 they accounted for only 29 percent, with a staggering 57 percent of the academic labor force consisting of full-time non-tenure-track and part-time faculty.[32] Dependent on tuition and revenue from wealthy benefactors, institutions of higher education have entered onto a path of seemingly permanent austerity, undermining the stability and power of faculty even as they continue to grow at the administrative level. Education is now a commodity produced by a large class of precarious academic labor, subject to a massive surveillance machinery.

Training as the Aim of the University

The defunding and privatization of higher education has been accompanied by a campaign to transform its purpose in accordance with elite interests. This is perhaps nowhere more evident than in the attempts of former Wisconsin Governor Scott Walker to revise the mission of the University of Wisconsin system, known as the "Wisconsin Idea." Walker sought to have mission imperatives to "search for truth" and "improve the human condition" removed and replaced with language calling for the system to "meet the state's workforce needs."[33] David Noble helpfully theorizes such changes in terms of a distinction between "training" and "education." Training, Noble suggests, involves the teaching of technical knowledge to meet preestablished ends set by others. Education, by contrast, seeks to integrate greater self-understanding with the autonomous choice of values.[34] The Neoliberal University, then, reconceives the purpose of higher education to be training a workforce rather than educating students.

This substitution of training as the preeminent aim of the university is not a partisan affair. Rather, it is the agreed upon common sense of both major political parties in the United States, most parties around the world, and, one can only imagine, large majorities of their constituencies. Former President Obama's "Skills for America's Future" program announced in October 2010 illustrates this point well. The program was explicit in its aim of allowing corporations to redesign tax-payer-funded community college curricula to meet their own job training needs, partnering with retailers like McDonald's and the Gap, Inc. In the White House press release, President Obama is quoted as saying, "We want to make it easier to join students looking for jobs with businesses looking to hire. We want to put community colleges and employers together to create programs that match curricula in the classroom with the needs of the boardroom."[35] The Neoliberal University is dedicated to training meant to supply private corporations with pliable and competent employees; it is not, as it once claimed to be, a privileged space of segregated study in pursuit of greater knowledge, moral cultivation, and growing autonomy.

For this reason, philosopher Steven Fesmire interprets contemporary higher education as embodying an "industrial model." Within the industrial model, as he writes, "[The job of education] is to manufacture skilled labor, and it is expected to do so in a way that is maximally efficient."[36] Within the neoliberal iteration of this model, students are imagined as occupying a host of contradictory roles. First, they appear as raw material or "input" to be worked upon by a standardized process or system. Material is fed in and emerges on the other side of the process or system as "output," a product with some "value-added." Students, then, are both material and product. Beyond this, however, they are viewed as customers or clients. In this role, students are pictured as calculating consumers who want "bang for their buck." The rational customer demands a high-quality product at the lowest possible cost and "the customer is always right." The product students are now imagined as purchasing, however, is an enhancement of their "human capital" which will be maximally profitable.[37] The student is not only a customer, then, but also an entrepreneur and a profit-seeking investor. Education is an "investment in the future," both for society and for the student. In sum, education is thought to be an industry, alongside, say, the automobile industry, and the student in the "knowledge factory" is conceived simultaneously as material to be worked upon, a product to be manufactured, and a shrewd investor/consumer responsible for using and enhancing their capital wisely. Likewise, for the state, the question is how best to invest resources in order to train a more productive workforce and secure jobs in a highly competitive international market.

The Instrumentalization and Commodification of Knowledge

The impacts of the neoliberal restructuring of the university, however, have reached not only the educational mission, but have also affected research and scholarship. As described by Slaughter and Rhoades, the previous model of knowledge production—what they refer to as the "public good knowledge/learning regime"—rewarded researchers who made new discoveries or contributed significantly to the scientific or scholarly enterprise with increased status and prestige. In opposition to this system, they explain, "The academic capitalist system is setting up an alternative system of rewards in which discovery is valued because of its commercial properties and economic rewards, broad scientific questions are couched so that they are relevant to commercial possibilities (biotechnology, telecommunications, computer science), knowledge is regarded as a commodity rather than a free good, and universities have the organization capacity (and are permitted by law) to license, invest, and profit from these commodities."[38] With declining state funding and increasing political pressure, colleges and universities have partnered directly with corporations to fill funding gaps and demonstrate their utility, which is understood almost exclusively in terms of direct market value. By doing so, they effectively take over corporate research and development functions, thereby socializing the costs and risks associated with such functions. Moreover, given their increasing dependence on funding from sources other than the state, private donors now play an outsized role on campuses across the United States, shaping all aspects of campus life in accordance with private interest and personal opinion.[39]

Academics, administrations, corporations, and governments have all come together to facilitate the emergence of a now-literal "marketplace of ideas" in which alienable knowledge-commodities are transformed into intellectual property and exchanged for profit. Ward describes this process in terms of three trends: First, there is the imposition of regimes of efficiency and economic rationality on knowledge production. Second, research results are transformed into private commodities through a number of legal mechanisms. And finally, outcomes and assessment regimes are implemented in order to adequately orient market behavior; producers must know the needs of the market and consumers must know the quality and types of products.[40] Central to this process, competition for grants and other forms of funding from outside the academy places new pressures on faculty to "pitch" their research as serving the aims and interests of funders and donors.[41] These transformations affect the direction of research because funding is now dictated by the demands of external markets. From the standpoint of neoliberalism, this is a good thing, since, as Ward explains the neoliberal point of view, "Only the market can discipline knowledge making and dissemination in a manner that makes it socially useful."[42] At the end of the day, the Neoliberal University favors and seeks to produce knowledge that is directly profitable to corporate partners and donors while disfavoring work that serves broader public aims or which has no utility outside itself.

The Centralization and Bureaucratization of University Administration

Commensurate with its transformed social function, the Neoliberal University has altered its internal administrative structures to reflect those of private enterprise, implementing a centralized bureaucratic structure staffed by a massive layer of administrators along with a self-propelling audit culture supposedly aimed at ensuring quality.[43] As described by business and accounting scholars Russell Craig, Joel Amernic, and Dennis Tourish, this involves the replacement of traditional "collegial control" of the university organization with what they call "bureaucratic control." Changes in the administrative structure of universities, then, are in line with the broader rise of the "New Public Management" and the reorganization of public institutions that has characterized neoliberalism globally.[44] Essentially, government functions have been cast as inefficient and wasteful then submitted to regimes of austerity and "accountability" in order to align their functioning with market discipline, which is presumed to be more efficient and better able to respond to the needs of the public, who are now conceived as individual consumers of government products and services.

In contrast to the hierarchical, military-style bureaucratic structures of the socialist and welfare states and the Fordist organization of labor that dominated the disciplinary societies of the twentieth century, however, neoliberal managerialism promotes a vision of state bureaucracy and post-Fordist production driven by ideas of competition, flexibility, and output-oriented performance metrics. In a somewhat dated analogy, sociologist Richard Sennett compares this new form of organization to an MP3 player. Like an MP3 player, and in contrast to the older organizational forms that characterized what Sennett terms "social capitalism," the new, flexible organization can be programmed or reprogrammed to accomplish specific tasks. Further, an MP3 player need not play songs in any particular sequence. Similarly, flexible organizations are not focused on any specific sequence of functions or performances—they sequence production to the short-term demands and signals of the market. In contrast to "fixed functions" and "linear development," the flexible organization is thus task-oriented and nonlinear. Finally, the MP3 player is incredibly centralized inasmuch as the song played is determined by the central processing unit. All other functions and operations are determined by and feed into this one, to which they must all be legible. Similarly, new communications technologies enable immediate surveillance and control by management, submitting worker operations to forms legible by the commanding bureaucracy. The center governs the social periphery, according to Sennett, by monitoring results in something very near real-time.[45]

As applied to higher education, the new organizational form has led to what sociologist Benjamin Ginsberg has characterized as the "fall of the faculty." Documenting, on the one hand, the massive increase in tuition cost in recent decades, Ginsberg notes, on the other hand, that there has not been a concomitant drop in the ratio of faculty to students. Instead, he shows, while the ratio of faculty to students has remained relatively constant, the ratio of administrators and related professional staff to students has decreased dramatically.[46] Despite neoliberal rhetoric of individual choice, responsibility, and increased efficiency, faculty in the Neoliberal University are ever less able to control their own labor or make effective decisions about curriculum even as resources are diverted from instruction and related activities toward maintaining and expanding administrative and managerial staff. Instead, they are submitted to the economic imperatives of corporate management oriented to the "bottom line" and disciplined through pervasive surveillance and accountability regimes. As Henry Giroux laments, "Within the logic of the new managerialism, there is little concern for matters of justice, fairness, equity, and the general improvement of the human condition insofar as these relate to expanding and deepening the imperatives and ideals of a substantive democracy."[47] Whether inside or outside the academy, neoliberalism shifts power away from those at the bottom or periphery of social hierarchies toward managerial elites.

Connected to these organizational changes is the emergence of a vast auditing enterprise aimed at producing quantifiable measures of performance outcomes and output. After all, markets can only be assumed to produce efficiencies in situations where consumers are able to collect and act on good information. How would students invest wisely if there were no good indicators of quality or efficiency? Plus, management can only control what it can see. In the case of the production of material goods, quantifiable evaluations of efficiency and quality make some sense. However, many other human activities, including most governmental and public services, are much more difficult to measure in such terms. For this reason, neoliberalism has demanded the creation of innumerable performance metrics and systems of accreditation and assessment—a phenomenon with which faculty in the Neoliberal University are only too familiar. Describing the emergent audit culture as a new "market Stalinism," Fisher writes, "New bureaucracy takes the form not of a specific, delimited function performed by particular workers but invades all areas of work, with the result that—as Kafka prophesied—workers become their own auditors, forced to assess their own performance."[48] Integrated into this "market Stalinism," professors in the Neoliberal University spend large parts of their day creating and deploying assessment metrics to demonstrate their effectiveness—time that might otherwise be spent on teaching, research, or mentorship. Furthermore, as many have documented, the measures not only draw attention away from productive work, they come to dominate it in such a way that one's goal becomes to meet whatever metrics have been identified; measures become targets. One must, for instance, "teach to the test," regardless of whether the test has anything to do with real education or is a reliable or accurate measure of student learning. Similarly, researchers compete to publish an appropriate quantity of articles in journals with the right level of "impact," often with little concern for the quality or depth of the contribution to the broader scholarly enterprise. In a perverse irony, the culture of performance metrics meant to rationalize labor and make it efficient comes to absorb and supplant labor itself in the proliferating exercise of "data collection" and pushes all involved to produce assessment reports that no one will ever read.

The Neoliberal University as Class Politics

Following Harvey and others in the Marxist tradition, this now-dominant neoliberal configuration of higher education should be seen within the context of the reassertion of bourgeois class power and control over labor.

Increasing tuition and rationing of public goods means that higher education is more exclusive, particularly out of reach for poor and working-class students and students of color. For this reason, Fabricant and Brier describe even public higher education as an "engine of inequality."[49] They list a host of related trends: diminishing grant aid, tuition increases, restricted access and declining completion for poor students and students of color, greater reliance on debt financing, external work obligations for students, and so on.[50] But unequal access to higher education is only one way in which the Neoliberal University functions to sort people and reproduce existing inequalities of class, race, gender/sex, sexuality, and so forth. Indeed, as Amy E. Stich and Carrie Freie explain, increased availability and participation of working-class people in higher education in the United States since the 1950s has been accompanied by intense stratification of institutions. According to Stich and Freie, "The most overt indication of this stratification is the concentration of low-income and working-class students within the lowest-ranking postsecondary institutions."[51] One might only add that students of color are over-represented among low-income and working-class students and that they are even more likely to find themselves in the lowest ranking institutions. The meaning of such stratification becomes clear if one acknowledges that education, in the sense identified by Noble, is reserved for those with the means to access elite schools. More affordable options—still beyond consideration for many—focus on training.

Training unto itself often serves to stifle rather than stimulate the sensibilities embodied in and instilled through education, thereby producing what Nussbaum calls "useful machines."[52] In this way, the narrow focus on training—and, it must be said, the encumbrance of major debt—achieves the political purpose of heading off broad-based democratic social movements that might challenge a system dedicated to unprecedented social inequality, perpetual warfare, global poverty, and perilous environmental devastation. Rather than an institution responsible for the expansion of democracy or equality, higher education is instead positioned as the industry responsible for (re-)producing the labor force required for the knowledge economy. In this sense, the Neoliberal University in the United States, though it ostensibly promises opportunity and success for all, serves in a much more direct way than in its predecessor as what Louis Althusser termed an "Ideological State Apparatus." Such institutions, according to Althusser, are responsible for reproducing dominant ideology and, with it, the relations of production characteristic of capitalist society. As he puts it, "[I]t is by apprenticeship in a variety of know-how wrapped up in the massive inculcation of the ideology of the ruling class that the *relations of production* in a capitalist social formation, i.e., the relation of exploited to exploiters and exploiters to exploited, are largely reproduced."[53] The Neoliberal University produces both the training and the relations of production necessary to the knowledge economy of late capitalism. It creates competent and pliable workers who "meet the state's workforce needs" while also naturalizing a social system that positions some as "labor," now explicitly conceived as "human capital," who may only meet their individual needs by producing profit for others.

The emphasis on training as the end of higher education, moreover, serves to shift responsibility for employment onto individual workers. This aligns with the broader trends of "devolution" of power and "responsibilization" of smaller social units identified as hallmarks of neoliberalism by Brown.[54] By shifting the burden of risk and investment away from private capitalist enterprises while simultaneously devolving responsibility to ever smaller units, neoliberalism reimagines human beings as "entrepreneurs of themselves" seeking to profit on individual investment through calculations of risk and reward. Relatedly, in her *The Lost Soul of Higher Education*, historian Ellen Schrecker cites a 1971 document produced by the U.S. Health, Education, and Welfare Department claiming that individualized student aid would provide for "a freer play of market forces" and "give individuals the general power of choice in the education marketplace."[55] In other words, federal student loans emerged at least in part as a mechanism to increase the role of individual choice and the market in education—which is to say, as a mechanism to devolve responsibility for education to individual students and to discipline them in this way, along with colleges and universities, to the market. While individual students are made responsible through such mechanisms, the state is likewise made responsible for "attracting and retaining good jobs" and for privatizing and commodifying previously public goods or those held in common; responsibilities that are typically shifted to smaller organizational units. The neoliberal state must act as a handmaid to elite economic interests.

Indeed, this shift of responsibility constitutes a massive government subsidy to bourgeois elites. By restructuring higher education to "meet workforce needs" and shifting the financial burden onto students, the costs of training employees are externalized. They are socialized in the form of government-funded educational institutions, grants, and low-interest loans. Yet they are simultaneously individualized in the form of student tuition and debt. Much as early Appalachian coal miners were indentured to their employers for the picks, helmets, lights, and other equipment necessary to perform their work, so, too, the workforce of our contemporary knowledge economy is indentured through federal and private loans for the training necessary to perform. In both cases, the employer benefits by shifting the costs of (re-)production onto workers. Of course, this means that responsibility for employment and the basic material goods that sustain human life belongs to workers, who are now understood as entrepreneurial enterprises competing in a global labor market. Those who invest well in their human capital will be rewarded by the market; those who invest poorly will be duly, and we are assured justly, punished. As Brown has eloquently outlined, the necessary complement of the mantra of the Great Recession, "too big to fail," is "too small to protect." She goes on, "Where there are only capitals and competition among them, not only will some win while others lose (inequality and competition unto death replaces equality and commitment to protect life), but some will be rescued and resuscitated, while others will be cast off or left to perish (owners of small farms and small businesses, those with underwater mortgages, indebted and unemployed college graduates)."[56] Banks and corporations may be "too big to fail," but individual workers and, indeed, whole nations are not; they are too small to save.

NOTES

1. See Alan Rappaport, "Philosophers (and Welders) React to Marco Rubio's Debate Comments," *The New York Times*, November 11, 2015, https://www.nytimes.com/politics/first-draft/2015/11/11/philosophers-and-welders-react-to-marco-rubios-debate-comments.

2. For a prime example of this kind of response, see Bryan W. Van Norden, *Taking Back Philosophy: A Multicultural Manifesto* (New York: Columbia University Press, 2017), 110ff.

3. In response to the influence largely of then-candidate Donald Trump, the GOP primaries were a major reason why Oxford Dictionaries named "post-truth" their "Word of the Year" in 2016. For a useful philosophical primer on the emergence of the concept of post-truth, see Lee McIntyre, *Post-Truth* (Cambridge, MA: MIT Press, 2018).

4. For data relating to the "crisis" and the general tenor of the response, see David Armitage, Homi Bhabha, Emma Dench, Jeffrey Hamburger, John Hamilton, Sean Kelly, Carrie Lambert-Beatty, Christie McDonald, Anne Shreffler, and James Simpson, "The Teaching of the Arts and Humanities at Harvard College: Mapping the Future" (Cambridge, MA: Harvard University, May 31, 2013). https://scholar.harvard.edu/files/jamessimpson/files/mapping_the_future.pdf. For criticism of the idea that the humanities are in decline that nonetheless takes concerns about crisis very seriously, see Michael Bérubé, "The Futility of the Humanities," *Qui Parle* 20, no.1 (Fall/Winter 2011): 95–107. Bérubé helpfully debunks misinterpretations of the widely circulated data cited by the Harvard report.

5. Tanya Loughead, *Critical University: Moving Higher Education Forward* (Lanham, MD: Lexington Books, 2015), 1.

6. Steven Johnson, "Colleges Lose a 'Stunning' 651 Foreign-Language Programs in 3 Years," *The Chronicle of Higher Education*, January 22, 2019, https://www.chronicle.com/article/Colleges-Lose-a-Stunning-/245526.

7. Adam Harris, "Alaska Still Hasn't Saved Its Universities," *The Atlantic*, September 3, 2019, https://www.theatlantic.com/education/archive/2019/08/alaskas-higher-education-system-still-trouble/596191.

8. Martha Nussbaum, *Not for Profit: Why Democracy Needs the Humanities* (Princeton, NJ: Princeton UP, 2010), 1–12.

9. Patricia Cohen, "In Tough Times, the Humanities Must Justify Their Worth," *The New York Times*, February 25, 2009, https://www.nytimes.com/2009/02/25/books/25human.html.

10. Margaret Spellings, *A Test of Leadership: Charting the Future of US Higher Education* (U.S. Department of Education, 2006), 4ff.

11. "Remarks by the President in the State of the Union Address," February 12, 2013, National Archives and Records Administration, https://obamawhitehouse.archives.gov/the-press-office/2013/02/12/remarks-president-state-union-address quoted in Wendy Brown, *Undoing the Demos: Neoliberalism's Stealth Revolution* (New York: Zone Books, 2015), 24–25.

12. See Loughead, *Critical University*. For an important predecessor, see Stanley Aronowitz, *The Knowledge Factory: Dismantling the Corporate University and Creating True Higher Learning* (Boston, MA: Beacon Press, 2000). For another, less radical or critical perspective, see Derek Bok, *Universities in the Marketplace: The Commercialization of Higher Education* (Princeton, NJ: Princeton UP, 2003).

13. David Harvey, *A Brief History of Neoliberalism* (Oxford: Oxford University Press, 2005), 2ff.

14. Steven C. Ward, *Neoliberalism and the Global Restructuring of Knowledge and Education* (New York: Routledge, 2012), 28–29. For an impressive and useful history of the movement, see Daniel Stedman Jones, *Masters of the Universe: Hayek, Friedman, and the Birth of Neoliberal Politics* (Princeton, NJ: Princeton UP, 2012).

15. Harvey, *A Brief History of Neoliberalism*, 19. See also Jodi Melamed, *Represent and Destroy: Rationalizing Violence in the New Racial Capitalism* (Minneapolis, Minnesota University Press, 2011), 39. Melamed will discuss what she terms "neoliberal sovereignty," which is the biopolitical ordering of populations for the sake of economic ends such as productivity.

16. *A Brief History of Neoliberalism*, 64ff.

17. See Michel Foucault, *The Birth of Biopolitics: Lectures at the Collège de France, 1978–1979*, eds. François Ewald, Alessandro Fontana, and Michel Senellart and trans. Graham Burchell (Basingstoke: Palgrave Macmillan, 2010); Brown, *Undoing the Demos*.

18. Sanford F. Schram, "The Knight's Move: Social Policy Change in an Age of Consolidated Power," in *Rethinking Neoliberalism: Resisting the Disciplinary Regime*, eds. Sanford F. Schram and Marianna Pavlovskaya (New York: Routledge, 2017), 215–216.

19. *Undoing the Demos*, 22.

20. Loughead identifies six key features of the corporatization of higher education in the United States: (1) the weakening of shared governance; (2) the increase of administration and decrease in full-time faculty; (3) the increasing importance of grants; (4) the lack of importance given to teaching; (5) the waning importance of the

humanities to undergraduate education; and (6) the rising commodification and cost of higher education in the United States. See *Critical University*, 1–36. I take it that we are largely in agreement and consider the differences more a matter of emphasis than fundamental vision.

21. For a useful history of the metaphor and related policies from an insider, see Bruce Bartlett, "'Starve the Beast': Origins and Development of a Budgetary Metaphor," *The Independent Review* XII, no. 1 (Summer 2007), 5–26.

22. Jeremy Pilaar, "Starving the Statehouse: The Hidden Tax Policies Behind States' Long-Run Fiscal Crises," *Yale Law and Policy Review* 37 (2018), 345–383.

23. Ibid., 351–359.

24. Michael Mitchell, Michael Leachman, and Kathleen Masterson, "A Lost Decade in Higher Education Funding: States Cuts Have Driven UP Tuition and Reduced Quality," Center on Budget and Policy Priorities, August 23, 2017, https://www.cbpp.org/sites/default/files/atoms/files/2017_higher_ed_8-22-17_final.pdf.

25. Robert B. Archibald and David H. Feldman, *Why Does College Cost So Much?* (New York: Oxford UP, 2011), 144–146.

26. Robert B. Archibald and David H. Feldman, "State Higher Education Spending and the Tax Revolt," *The Journal of Higher Education* 77, no. 4 (July/August 2006), 618–644.

27. Michael Fabricant and Stephen Brier, *Austerity Blues: Fighting for the Soul of Public Higher Education* (Baltimore, MD: Johns Hopkins UP, 2016), 22.

28. Jennifer Ma, Sandy Baum, Matea Pender, and Meredith Welch, "Trends in College Pricing 2017," College Board, October 2017, https://research.collegeboard.org/pdf/trends-college-pricing-2017-full-report.pdf.

29. Nigel Chiwaya, "The Five Charts Show How Bad the Student Loan Debt Situation Is," *NBC News*, April 24, 2019, https://www.nbcnews.com/news/us-news/student-loan-statistics-2019-n997836.

30. Noam Chomsky, "On Academic Labor," *Counterpunch*, February 28, 2014, https://www.counterpunch.org/2014/02/28/on-academic-labor/.

31. American Association of University Professors (AAUP), "Data Snapshot: Contingent Faculty in US Higher Ed," https://www.aaup.org/sites/default/files/10112018%20Data%20Snapshot%20Tenure.pdf.

32. American Association of University Professors (AAUP), "Academic Labor Force Trends, 1975–2017," https://www.aaup.org/sites/default/files/Academic_Labor_Force_Trends_1975-2015_0.pdf.

33. Molly Beck, "Scott Walker Sought Changes to Wisconsin Idea, Emails Show After Judge Orders Release of Records," *Wisconsin State Journal* (Madison, WI), May 28, 2016, https://madison.com/wsj/news/local/govt-and-politics/scott-walker-sought-changes-to-wisconsin-idea-emails-show-after-judge-orders-release-of-records/article_268eb62f-d548-5a2d-a2f0-ca977dac2346.html.

34. David Noble, *Digital Diploma Mills: The Automation of Higher Education* (New York: Monthly Review Press, 2002), 2. See also Aronowitz, *The Knowledge Factory*, 1ff. Aronowitz distinguishes between "learning," "education," and "training," associating the term "education" with assimilation into a national culture. Certainly, the development of autonomy identified as "education" by Noble and the

kind of assimilation identified as "education" by Aronowitz are both related, if contradictory, legacies of the Enlightenment and its competing goals for institutions of higher education or higher learning, as Aronowitz might insist.

35. "President Obama to Announce Launch of Skills for America's Future," October 4, 2010, National Archives and Records Administration, https://obamawhitehouse.archives.gov/the-press-office/2010/10/04/president-obama-announce-launch-skills-america-s-future. See also Loughead, *Critical University*, 20–21.

36. Steven Fesmire, "Democracy and the Industrial Imagination in American Education," *Education and Culture* 32, no. 1 (2016): 53–61. See also Aronowitz, *The Knowledge Factory*. Clearly, Aronowitz's dominant metaphor—the university as factory—is a vivid means of depicting what Fesmire describes as the "industrial model." As Aronowitz writes, "Most colleges and universities are part of an academic system in American society whose success is measured by, among other criteria, how much it contributes to the economy" (11). As I will show in chapter 2, Fesmire's and Aronowitz's analysis is incomplete insofar as it fails to conceptualize the logic of the system in terms of performance optimization—not only production of useful goods, but the production of technologies that yield "return on investment."

37. See David Lea, "The Future of the Humanities in Today's Financial Markets," *Educational Theory*, 64, no. 3 (June 2014): 261–283. Most important: "In accordance with the market conceptualization of relationships, students are both consumers and ultimately products within a system" (278). See also chapter 2.

38. Sheila Slaughter and Gary Rhoades, *Academic Capitalism and the New Economy: Markets, State, and Higher Education* (Baltimore: Johns Hopkins University Press, 2010), 107.

39. As documented by the activist group Unkoch My Campus, the billionaire Koch brothers have used the opportunity to infiltrate academe across the country by establishing privately funded centers. See "Higher Education," *Unkoch My Campus*, http://www.unkochmycampus.org/highereducation, accessed November 30, 2020. The discipline of philosophy has been central to their efforts with programs, like that at Bowling Green State University, accepting large donations for the establishment of programs in philosophy, politics, economics, and law. See, for example, Justin Weinberg, "Bowling Green Receives $1.6 Million to Expand Philosophy, Politics, Economics, and Law Program," *Daily Nous*, August 5, 2019, https://dailynous.com/2019/08/05/bowling-green-receives-1-6-million-philosophy-politics-economics-law.

40. *Neoliberalism and the Global Restructuring of Knowledge and Education*, 102ff.

41. See Loughead, *Critical University*, 11–13.

42. *Neoliberalism and the Global Restructuring of Knowledge and Education*, 104.

43. For the *locus classicus*, see Cris Shore and Susan Wright, "Audit Culture and Anthropology: Neo-Liberalism in British Higher Education," *The Journal of the Royal Anthropological Institute* 5, no. 4 (1999): 557–575. For an update from the same authors, see Cris Shore and Susan Wright, "Audit Culture Revisited: Rankings, Ratings, and the Reassembling of Society," *Current Anthropology* 56, no. 3 (June 2015): 421–444.

44. Russell Craig, Joel Amernic, and Dennis Tourish, "Perverse Audit Culture and Accountability of the Modern Public University," *Financial Accountability &*

Management 30, no. 1 (February 2014): 8–9. See also Ward, *Neoliberalism and the Global Restructuring of Knowledge and Education*, 46–73.

45. Richard Sennett, *The Culture of the New Capitalism* (New Haven, CT: Yale UP, 2006), 47–58.

46. Benjamin Ginsberg, *The Fall of the Faculty* (New York: Oxford UP, 2011), 26–27.

47. Henry Giroux, *Neoliberalism's War on Higher Education* (Chicago, IL: Haymarket Books, 2014), 272.

48. Mark Fisher, *Capitalist Realism: Is There No Alternative?* (Winchester, UK: O Books, 2009), 51.

49. *Austerity Blues*, 117ff.

50. Ibid., 122–127.

51. Amy E. Stich and Carrie Freie, "Introduction: The Working Classes and Higher Education: An Introduction to a Complicated Relationship," in *The Working Classes and Higher Education: Inequality of Access, Opportunity and Outcome* (New York: Routledge, 2016), 2.

52. *Not for Profit*, 2.

53. Louis Althusser, "Ideology and Ideological State Apparatuses (Notes towards an Investigation)," in *Lenin and Philosophy and Other Essays*, trans. Ben Brewster (New York: Monthly Review Press, 1971), 156.

54. *Undoing the Demos*, 133.

55. Quoted by Ellen Schrecker in *The Lost Soul of Higher Education: Corporatization, the Assault on Academic Freedom, and the End of the American University* (New York: The New Press, 2010), 161.

56. *Undoing the Demos*, 72.

Chapter 2

The Performativity of Neoliberal Philosophy

In the introduction, I outlined the contours of the Neoliberal University. The Neoliberal University, I showed, is shaped by four central trends: (1) defunding higher education and conceiving it as a private commodity, (2) viewing training as the preeminent aim of the university, (3) the instrumentalization and commodification of knowledge, and (4) the centralization and bureaucratization of administration. Following McCumber's method, my argument throughout this work is that these changes to higher education in the United States have resulted in a paradigm shift in philosophy. The political and institutional pressures on philosophy within the Neoliberal University have led to the emergence of what I call Neoliberal Philosophy.

In this chapter, I further develop the thesis that these trends have impacted philosophy and explain how they have engendered Neoliberal Philosophy. I begin by drawing on the work of Lyotard to develop an account of the "performativity" of philosophy within the Neoliberal University. Lyotard's seminal work, *The Postmodern Condition*, predicted massive changes to the institution of the university and the significance and role of philosophy within the postmodern era. Without recourse to legitimating metanarratives, Lyotard contended, science cannot rely on philosophy for the social authority through which it was previously able to govern other discourses and claim an exclusive right to knowledge—along with a share of social resources. Since it can no longer offer a foundation for science in the form of a grand narrative, philosophy takes a place alongside science with no special claim to higher authority.[1] And, just like science, philosophy is called upon to legitimate itself according to external, economic criteria. Philosophy must perform. It is within this broader social context that philosophy is led to market itself as providing critical thinking skills that are supposedly desired by employers and knowledge which is applicable to more directly profitable enterprises. Much like scientists and other researchers, philosophers and philosophy departments in the United States therefore face the demand that they legitimate themselves by demonstrating their ability to meet external economic metrics. This demand, I argue, has the effect of forcing individuals and departments to reconceptualize and reorganize their curricula, pedagogy, and research agendas.

PERFORMATIVITY AND PHILOSOPHY

In the broadest strokes, Lyotard's discussion of postmodernism is quite well known.[2] Some four decades after his theorization, the term "postmodernism" is used most frequently as a pejorative, it seems. Still, Lyotard's ideas remain powerful as a diagnosis of the contemporary state of the academy. They also provide a helpful means by which to account for the changes that philosophy has undergone within the Neoliberal University. Famously, Lyotard defines postmodernity in terms of "incredulity toward metanarratives."[3] As Nicholas C. Burbules notes, the incredulity Lyotard identifies is all too often misinterpreted as conscious rejection. It is more appropriately understood as an inability to believe wholeheartedly—a loss of conviction.[4] We are stuck with cultural frames of reference and narratives that can nonetheless no longer claim our unconditional allegiance. The metanarratives that have functioned within modernity to place science in a position of epistemic supremacy strike us as hollow or outdated, even if it is also true that we cannot think entirely outside them. Indeed, following Friedrich Nietzsche, Lyotard suggests that it is the supremacy of science itself that comes to undermine these grand narratives. In these circumstances, without an external discourse of legitimation, Lyotard argues, knowledge is judged according to criteria of "performativity."[5]

To explain his concept of performativity, Lyotard begins with a discussion of the "pragmatics" of scientific research.[6] According to Lyotard, fundamental features of scientific practice are altered in postmodernity. He identifies two central changes. First, there is an increase in the methods of scientific argumentation. Lyotard follows Gaston Bachelard in observing that the method of science is not unitary, as classically expounded by Aristotle, René Descartes, or J.S. Mill. Good scientific reasoning, he thinks, takes many incompatible forms which cannot, finally, be described in terms of a single, consistent canon or set of rules.[7] In such a situation, he writes,

> The principle of a universal metalanguage is replaced by the principle of a plurality of formal or axiomatic systems capable of arguing the truth of denotative statements; these systems are described by a metalanguage that is universal but not consistent. What used to pass as paradox, and even paralogism, in the

knowledge of classical or modern science can, in certain of these systems, acquire a new force of conviction and win the acceptance of the community of experts.[8]

In effect, Lyotard argues for the disunity of science, at least in its postmodern form. Second, he suggests that the processes by which scientific statements are demonstrated as true have become much more sophisticated, generally requiring new and expensive technological means.[9] The important point here is that science is technologically mediated to an unprecedented degree, so that the work of conducting a scientific study or observation requires advanced computing and other devices. In postmodernity, science is nearly inconceivable without advanced technology. Postmodern science is therefore technoscience.[10] Rather than the modernist image of a unitary system of knowledge, there is now a multiplicity of technosciences which cannot be reduced one to the next or fully translated into the terms of a higher order discourse. In the process, the distinctions and oppositions characteristic of modernity (e.g., those between culture and nature or politics and science) become blurred.

The second thesis in particular has implications for the politics and economics of knowledge. After all, the technosciences require massive social expenditure in order to fund their research. As Lyotard elaborates, "A new problem appears: devices that optimize the performance of the human body for the purpose of producing proof require additional expenditures. No money, no proof—and that means no verification."[11] Integrated with and mediated by high technology, scientific research is absorbed into the broader productive economy as a site of social investment and expenditure. At the same time, the economy, particularly in the Western metropolitan centers of global capitalism, is itself increasingly technologically mediated and integrated into the very production of knowledge. Postmodernity therefore sees the rise of the "knowledge economy."[12] Lyotard follows Karl Marx very closely in considering the reasons for and implications of this fact. Essentially, investment in technology serves to optimize production by increasing efficiency, therefore reducing the average labor-time necessary to produce any given commodity. Automation and other labor-saving technologies, generally speaking, increase profit by maximizing output relative to input. It is this logic of optimization through technologically produced efficiencies—what I term "technologies of optimization"—that Lyotard highlights with the concept of performativity.

The broad logic of performativity, then, is "return on investment," where investment is aimed at optimizing the ratio between given inputs and related outputs. As they are increasingly technologically mediated and dependent on funding, the technosciences are submitted to the criterion of performativity. On the one hand, they are an economic factor in their own right, becoming, as Lyotard puts it, a "force of production."[13] On the other hand, owing to a "generalized spirit of performativity," they too are submitted to this criterion.[14] Within this "generalized spirit," that which performs, that which optimizes through enhanced productivity, is good and that which does not perform is bad. As Kirsten Locke summarizes, "Performativity as a kind of logic and in relation to discursive effects, is a *normative* force on systems: inefficiency is not, and will not, [sic] be tolerated in efficient systems."[15] A worthy investment in the technosciences is one that will produce the greatest return by enhancing the functioning of the system, its efficient transformation of input into output. Economic discourses, discourses of investment, optimization, and maximized efficiency, come to govern scientific practice so that only those forms or directions of research that promise to increase profit or augment power are funded. Lyotard therefore writes,

> The production of proof, which is in principle only part of an argumentation process designed to win agreement from the addressees of scientific messages, thus falls under the control of another language game, in which the goal is no longer truth, but performativity—that is, the best possible input/output equation.[16]

Scientific truth is subordinated to power and profit.

For the purposes of understanding Neoliberal Philosophy, it is important to recognize that, under the totalizing dominance of economic discourses, those forms of research that do not promise to perform are not funded and, through economic starvation, they are either left to slowly languish or are more directly committed to the flames. It is not so much that whatever is profitable is true or that the truth is always profitable; rather, only research that promises profit and which serves to augment power can be successful since only such research will be funded. As alluded to in the introduction, however, performativity should not be conceived merely as a constraint on an otherwise independent process of research. Rather, it is itself productive in that it spurs research in directions that are perceived as potentially lucrative investments.

As applied to education, performativity has a number of important consequences, which will be explored in greater depth throughout the remainder of this chapter. Within the framework of performativity, according to Lyotard, higher education is understood as an investment that must contribute to the optimization of the social system as a whole. "Accordingly," he writes, "it will have to create the skills that are indispensable to that system."[17] He divides these skills into two broad types: (1) those aimed at enhancing the position of the nation-state in its competition with others worldwide and (2) those aimed at meeting the essential needs of the society internally.[18] In either instance, education is conceived as an investment and the goal is to optimize the ratio of input to output. The question posed at the level of the nation-state is how best to invest in higher education in order to maximize the returns in the form of economic growth and to remain competitive globally—that is, how to produce technologies of optimization. As I have already suggested in chapter 1, these are the criteria used by policy makers at all levels in funding decisions and policy regarding education in the era of neoliberalism. Ultimately, the university comes to serve a number of functions when the criterion of performativity is applied. It retains the older function of professional training for those who will join the elite professions. Yet, simultaneously, it is required to train a new class of "intellectuals" whose work will be particularly oriented toward the knowledge economy. Finally, in this functional role and in an environment of increasing technological change and technologically produced unemployment, higher education serves the purpose of continuing adult education and credentialing.[19]

Robin Usher notes an important implication of the concept of performativity that is necessary to the analysis to come, though it is not clearly articulated by Lyotard. Namely, social actors in a world of generalized performativity must *perform their performativity*.[20] The worthiness of an investment, its possibility for payoff, has to be communicated and must therefore become part of a broader symbolic economy or semiotics. This point applies as much to corporations as it does to universities and the academics within them. As Usher puts it, "By consuming the signs with which the knowledge they produce is endowed, universities communicate or 'show' something about themselves and thus position themselves (and equally are themselves positioned) in relation to other universities, government, business and communities."[21] He uses the example of research funding to explain the point. Winning a grant has value in terms of its absolute dollar amount and the knowledge that will then be produced through it. But, perhaps as important, it also communicates to outside actors that one is "research active" and therefore worthy of further investment, indeed worthier than other possible investments. Usher concludes, "Research performance assessment regimes can be seen therefore as a technology that responds to performativity's demand to 'tell and show' to various audiences, the so-called 'stake-holders' outside as well as within the disciplines."[22] The demand of the criterion of performativity is that one must optimize functioning in order to produce return on investment. But the fact of optimization is insufficient unto itself—it must be transformed into a symbol within a broader symbolic economy. One must enter into the economic discourse of performativity and its semiotic universe to demonstrate performativity. It is this performance of performativity that I have in mind in what follows when I discuss "marketing" as a strategy of individual philosophers and philosophy departments.

In chapter 1, I discussed Fesmire's analysis of the "industrial model" of education. Within this model, Fesmire argues, education is conceived as a sector of the economy which is tasked with contributing to the broader economy through the "manufacture" of skilled labor.[23] With Lyotard's concept of performativity in hand, we may now further clarify this point. The role of education is understood, not only as the manufacture of ready-made goods, as perhaps suggested by Fesmire's analysis, but as the production of technologies of optimization. Broadly speaking, higher education is tasked with training workers who offer maximal gains to productivity relative to training costs and who have the capacity to increase productivity over time with greater investment in their knowledge and skills. Just like workers, higher education must itself, furthermore, perpetually update to remain competitive through optimization. The watchword is "continuous improvement." Everyone will do more with less. Within this context, actors at all levels must market themselves to appear worthy of investment—that is, demonstrate value as a contribution to output relative to other potential investments.

Clearly, the situation of philosophy as a discipline is especially tenuous in these circumstances. The contribution of the technosciences to the optimal functioning of society, understood in narrowly economic terms, is relatively plain for all to see. Those disciplines certainly seem to be a worthy investment. Thus the recent enthusiasm for so-called STEM education. Why, however, should society invest in philosophy when the return on investment in terms of optimal functioning would clearly be greater if the resources were directed elsewhere? Indeed, what does philosophy contribute to the functioning of society in the first place? How does it provide the skills necessary to meet "workforce needs" internally and enhance the "global competitiveness" of the nation-state externally?

These questions become more urgent if we follow Lyotard in recognizing the obsolescence of the metanarratives structuring modernity. In Lyotard's analysis, we must recall, the traditional role of philosophy was to provide the narrative basis necessary to legitimate science, which was understood as a unified system of knowledge. However, within the postmodern context, this demand for legitimation is no longer relevant. The methodological pluralism of the sciences discussed above means that the knowledge produced by the technosciences need not conform to any external canon or set of rules. The sciences are epistemically autonomous. Moreover, the social legitimacy of the sciences is guaranteed not by an appeal to an overarching narrative or transcendent value but precisely by their performativity. Hence, Lyotard writes, "Speculative or humanistic philosophy is forced to relinquish its legitimation duties, which explains why philosophy is facing a crisis wherever it persists in arrogating such functions and is reduced to the study of systems of logic or the history of ideas where it has been realistic enough to surrender them."[24] Rather than standing above the fray of scientific research to provide a universal, integrative discourse of legitimation, philosophy takes place alongside them on epistemically flattened terrain. Divested of its traditional role, philosophy is forced to submit to the criterion of performativity.

Following McCumber, I observed in the introduction that philosophy departments and the individual philosophers within them act strategically to preserve and enhance their relative position and to ensure their survival and autonomy. In McCumber's account, such strategic action took the form primarily of what he called "stealth" in the Cold War era. Essentially, philosophers and research programs that would "fly under the radar" of religious and McCarthyist critics were favored.[25] Indeed, as he documents, administrators at the university and the department levels took it upon themselves to preemptively police and surveil colleagues and potential hires in an effort to avoid more draconian interventions.[26] By contrast, philosophers now face a new strategic imperative in the Neoliberal University: They must market themselves in order to appear worthy of investment. With Lyotard's conception of performativity in place, we are now in a better position to examine the significance of this reality. Situated on an even epistemic playing field with the technosciences, philosophy is judged according to the criterion of performativity. It must therefore enter into the semiotic universe of economic discourse and communicate how it contributes to the enhanced productivity of the social whole. It must perform its performativity. At the same time, the social whole is reimagined in strictly economic terms and dissolved into a multitude of competing, responsibilized enterprises functioning at varying scales. Ultimately, in a competitive educational marketplace dedicated to providing the training necessary for enhanced productive employment, philosophy must market itself as providing the skills required for success in this new economy.

As I will show in the remainder of this chapter, such marketing increasingly shapes philosophical pedagogy. I turn to the effects of these imperatives on research, scholarship, and the production of knowledge more broadly in the upcoming chapter. In the remaining sections, I focus on the ways that marketing, in the sense of the performance of performativity, plays out in philosophy in its educational role. What does philosophy claim to contribute to the optimization of the functioning of society and how does it demonstrate and communicate this claim to its various audiences understood as potential investors? Before I can fully answer this question, however, a first look is required at human capital theory and its role in the construction of the Neoliberal University.

HUMAN CAPITAL AND TECHNOLOGIES OF OPTIMIZATION

The idea of education as producing technologies of optimization is the central thread of what is known as "human capital theory," possibly the most significant driver of education policy globally and in the United States today. As underscored by then-Secretary of Education Arne Duncan in remarks to the World Bank in 2011, "Education today is inseparable from the development of human capital."[27] The theory of human capital begins from the assumption, known as the Marginal Productivity Theory of Distribution, that workers' wages are equal to the marginal product of their labor. The likely originator of this thesis, J.H. von Thünen, stated the idea as follows: "The wage is equal to the extra product *of* the last labourer who is employed in a large enterprise."[28] A profit-maximizing firm could not pay more in total wages than what is necessary to increase marginal product. After all, it would profit more if it did not do so. On the other hand, it could not pay less without decreasing its output, thereby again decreasing its profit. From this assumption, it is supposed to follow that increases in worker productivity are met with increases in wage. In a competitive labor market, workers who are more productive, whose employment contributes more to the marginal product, will be paid more.

The theory of human capital builds on this thesis regarding marginal productivity. The central idea of human capital theory is that enhancements to human capital increase workers' marginal productivity. As defined by Angel Gurría, secretary general of the Organisation of Economic Co-operation and Development (OECD), human capital is the "knowledge, skills, competencies, and attributes that allow people to contribute to their personal and social well-being, as well as that of their countries."[29] It is through the utilization or activation of human capital that workers' labor contributes to commodity production and thus to a thriving personal and national life. According to neoliberal economic theory, the failure to account for human capital hobbled classical economic theory. In his foundational, "Investment in Human Capital," T.W. Schultz proclaims,

> The failure to treat human resources explicitly as a form of capital, as a produced means of production, as the product of investment, has fostered the retention of the classical notion of labor as a capacity to do manual work requiring little knowledge or skill, a capacity with which, according to this notion, laborers are endowed about equally. This notion of labor was wrong in the classical period and it is patently wrong now.[30]

In other words, the theory of human capital considers the worker not merely as labor, as a "factor of production," but as a "produced means of production," which can be enhanced and optimized for maximal output. A simple example: the labor of most secretaries requires some minimum ability to use word processing applications, such that secretaries with an enhanced ability to do so may be more productive and secretaries falling below a minimum threshold may be entirely unproductive. The skill of word processing, then, contributes to productivity and is therefore human capital which might be optimized or enhanced—for instance, through training courses, daily exercises, or regular upskilling of one kind or another. A rational firm will invest in such enhancements, according to human capital theory, to maximize the marginal productivity of secretaries they employ. Yet classical liberal economics largely overlooked this.[31] In contrast, Schultz, Gary Becker, and other proponents of human capital theory set out to explain such investments and their broader economic impact.

For Becker, the most famous proponent of human capital theory, a profit-maximizing firm would invest neither more nor less in human capital than would contribute to greater productivity in the future. He expresses this in the equation: $MP_0' + G = W_0 + C$.[32] This equation requires some unpacking. MP_0' represents the difference between what could have been produced had the worker continued working rather than training and what is actually produced given that the worker is engaged instead in training. Broadly, G represents the return on the investment—namely, the difference between future receipts and future outlays. Thus, the left-hand of the equation represents the net marginal productivity of the worker. On the right-hand side, there are the costs to the firm. W_0 represents wages and C represents the opportunity costs and expenditures required for the training. As explained by Becker, "If training were given only during the initial period, expenditures during the initial period would equal wages plus the outlay on training, expenditures during other periods would equal wages alone, and receipts during all periods would equal marginal products."[33] Ultimately, the rational, profit-maximizing firm would invest in the human capital of the worker precisely to the extent that the value of increased future marginal productivity was equal to the value of all related costs.[34]

The relationship between capitalist firms investing in on-the-job training and education may seem somewhat obscure. A first step in recognizing the connection is to recall the transformation in *homo economicus* identified by Foucault as central to neoliberalism. Like its antecedent and namesake, Foucault argues, neoliberalism places a vision of the individual human being as *homo economicus* at its center. Unlike classical liberal economics, however, the neoliberal conception of *homo economicus* is radically altered. In classical liberalism, this figure is represented as one who is driven to satisfy needs through exchange on the marketplace. By contrast, in the neoliberal vision *homo economicus* is recast as one who acts, in Foucault's terms, as an "entrepreneur of himself." This person is both a capitalist and also human capital to be productively utilized.[35] The driving aim of liberal thought, whether classical or neo-, is to free *homo economicus* from meddlesome interference by the state and by this means to promote the greatest good. Within the classical framework, this was to have taken place through the satisfaction of needs by means of market exchange. In the neoliberal context, by contrast, competition between profit-seeking "firms" is thought to drive innovation, create new markets, and promote greater productivity.

Like the firm employing them, then, the worker is also considered to be, in Becker's analysis, an entrepreneurial enterprise seeking to maximize earnings through the utilization of human capital. Just as the capitalist employing the worker seeks to maximize the worker's productivity in order to produce profit, so, too, the worker seeks to maximize their own productivity in order to command increased wages. For example, a secretary may invest in training software or classes in order to improve their word processing skills and thereby command a higher wage in the labor market. All the equations which are supposed to describe the behavior of the rational capitalist firm are thus also taken to describe the behavior of the worker; the worker is an entrepreneur investing in their sole asset, their human capital, and their return on investment amounts to maximization of earnings, whether in the form of "money income" or in the form of "psychic income," as Becker explains.[36] His analysis, he writes, is "from the viewpoint of workers."[37] The worker is both, then, a form of capital that can be enhanced—a "produced means of production," a technology of optimization—and simultaneously a capitalist seeking to maximize return on investment. Foucault explains this shift as follows: "[W]e adopt the point of view of the worker and, for the first time, ensure that the worker is not present in the economic analysis as an object—the object of supply and demand in the form of labor power—but as an active economic agent."[38]

Human capital theory takes for granted the substitution of training for education discussed in chapter 1. "Schooling," as Becker is wont to call it, is an investment in human capital with the purpose of accruing a future return on investment in the form of increased marginal earnings and this is achieved through gains in productivity. The ends of training are external to the process and consist in the enhancement of labor for the purpose of its profitable exploitation by both the capitalist and the worker. The training offered in a school differs from on-the-job training only in that the primary function of the school is to produce such knowledge or skills; that is, the school is a kind of "knowledge factory" for the manufacture of human capital, a producer of technologies of optimization.[39]

In considering whether to invest in "schooling," the rational worker will act to maximize earnings through investments in human capital that maximize their productivity. Becker expresses this with the equation: $W = MP - k$. The left-hand side of the equation, W, represents the worker's net earnings; it is the difference between what could have been earned if the person had skipped schooling and what is actually earned while in school. The right-hand side is the worker's marginal product (MP) minus the total direct costs (k) of "schooling." Given that they are rational and seek to maximize their earnings, a worker will forego investment in schooling only if their net earnings would otherwise exceed the value of the gains in marginal product (substitutable for the marginal wage), factoring in the direct costs associated. Likewise, were their present net earnings less than the value of such gains, they would forego some present earnings to invest them in education.[40] To summarize human capital theory, education increases marginal productivity by enhancing human capital, thereby increasing earnings. As succinctly outlined by Simon Marginson, for human capital theory, "Education, work, productivity and earnings are seen in a linear continuum. When educated students acquire the embodied productivity (the portable human capital) used by employers, graduate earnings follow."[41] The present is always an opportunity for investment, from this perspective, and one must invest prudently in education in order to ensure that the future is one of growth and maximized prosperity, whether in the form of money or "psychic income."

Importantly, the theory is applied not only to individuals, but to social actors at all scales. It is taken, therefore, not only as a theory of individual earnings, but also as a theory of economic development and growth at the macro scale. To see why, one must note that, according to classical liberal economic theory, total product is the result of "four factors of production": land, capital, entrepreneurship, and labor. For there to be greater total product, at whatever scale, there must be an increase somewhere in the inputs, in the factors of production. From this, one may reason that growth in capital relative to labor, would result in an increase in capital-intensive production—the means of production being now in greater supply and cheaper than labor itself. But in the 1950s and 1960s, Schultz and others observed that this was not what had occurred in the United States in the early part of the twentieth century. Rather, despite general economic growth, capital seemed to be employed *less intensively*. How was this possible, they asked? Furthermore, as Schultz noted, "The income of the United States has been increasing at a much higher rate than the combined amount of land, man-hours worked and stock of reproducible capital used to produce the income."[42] Again, how could such massive growth in product be explained in relation to the relatively low dynamic growth in inputs from the three factors of land, labor, and capital? To the progenitors of human capital theory, the answer—or at least an answer—seemed apparent. Human capital had not been accounted for. As Schultz explained in his "Reflections on Investment in Man,"

> the inclusion of human capital will show that the ratio of *all* capital to income is not declining. Producer goods—structures, equipment, and inventories—a particular stock of capital has been declining relative to income. Meanwhile, however, the stock of human capital has been rising relative to income.[43]

The secret to sustained economic growth was not increasingly capital-intensive production, at least not in the sense of physical capital. It was instead to be found in increased human capital; production had become increasingly knowledge- and skills-intensive.

Despite its many failings, this theory is the mainstream of economic thought. Given the "general spirit of performativity," the mainstream of economic theory is also the governing form of rationality in our time. Global institutions focused on economic development, from the OECD to the World Economic Forum to the World Bank, are devoted to the enhancement of human capital.[44] The essential pieces of the framework produced by Becker and Schultz remain intact. To take only one example, the World Bank now offers a "Human Capital Index" that measures the differences between actual productivity and possible productivity for countries on the basis of various metrics concerning investment in human capital.[45] As explained in the description for the video introducing the project to the public, "We can end poverty and create more inclusive societies by developing human capital."[46] The video itself tells the story of "Anna," explaining that investments in health and education will shape not only her life but also that of her generation, her country, and the world as a whole. Regarding human capital, the video asserts, "The math is simple, but powerful."[47] This reduction of economic growth and development—not to mention Anna's life—to a simple math problem that reproduces at every scale, however, is almost absurdly inadequate. Nonetheless, as Foucault enabled us to see, it is indeed *powerful*. Why, for example, are some countries economically developed while others are not? Do the math.

In accord with the "general spirit of performativity," as Foucault argues, this neoliberal thinking generalizes a conception of the economic across social domains and views economic explanation as valid for human behavior tout court. There are a number of intellectual operations underlying this totalization. First, it cleaves economic behavior from other domains or aspects of human life; this allows the identification and sequestration, so to speak, of an object or region of study which may then be called "the economy." As Brown makes clear, this requires that economic activity be construed in relation to a constitutive outside—that which is "non-economic."[48] One is then able to abstract *homo economicus* from the concrete individuals occupying a multitude of roles in the world and whose actions or behavior might be guided in any given instance by non-economic beliefs, motives, or desires. Importantly, as Brown indicates, "the economy" is not therefore a transhistorical object or an eternal essence. Rather, it is historical through and through. Next, the totalization of the economy extends the abstract image of *homo economicus* produced through the first operation across domains, thereby reducing all of that which was previously bracketed as non-economic to this newly formed abstraction. For example, child rearing may now be conceptualized as an economic activity, but only after having been initially bracketed from consideration as "non-economic." A final operation involves the collapse of the descriptive, explanatory, and normative so that appeals to *homo economicus* are taken simultaneously as descriptions of basic human nature, explanations of various behavior and phenomena, and finally norms of rationality to which one ought to conform. The individual human being is (economically) rational and the phenomena of individual and collective life can be explained by this innate (economic) rationality. Those who behave irrationally (from an economic perspective) are defective, and competition should and will punish accordingly.[49]

Brown's revisions and criticisms of Foucault are important here. She points out some significant oversights in Foucault's treatment of neoliberalism. First, Foucault emphasizes the concept of "interest" and the characterization of *homo economicus* as self-interested. As Brown notes, however, and the above discussion of the collapse of scales should help to explain, self-sacrifice is now a significant demand placed on the neoliberal subject.[50] Much as then-President George W. Bush encouraged Americans to go shopping in the aftermath of the 9/11 attacks, thereby coordinating individual interest and economic activity with the explicit aim of national economic recovery, so, too, neoliberal subjects are coordinated to the demands of ever-greater national output through the mechanisms of prudent self-investment. Even so, sacrifice is routinely demanded for the sake of "the economy" or some sector thereof. We must all chip in to preserve that which is "too big to fail." And what professor has not been enjoined to give more in order to meet the needs of students, prepare them for a brighter future, and ensure the competitiveness of the institution? We must all sacrifice at the altar of optimization in the name of greater prosperity.

Brown also highlights Foucault's failure to take *homo politicus* seriously. Foucault analyses the subject envisioned by liberalism as divided into two. On one side, this person is the economic subject identified by liberal economic theory as *homo economicus*. On the other side, this person is the juridical-legal subject of rule. It is only insofar as a person is both that the basic issue of liberal thought can emerge—namely, the limits to juridical-legal intervention into the economic activities of market actors. The goal for liberal theory is to draw the boundary beyond which juridical-legal authority may not be exercised over *homo economicus*. Brown argues convincingly, however, that through its entwinement with emergent democracy, liberalism already bears within itself a relation to the human being as a "political animal," understood as a being who is engaged along with others in self-rule and collective decision-making. As she writes, "This subject, *homo politicus*, forms the substance and legitimacy of whatever democracy might mean beyond securing the individual provisioning of individual ends; this 'beyond' includes political equality and freedom, representation, popular sovereignty, and deliberation and judgment about the public good and the common."[51] For Brown, in contrast to Foucault, this question is central: To what extent does neoliberalism allow a conception of the economic to subsume or eclipse the political? This reduction of the political to the economic is characteristic of the kind of one-dimensionality that I will discuss in the next chapter.

Finally, and equally importantly, Foucault repeats the erasure of gender (and one ought to add race, sexuality, and so on) characteristic of the liberal conception of *homo economicus*.[52] On the one hand, for Brown, the failure to gender *homo economicus* serves to make women and women's labor invisible. It treats the male head of household as an independent and autonomous subject who exists outside of relations of care and reproduction even as it evacuates power from the domestic sphere—an obvious fiction well documented by feminists. But Brown goes beyond this to point out that this fiction has practical effects within neoliberalism: namely, the intensification and transformation of women's labor. As she explains, women are faced with a dilemma: "Either women align their own conduct with this truth, becoming *homo economicus*, in which case the world becomes uninhabitable, or women's activities and bearing as *femina domestica* remain the unavowed glue for a world whose governing principle cannot hold it together, in which case women occupy their old place as unacknowledged props and supplements to masculinist liberal subjects."[53] By erasing gender and other dimensions of identity, including their imbrication with profit and the social division of labor, neoliberalism not only covers over identity-based oppressions, it further reproduces them in an intensified and altered form.[54] A single woman of color who is a working mother, for instance, must make different "investment choices" based on what is likely to "pay off" given her resources and social position than a white male counterpart with no children. To the extent that she acts as a competitive economic agent, she must either neglect obligations to care for her children or work day and night to simultaneously augment her human capital—despite her more limited employment prospects and guaranteed lower pay—while also "investing" time, energy, and scarce financial resources into her children. From the neoliberal perspective, such a person, should they fail to compete, is essentially detritus, an obsolescent form of humanity.

With the rise of neoliberalism, a normative conception of human existence thus emerges predicated on the dual image of the human being as both an entrepreneur of themselves and as human capital. The dominance of this form of economic rationality has led to what education scholar Mark Garrison has called the "skillsification of education."[55] As Garrison remarks, "Even a casual observation of education policy discourse would reveal the extent to which any possibly valued human attribute is now rendered as a skill."[56] In general, human capital theory will refer to an indefinite list of qualities that might be understood as human capital—generally to include such entities as "knowledge, skills, competencies, and attributes." These terms, however, float relatively free of any substantive definition and are largely understood and measured operationally by their supposed effects—namely, enhanced performativity. In education policy discourse and increasingly among the general public, the dominant form of human capital produced by the training offered in schools is understood as a "bundle of skills."[57] Thus, for example, in its *New Vision for Education* report, the World Economic Forum provides a list of the skills needed for the twenty-first century, which are divided into categories of "foundational literacies," "competencies," and "character qualities."[58] The report explains, "To thrive in today's innovation-driven economy, workers need a different mix of skills than in the past."[59] It goes on to discuss the possible contribution of new technologies to achieving the required enhancement. Here again, schools are imagined as factories for the manufacture of human capital, the production of technologies of optimization. Such technologies largely take the form of performance-oriented skills and can itself be enhanced through the application of technologies of optimization. This broad vision is a consequence of the dominance of performativity as articulated through human capital theory. It was already predicted by Lyotard:

> Having competence in a performance-oriented skill does indeed seem saleable in the condition [in which grand narratives of legitimation are no longer the principal driving force behind interest in acquiring knowledge], and it is efficient by definition. . . . This creates the prospect for a vast market for competence in operational skills.[60]

For investors in human capital, the significant question they must pose is: What skills may I invest in to produce the greatest return on investment? And social actors at all scales are imagined as enterprising investors in human capital.

CRITICAL THINKING AS HUMAN CAPITAL

Human capital theory conceives of students as entrepreneurs of themselves. Students enter into a marketplace of educational commodities purportedly designed to increase their marginal productivity and they must invest wisely; that is, spend their time, foregone earnings, and tuition dollars on developing the bundle of skills desired by potential future employers. But it is not only students who must make such investments. Educational institutions, states, and indeed social actors at all scales must consider where and how to invest in order to remain competitive, attract corporations, retain jobs, and ensure future economic growth and development. Likewise, lacking any further claim to legitimacy, academic philosophy must enter into the semiotic universe of such economic discourse and communicate its value as an investment. In this context, philosophy performs its performativity. It markets itself. Academic philosophy is now called upon to show that it can produce technologies of optimization, thereby providing return on investment. To survive in the context of the Neoliberal University, where education is considered a private consumer good and is conceived as training, philosophy sells critical thinking skills.[61] As I will show, this marketing of philosophy ultimately comes to shape curricula and pedagogy.

The centrality of such marketing efforts and their strategic rationale can be gleaned from the website of the American Philosophical Association (APA), the central disciplinary organization for philosophers in the United States. One finds there a "Department Advocacy Toolkit" designed to aid departments in advocating for philosophy on their campus and in their community. As explained on the APA website, "Motivated by our belief in the value of philosophy, the Department Advocacy Toolkit is intended to provide strategies that might be useful to programs that are at risk, programs hoping to insulate themselves against future risk, and programs aiming to strengthen and/or expand."[62] Clearly, philosophy is regarded as a foolish investment by many. So at-risk departments must answer the questions and concerns of potential investors and consumers. *What can you do with a philosophy degree? How much can you make? How does philosophy contribute to meeting the state's workforce needs?* These are the questions that the toolkit is supposed to help philosophy departments answer publicly to its "stakeholders."

The authors of the "Department Advocacy Toolkit" insist on the value of philosophy, which they explain by reference to the APA's "Statement on the Role of Philosophy in Higher Education." Regarding the value of philosophy, they quote from the statement as follows:

> The discipline of philosophy contributes in an indispensable way to the realization of four goals that should be fundamental to any institution of higher

learning: instilling habits of critical thinking in students; enhancing their reading, writing, and public speaking skills; transmitting cultural heritages to them; stimulating them to engage fundamental questions about reality, knowledge, and value.[63]

Indeed, these four contributions are only the ones considered most fundamental. The authors extend the list further by noting that philosophy plays an important role in the core curriculum at most institutions, engages productively with other disciplines, whether as part of interdisciplinary programs or through reflection on their basic concepts and methods, and contributes to society more broadly through engagement with various public audiences beyond the confines of campus.[64]

Importantly, the statement eventually turns to the question of how one might measure success for philosophy programs. It cautions against the use of metrics related to grants and enrollments since philosophical research is relatively inexpensive and unlikely to require or seek out large grants. Plus, incoming undergraduates often lack prior exposure to philosophy. Instead, the statement indicates that "employment prospects" should be the chief measure of programmatic success. The authors write, "Because the cost of a college education continues to rise, quite often more rapidly than inflation, students want their investment to pay off by improving their prospects of employment."[65] Whatever their value or contribution to higher education may be, the success of philosophy programs should be measured in terms of the "marketable skills" that they provide to students. While certainly not incommensurable or contradictory, this view of how to measure success sits uneasily alongside the central claims concerning the value of philosophy which are also quoted in the toolkit. How does asking fundamental questions translate into increased productivity? It seems to me at least that there is a good case to be made that the situation is quite the opposite.

Within the toolkit, there is a section called "Marketing Philosophy," which opens by emphasizing the importance of marketing. The authors explain, "Philosophers tend not to think much about selling ourselves or our profession. But as with any major or profession, students are interested in hearing about who studies philosophy and what that person does with his or her major."[66] The strategic imperative for a program that is at risk or may be in the future, or even a program that seeks to strengthen itself, is to market philosophy to, among other potential investors or consumers, prospective majors. Once again, one finds an emphasis on the marketable skills—human capital, technologies of optimization—that philosophy purportedly provides. Thus, the APA offers a page of "Resources for Undergraduates."[67] The resources amount to a list of hyperlinks divided into three main sections: "Why Study Philosophy?," "Resources," and "After Graduation." All three sections link to arguments for the "return on investment" from a philosophy degree, with the "Why Study Philosophy?" section in particular hosting multiple links to a genre of webpage that I will designate with the acronym WSP. The link provided to the Department of Philosophy at the University of North Carolina (UNC), for example, opens by insisting that the best reason to major in philosophy is "because you love it."[68] But, predictably, it shifts immediately to a discussion of brass tacks. Here again, one finds a nearly overwhelming number of links to various articles. By the end of the page, one arrives at the bottom-line question: "How much money do philosophy majors make?"

While it may be true that many philosophy departments and programs lack a webpage that fits squarely within the WSP genre, it is also noteworthy that the general strategy of marketing philosophy by reference to critical thinking skills, employability, and return on investment in the form of increased earnings is very widespread. Consider the two programs that are the most highly ranked by the *Philosophical Gourmet Report* (PGR).[69] The Philosophy Department at New York University (NYU), ranked first, assures interested students that "In a world where many college graduates will have more than one career, and specific job skills will continually become obsolete, employers increasingly value the all-purpose skills of analysis and expression that are taught in philosophy."[70] Like many others, they also mention that philosophy majors tend to score higher on various standardized tests required for admission into law school, medical school, and so on. Similar to UNC, the department at Rutgers University, ranked second, takes the common alternative approach of offering a list of links. Among the links, one finds a WSP page hosted by the Andrew W. Mellon Foundation with an interview profiling "legendary investor" Bill Miller.[71] The Mellon Foundation profile links back to the APA Blog, which features an interview with Miller in which he attributes his success as an investor to the critical thinking skills he learned as a philosophy student.[72] Through such profiles students are invited to an aspirational imagining of themselves as "maverick investors," innovative entrepreneurs who "think outside the box" to creatively envision "the next big thing." The "next big thing," it goes almost without saying, will be a "disruptive" high-tech "innovation" from Silicon Valley. In any case, these very influential departments are clearly concerned to market philosophy as offering enhancements to human capital.

These programs are well funded and large. They face very little risk of losing the support of their respective administrations. They are housed within universities with very large endowments and a great deal of public support. Yet they market themselves to students in much the way advised by the APA for programs that are "at risk": philosophy provides human capital in the form of critical thinking and other skills that pay off in higher earnings after graduation and are necessary within the knowledge economy. One may still insist that philosophy is valuable for a number of other reasons. Nonetheless, the necessity remains that programs and departments *perform their performativity*.

Philosophy departments and programs throughout the country thereby participate in the skillsification of education, marketing themselves as distinctly suited to produce critical thinking skills. In this, they not only resonate with the broader skillsification phenomenon, but more importantly present themselves as providers of the skills that are viewed by many as the most significant human capital within the knowledge economy. As emphasized by "21st Century Skills" gurus Bernie Trilling and Charles Fadel, "Critical thinking and problem solving are considered by many to be the new basics of 21st century learning."[73] Why are these skills so important? Trilling and Fadel explain that the "new world of work is demanding higher levels of expert thinking and complex communicating."[74] Critical thinking, problem solving, communication, and collaboration are therefore "the key learning and knowledge work skills that address these new work skill demands."[75] In higher education, this outlook is further represented, among other places, in the "essential learning outcomes" touted by the Association of American Colleges and Universities (AAC&U).[76] According to the report of the AAC&U's most recent survey of business executives and hiring managers, titled "Fulfilling the American Dream: Liberal Education and the Future of Work,"

> When hiring, executives and hiring managers place a high priority on graduates' demonstrated proficiency in skills and knowledge that cut across majors, and hiring managers are closely aligned with executives in the importance that they place on key college learning outcomes. The college learning outcomes that both audiences rate as most important include oral communication, critical thinking, ethical judgment, working effectively in teams, working independently, self-motivation, written communication, and real-world application of skills and knowledge.[77]

It is no accident, then, that the APA "Department Advocacy Toolkit" identifies "critical-thinking and problem-solving skills and qualities," "oral and written communication skills and qualities," and "teamwork, collaboration, and leadership skills" as among the "skills and competencies" produced by the study of philosophy, linking to the AAC&U's Valid Assessment of Learning for Undergraduate Education or "VALUE" rubrics, among other resources.[78]

It could be thought that the teaching of critical thinking and other skills is salutary since it prepares students for life beyond college, producing in them qualities that will be useful to them far beyond the context of the study of arcane philosophical texts. In this way, marketing philosophy as producing critical thinking skills would only highlight the important work that an education in philosophy does even for non-majors, who will not likely remember Descartes's name or be able to summarize or analyze the Cartesian Circle even months after their philosophy class. Philosophy departments benefit because they are able to continue to attract "investment." Students benefit because they are able to continue developing the important skills philosophy imparts, enhancing their marginal productivity. The nation benefits because it has a highly competitive workforce capable of winning the global competition for jobs. The invisible hand strikes again.

The problem with this point of view emerges more fully, when one considers the disappeared social relations that support the skills market. In this marketplace, critical thinking and associated skills appear as items of exchange, the value of which is determined not by "use" but instead by their value as commodities. The production and distribution of critical thinking are guided neither by need nor by pleasure nor by virtue. Rather, as commodities, skills are produced and distributed to serve the market, ultimately for the production of profit. Moreover, whether or not it is true that philosophy enhances students' critical thinking, and however one conceives critical thinking, this now-commodified skill is supposed to be utilized within a context in which the general spirit of performativity prevails unquestioned. Whatever it is that one thinks about, and whatever one's purpose in thinking, performativity is to remain the taken-for-granted background—the ultimate value—that guides all thought in advance.

As Marianna Papastephanou and Charoula Angeli make clear, these changes result in an increasing emphasis on what they call, following Jürgen Habermas, "strategic-purposive rationality."[79] Critical thinking becomes a form of strategic-purposive rationality insofar as it is oriented to the assessment of efficiency in the utilization of means to achieve desired ends, rather than the evaluation of ends themselves. It thus treats others from a strategic perspective, as either conducive toward or an obstacle to the goal of the efficient realization of a given purpose. To establish this point, Papastephanou and Angeli distinguish between two dominant conceptions of critical thinking: the rationalist and the technicist.[80] In explanation, they write, "The rationalist perspective assumes the highest critical distance from emotions, context and prejudice and almost no distance at all from what it perceives as universally valid criteriology."[81] That is, the rationalist view posits that there is a universal definition of critical thinking and that it involves "objectivity," in the sense of the neutralization of bias of whatever kind. Papastephanou and Angeli are rightly critical of this rationalist conception for its willingness to treat the criteria for thinking critically as universally valid and objective. As they write, "Some criteria may appear to [a community of thinkers be it a lifeworld or scientific community] as self-evident, axiomatic, universal, but whether they are indeed so is never, or rarely, conclusive."[82] It should be further clear that such criteria function as a form of what I called discipline policing in the introduction. That is, given that there is no universal agreement regarding the definition or criteria by which one might judge critical thinking, asserting such criteria is not really to define critical thinking. It is to bring thinking into line with a particular normative conception. It insists on norms of legitimacy that one must appeal to in a culture of legitimation.[83]

Perhaps more important, however, the broad social context within which critical thinking takes place is taken for granted. Why does one think (critically)? For what purpose or to what end? What values, desires, or emotions guide and motivate (critical) thinking? In connection with this point, Loughead invokes the work of Simone de Beauvoir, who pointed to the contradictions in the attitude of what she termed the "critic." Insofar as the position of the "critical thinker" unwittingly serves values which it refuses to take responsibility for or regard as freely chosen, according to Beauvoir, it falls into the trap of what she calls "seriousness." That is, the critical thinker may act in bad faith by reifying their own subjective values, treating them as objectively given laws and, thus, concealing their own "choice" or "freedom." As Beauvoir puts it, "Instead of the independent mind he claims to be, [the critic] is only the shameful servant of a cause to which he has not chosen to rally."[84] Of students who have been taught the rules of logic and the attitude of objectivity, Loughead thus writes, "they might just wield a limited tool; able only to critique others when they commit some logical fallacy, but not able to think about what they are doing, why it is relevant, who and what power it serves and why."[85] Put somewhat paradoxically, one is hardly thinking (critically) if one fails to interrogate and take responsibility for the values and related desires and emotions that guide (critical) thinking or imagines that thought can somehow be lifted above or outside the social world and matrices of power within which it occurs.

In contrast to this rationalist vision, the technicist conception of critical thinking views it in terms of the capacity to solve problems and achieve desired ends. As Papastephanou and Angeli explain, this perspective, "reinstates situatedness and appropriates it only for the sake of optimizing outcomes."[86] This conception of critical thinking removes it from the presumed objectivity and reliance on putatively universally valid criteria of the rationalist conception. Instead, it situates the critical thinker within a system of values and activities in which they are already involved, justifying its canon of rules only in terms of the ends of the thinker. For this very reason, however, it falls into much the same trap as the rationalist view. It fails to question the social system and values that produce the ends to which critical thinking is applied. Papastephanou and Angeli provide a vivid example: "If applied to a specific domain, e.g., the army industry, this entails more or less that an employee is a critical thinker when she performs successfully the undertaken tasks and perhaps accomplishes modifications that will refine the tasks and effect a better outcome (e.g. a 'smart' bomb)."[87] In a sense, one can say that, for the technicist, critical thinking is value-neutral—after all, it amounts to the capacity, within context, to achieve one's desired ends and places no particular constraint on which ends one ought to pursue. In another sense, however, it is value-saturated. It commands performativity itself as an absolute value and fails to acknowledge that the ends pursued (indeterminate as they may be) are set in advance by the taken-for-granted social framework. That this dominant technicist conception has largely eclipsed the rationalist conception is evident in the frequent coupling of critical thinking with "problem-solving," a term that places obvious emphasis on the achievement of desired ends within a given practical context.

What does this tell us about Neoliberal Philosophy? Academic philosophy now markets itself as offering critical thinking skills. But, in a world in which the figure of *homo economicus* dominates our understanding of human life, such skills are subsumed by the economic calculations of the entrepreneurial self. In fact, this process is taken for granted and reiterated by the very strategy of marketing, which presupposes that the student is a consumer and an entrepreneur. Philosophy must sell itself in order to attract investment, it must perform performativity. It therefore offers critical thinking skills as human capital on the skills market. Within this framework, the teaching of critical thinking, however conceived, is subordinated to the demands of optimization. The motivational context and ends of thinking, the social system and values underwriting it, are taken for granted. Given the prior assumption of *homo economicus* these values are clear enough. The goal is to increase marginal productivity through optimization of production and one seeks this in order to increase earnings individually and ensure economic growth at larger scales. Earnings and growth are in themselves and absolutely valid ends. The purpose of critical thinking is given in advance and the value framework that poses this end remains itself occluded and unquestionable.

Sociologist Chris McMillan therefore describes critical thinking as the "pedagogical logic of late capitalism." Following Frederic Jameson and Slavoj Žižek, McMillan points to the capacity of capitalism to incorporate and co-opt apparently subversive tendencies or obstacles. "The resiliency of capitalism," he writes, "can then be explained by its recuperative capacity to not only include that which transgresses its boundaries, but to profit from it."[88] The knowledge economy calls for destruction but also for creation, it calls for new subjects who bring to the contemporary deluge of information and the exponential magnification of technical capacity abilities to analyze, interpret, and evaluate. "Yet," as McMillan explains, "while an 'edgy' and 'high-tech' capitalist economy encourages creativity and disruption, it is only to the extent that this mode of criticality enhances profitability: questioning the very principle of profit remains unprofitable."[89] In short, Neoliberal Philosophy adopts the pedagogical logic of late capitalism.

NOTES

1. Robert Frodeman and Adam Briggle discuss this development in terms drawn from early phenomenology. In their account, philosophy is now a "regional ontology"—that is, it involves knowledge of a special domain of entities or entities under a particular aspect (e.g., qua material). This would be in contrast to attempts to situate philosophy over and above other forms of inquiry as "transcendental phenomenology" or "fundamental ontology." See Robert Frodeman and Adam Briggle, *Socrates Tenured: The Institutions of 21st-Century Philosophy* (New York: Rowman & Littlefield, 2016), Kindle, 3. Justin Pack also describes what he terms the "hegemony of science" in the modern university, where all disciplines gain their epistemic legitimacy by presenting themselves as or claiming some proximity to the natural sciences. See Justin Pack, *How the Neoliberalization of Academia Leads to Thoughtlessness: Arendt and the Modern University* (Lanham, MD: Lexington Books, 2018), 83ff.

2. See Richard Edwards, "All Quiet on the Postmodern Front?" *Studies in Philosophy and Education* 25, no. 4 (July 2006), 273–278. Edwards nicely summarizes the literature and its relation to philosophy of education as well as the later history of the term during the first decade of the twenty-first century.

3. Jean-François Lyotard, *The Postmodern Condition*, trans. Geoff Bennington and Brian Massumi (Minneapolis: University of Minnesota Press, 1984), xxiv.

4. Nicholas Burbules, "Postmodernism and Education," in *The Oxford Handbook of Philosophy of Education*, ed. Harvey Siegel (New York: Oxford UP, 2009): 524–534; see also Robin Usher, "Lyotard's Performance" *Studies in Philosophy in Education* 25, no. 4 (July 2006), 280.

5. *The Postmodern Condition*, 41ff.

6. Lyotard relies heavily on Wittgenstein and the concept of "language-games" throughout *The Postmodern Condition*. While his interpretation of Wittgenstein is questionable in some important respects, the broad use that Lyotard makes of Wittgenstein's work is valuable. See Ludwig Wittgenstein, *Philosophical Investigations, Revised Fourth Edition*, eds. P.M.S. Hacker and Joachim Schulte and trans. G.E.M. Anscombe, P.M.S. Hacker, and Joachim Schulte (Malden, MA: Blackwell Publishing, 2009).

7. For a famous exposition and defense of "epistemological anarchism," which is likewise influenced by Wittgenstein, see Paul Feyerabend, *Against Method, Third Edition* (London: Verso Books, 1993).

8. *The Postmodern Condition*, 43–44.

9. Ibid., 41.

10. For a quite helpful introduction to the concept of technoscience, see Don Ihde, *Postphenomenology and Technoscience: The Peking University Lectures* (Albany, NY: SUNY Press, 2009), 40–41. For an important classic work discussing

technoscience and postmodernity, see Donna J. Harraway, *Modest_Witness@Second_Millenium.FemaleMan_Meets_OncoMouse™: Feminism and Technoscience* (New York: Routledge, 1997). As she writes, "Technoscience extravagantly exceeds the distinction between science and technology as well as those between nature and society, subjects and objects, and the natural and artifactual that structured the imaginary time called modernity" (3).

11. *The Postmodern Condition*, 45.

12. For the classic work on this, see Michael Gibbons, Camille Limoges, Helga Nowotny, Simon Schwartzman, Peter Scott, and Martin Trow, *The New Knowledge Production: The Dynamics of Science and Research in Contemporary Societies* (Los Angeles: Sage, 1994). See also chapter 3.

13. *The Postmodern Condition*, 45.

14. Ibid.

15. Kirsten Locke, "Performativity, Performance, and Education," *Educational Philosophy and Theory* 47, no. 3 (2015), 248.

16. *The Postmodern Condition*, 46.

17. Ibid., 48.

18. See also Herbert Marcuse, "Lecture on Education, Brooklyn College, 1968," in *Marcuse's Challenge to Education*, eds. Douglass Kellner, Tyson Lewis, Clayton Pierce, and K. Daniel Cho (Lanham, MD: Rowman & Littlefield, 2009), 34. Marcuse discusses the material basis for the expansion of higher education as well as the containment of its prospects through anti-intellectualism. While certainly not as detailed, Marcuse's basic thesis is strikingly similar to that of Christopher Newfield. See Christopher Newfield, *Unmaking the Public University: The Forty Year Assault on the Middle Class* (Cambridge, MA: Harvard University Press, 2008).

19. See Ibid., 49.

20. I thank Rachel Walsh for emphasizing to me in personal conversation the importance of this aspect of the theory of performativity in theorizing the contemporary state of American academia.

21. "Lyotard's Performance," 285.

22. Ibid., 286.

23. See Steven Fesmire, "Democracy and the Industrial Imagination in American Education," *Education and Culture* 32, no. 1 (2016): 53–61.

24. *The Postmodern Condition*, 41.

25. John McCumber, *The Philosophy Scare: The Politics of Reason in the Early Cold War* (Chicago: University of Chicago Press, 2016), 25ff.

26. McCumber describes vividly the fallout from the California Oath Controversy and the subsequent adoption of what he terms the "California Plan," which involved cooperation at three levels (department, university, and state) to ensure that potential communists or "subversives" were prevented from working as faculty at the University of California. As McCumber writes, "The stated aim of the Plan was to make sure that no subversives were hired to teach at any institution of higher education in the state of California" (123).

27. "Improving Human Capital in a Competitive World—Education Reform in the U.S.," March 3, 2011, U.S. Department of Education, https://www.ed.gov/news/speeches/improving-human-capital-competitive-world-education-reform-us.

28. Quoted in John Pullen, *The Marginal Productivity Theory of Distribution: A Critical History* (New York: Routledge, 2010), 14. Emphasis in original.

29. Angel Gurría, Foreword to *Human Capital: How What You Know Shapes Your Life*, by Brian Keely (Paris: OECD Publishing, 2007), 3. Retrieved from: https://read.oecd-ilibrary.org/education/human-capital_9789264029095-en#page1.

30. Theodore W. Schultz, "Investment in Human Capital," *The American Economic Review* 51, no. 1 (March 1961), 3.

31. Of course, this is not entirely true. Schultz himself mentions Adam Smith, J.H. von Thünen, and Irving Fisher as predecessors. See Ibid., 2–3.

32. See Gary S. Becker, "Investment in Human Capital: Effects on Earnings," in *Human Capital: A Theoretical and Empirical Analysis, with Special Reference to Education, Second Edition* (Chicago: University of Chicago Press, 1975), 16–19. As the subscript "0" indicates, the equation represents the special case in which investment occurs only in the "initial period." Becker goes on to provide the equations to calculate equilibrium given continuous investment over some time period.

33. Ibid., 18.

34. Becker further offers and formalizes a number of caveats. As he summarizes, "Firms would benefit more from on-the-job investment the more specific the productivity effect, the greater their monopsony power, and the longer the labor contract; conversely, the benefit would be less the more general the productivity effect, the less their monopsony power, and the shorter the labor contract" (Ibid., 42).

35. Michel Foucault, *The Birth of Biopolitics: Lectures at the Collège de France, 1978–1979*, eds. François Ewald, Alessandro Fontana, and Michel Senellart and trans. Graham Burchell (Basingstoke: Palgrave Macmillan, 2010), 225–226.

36. See Gary S. Becker, "Introduction to the First Edition," in *Human Capital: A Theoretical and Empirical Analysis, with Special Reference to Education, Second Edition* (Chicago: University of Chicago Press, 1975), 9.

37. Gary S. Becker, "Investment in Human Capital: Rates of Return," in *Human Capital: A Theoretical and Empirical Analysis, with Special Reference to Education, Second Edition* (Chicago: University of Chicago Press, 1975), 46.

38. *The Birth of Biopolitics*, 223.

39. "Investment in Human Capital: Effects on Earnings," 37.

40. Ibid., 37–39.

41. Simon Marginson, "Limitations of Human Capital Theory," *Studies in Higher Education*, 44. No. 2 (2019), 287.

42. "Investment in Human Capital," 6. See also Theodore W. Schultz, "Reflections on Investment in Man," *Journal of Political Economy* 70, no. 5, Part 2 (1962), 1–8.

43. "Reflections on Investment in Man," 1.

44. See, for example, World Economic Forum (WEF), *The Global Human Capital Report: Preparing People for the Future of Work* (Geneva, Switzerland: World Economic Forum, 2017), http://www3.weforum.org/

docs/WEF_Global_Human_Capital_Report_2017.pdf or the previously cited, *Human Capital: How What You Know Shapes Your Life* from the OECD.

45. "Human Capital Project," Worldbank.org, World Bank Group. Accessed August 15, 2020. https://www.worldbank.org/en/publication/human-capital.

46. *What Is the World Bank's Human Capital Index?*, World Bank Group, October 10, 2018, video, runtime 2:59, https://www.youtube.com/watch?v=iCUIAQkOwKw.

47. Ibid.

48. Wendy Brown, *Undoing the Demos: Neoliberalism's Stealth Revolution* (New York: Zone Books, 2015), 81–83.

49. I will discuss the connection between this line of reasoning and theodicy in chapter 5. For more on theodicy and its relation to colonialism and development discourses, see Lewis Gordon, *Disciplinary Decadence: Living Thought in Trying Times* (New York: Routledge, 2016), 40 and 91ff.

50. *Undoing the Demos*, 84.

51. Ibid., 87.

52. Ibid., 99–107.

53. Ibid., 104–105.

54. See chapter 4 for a much lengthier discussion of this theme.

55. Mark Garrison, "Resurgent Behaviorism and the Rise of Neoliberal Schooling," in *The Wiley Handbook of Global Educational Reform*, eds. Kenneth J. Saltman and Alexander J. Means (Hoboken, NJ: Wiley Blackwell, 2019), 338ff. Garrison helpfully links the neoliberal educational agenda and its exercise of power to behaviorism. On this point, see also *Birth of Biopolitics*, 269–270.

56. "Resurgent Behaviorism," 338.

57. See Bonnie Urciuoli, "Skills and Selves in the New Workplace," *American Ethnologist* 35, no. 2 (May 2008), 211–228.

58. World Economic Forum (WEF), *New Vision for Education: Unlocking the Potential of Technology* (Geneva, Switzerland: World Economic Forum, 2015), 2–3. http://www3.weforum.org/docs/WEFUSA_NewVisionforEducation_Report2015.pdf.

59. Ibid., 2.

60. *The Postmodern Condition*, 51.

61. This is not to deny that philosophers and philosophy departments claim to offer other skills. In fact, the list is quite long. However, it seems to me that critical thinking is the most significant in emphasis and the one to which the discipline attempts to lay the most direct claim. For example, while philosophy certainly claims to provide students with "communication skills" it does not attempt to claim that it does so to a greater extent or with more direct curricular emphasis than, say, departments of rhetoric and composition.

62. "Department Advocacy Toolkit," American Philosophical Association, accessed September 2, 2020, https://www.apaonline.org/page/deptadvocacytoolkit. The original text is all bold for emphasis. In chapter 3, I discuss the invocation of "risk" as it relates to what Michael Peters calls "actuarial rationality." See Michael Peters, "The New Prudentialism in Education: Actuarial Rationality and the Entrepreneurial Self," *Educational Theory* 55, no. 2 (2005), 134.

63. Committee on the Status and Future of the Profession, "Department Advocacy Toolkit" (Newark, DE: American Philosophical Association, 2019), 6. https://www.apaonline.org/page/role_of_phil. Quotation is italicized in the original for emphasis. Regarding the transmission of "cultural heritages," see chapter 4.

64. Committee on the Status and Future of the Profession, "Statement on the Role of Philosophy in Higher Education," American Philosophical Association, accessed September 2, 2020. https://www.apaonline.org/page/role_of_phil. For more on philosophy aimed at public audiences, see chapter 3.

65. Ibid.

66. "Department Advocacy Toolkit," 33.

67. "Resources for Undergraduates," American Philosophical Association, accessed September 2, 2020. https://www.apaonline.org/page/undergrad_resources.

68. "Why Major in Philosophy?" Philosophy Department, University of North Carolina at Chapel Hill, accessed September 2, 2020. https://philosophy.unc.edu/undergraduate/the-major/why-major-in-philosophy. See also Miya Tokumitsu, *Do What You Love: And Other Lies about Success and Happiness* (New York: Regan Arts, 2015). As well as "In the Name of Love," *Jacobin*, January 12, 2014. https://www.jacobinmag.com/2014/01/in-the-name-of-love. Tokumitsu notes, "There's little doubt that 'do what you love' (DWYL) is the unofficial work mantra of our time. The problem is that it leads not to salvation, but to the devaluation of actual work, including the very work it pretends to elevate—and more important, the dehumanization of the vast majority of workers" ("In the Name of Love"). I discuss the idea of "doing what you love" in depth in chapter 5.

69. Berit Brogaard and Christopher A. Pynes, eds., "The Overall Rankings," *The Philosophical Gourmet Report*, accessed September 2, 2020. https://www.philosophicalgourmet.com.

70. "Studying Philosophy at NYU," Department of Philosophy, New York University, accessed September 2, 2020. https://as.nyu.edu/philosophy/undergraduate/studying-philosophy-at-nyu.html.

71. See "Why Philosophy?" Department of Philosophy, Rutgers University, accessed September 2, 2020. https://mellon.org/shared-experiences-blog/why-study-philosophy. The link takes you to "Why Study Philosophy?" Andrew W. Mellon Foundation, February 2019, accessed September 2, 2020.

72. "Interview with Former Philosophy Graduate Student and Investor Bill Miller," *Blog of the APA*, accessed September 2, 2020. https://blog.apaonline.org/2018/03/02/interview-with-former-philosophy-graduate-student-and-investor-bill-miller.

73. Bernie Trilling and Charles Fadel, *21st Century Skills: Learning for Life in Our Times* (San Francisco, CA: Jossey-Bass, 2009), 50.

74. Ibid., 49.

75. Ibid.

76. "Essential Learning Outcomes," Association of American Colleges and Universities (AAC&U), accessed September 4, 2020. https://www.aacu.org/essential-learning-outcomes.

77. Hart Research Associates, "Fulfilling the American Dream: Liberal Education and the Future of Work: Selected Findings from Online Surveys of Business

Executives and Hiring Managers" (Washington, DC: Association of American Colleges and Universities, 2018), 3. https://www.aacu.org/sites/default/files/files/LEAP/2018EmployerResearchReport.pdf.

78. "Department Advocacy Toolkit," 45–47. For the AAC&U's "Value Rubrics," see Terrel Rhodes, *Assessing Outcomes and Improving Achievement: Tips and Tools for Using Rubrics* (Washington, DC: Association of American Colleges and Universities, 2010).

79. Marianna Papastephanou and Charoula Angeli, "Critical Thinking Beyond Skill," *Educational Philosophy and Theory* 39, no. 6 (2007): 604–621. See also Jürgen Habermas, *The Theory of Communicative Action, Volume 1: Reason and the Rationalization of Society* (Boston, MA: Beacon Press, 1984), 273ff. For a similar discussion drawing on Hannah Arendt, see *How the Neoliberalization of the Academy Leads to Thoughtlessness*, 63ff.

80. Relying on Raymond Williams's concept of "keywords," Urciuoli writes of skills terms as "strategically deployable shifters." In "Skills and Selves in the New Workplace," she explains, "Skills-related terms are semantically variable, they tend to cluster, and they tend to expand with new conceptual formations" (214). See also Chris McMillan, "'I've Learned to Question Everything': Critical Thinking, or, the Pedagogical Logic of Late Capitalism," *Journal of Critical Education Policy Studies* 16, no 1 (April 2018): 1–29. Words like "critical thinking" often function as empty signifiers that can be strategically deployed for a variety of purposes. McMillan: "The empty signifier unifies a field of meaning by allowing a range of differences to invest in the same term" (7). Finally, see Tim Moore, "Critical Thinking: Seven Definitions in Search of a Concept," *Studies in Higher Education* 38, no. 4 (2013), 506–522. Moore emphasizes both the variety and the commonalities in the various ways that educators across disciplines use the term critical thinking, referring to the work of both Raymond Williams and Ludwig Wittgenstein in the process.

81. "Critical Thinking Beyond Skill," 605.

82. Ibid., 616.

83. See Kristie Dotson, "How Is This Paper Philosophy?" *Comparative Philosophy* 3, no. 1 (2012), 3–29.

84. Ibid., 69.

85. Tanya Loughead, *Critical University: Moving Higher Education Forward* (Lanham, MD: Lexington Books, 2015), 61. See also Simone de Beauvoir, *The Ethics of Ambiguity*, trans. Bernard Frechtman (New York: Citadel Press, 1976), 68–69.

86. "Critical Thinking Beyond Skill," 607.

87. Ibid., 608.

88. "'I've Learned to Question Everything,'" 20.

89. Ibid., 4

Chapter 3

The One-Dimensionality of Neoliberal Philosophy

In chapter 1, I articulated four central features of the Neoliberal University: (1) defunding higher education and reframing it as a private consumer good, (2) reconceiving the purpose of higher education as training rather than education, (3) the instrumentalization and commodification of knowledge, and (4) the centralization and bureaucratization of university administration. In discussing the performativity of Neoliberal Philosophy in the previous chapter, I focused on the way that philosophical education is rendered into a private consumer good in the form of training in critical thinking skills. Through this pedagogy, I argued, Neoliberal Philosophy fails to interrogate the broad social system, values, and motivations that lead one to think critically, imagining such thinking as a "transferable skill" that can be applied to any task or problem equally. Critical thinking is as useful for building the weapons systems of tomorrow as it is for solving world hunger. Primarily, of course, the problems and tasks to which such skills will be applied are those set by employers in the knowledge economy of the twenty-first century.

How did we get here? Within the Neoliberal University, I have argued, philosophy must perform its performativity. It must market itself as a good investment by demonstrating to "stakeholders" that it produces technologies of optimization. This marketing strategy transforms philosophical education insofar as it redounds upon philosophical pedagogy and curriculum with the demand that philosophy optimize productivity by enhancing the human capital of students. Critical thinking pedagogies, shaped by the imperative to perform, can demonstrate philosophy's value only by touting increases to productivity within the knowledge economy. The apparently subversive force of critique is absorbed into the optimizing logic of late capitalism. In this chapter, I turn my focus to the marketing of philosophical knowledge and research. What is the value of the philosophical knowledge produced by scholars? How does this conception of the value of philosophical knowledge affect the practice of philosophy and the subjectivity and self-conception of philosophers?

To answer these questions, I turn to Herbert Marcuse's 1964 classic, *One-Dimensional Man* and his 1955 *Eros and Civilization*. Combining insights from Sigmund Freud, G.W.F. Hegel, and Marx, Marcuse set out to theorize the sterile conformity and self-congratulatory consumerism of American culture in the mid-century. His brilliant, if bleak, critique sought to unearth the structures of repression underlying the facade of democracy, freedom, and affluence so integral to the national mythos of the U.S. and its citizens. For Marcuse, modern affluent society had managed to contain class conflict by integrating workers into its structure and sharing its immense wealth. These developments produced what he called a "Happy Consciousness" characterized by "one-dimensional thought." Much as this mid-century Happy Consciousness equated its freedom with consumer choice, so, too, a contemporary form of Happy Consciousness prevails in which freedom is rendered as the capacity to calculate risk and return and prudently invest in oneself, to exercise an "actuarial rationality." Both those outside the academy and those within it are encouraged to be, in Foucault's apt phrase, "entrepreneurs of themselves." Philosophers now market themselves as producers of investment-worthy knowledge commodities whose exchange value in the knowledge economy pays off in income or returns of one kind or another. Increasingly, what I will call "philosophical desire" is therefore oriented away from the internal and/or eternal goods that characterized the traditional pursuit of wisdom and toward the enjoyment of branded self-images created in pursuit of academic celebrity.

PERFORMATIVITY AND THE PERFORMANCE PRINCIPLE

To begin, it will be helpful to connect the previous discussion of "performativity" with Marcuse's theorization of what he calls the "performance principle." In *Eros and Civilization*, Marcuse develops a historicized version of Freudian psychoanalysis in order to link it with a Marxist conception of alienation. I will here only briefly trace the outlines and highlight the aspects of Freud's theory that are necessary for an understanding of Marcuse's revision. According to Freud, human psychology is primarily governed by what he considers an "economics of the libido."[1] That is, speaking very broadly, human beings seek to produce in themselves the greatest balance of pleasure and satisfaction over pain and dissatisfaction. Thus, for Freud, the "pleasure principle," which he also terms *Eros*, drives human behavior. Even so, painful disappointment, the imperatives of self-preservation, and long-term satisfaction set limits on the immediate satisfaction of libidinal urges. One is thus confronted by the demand to regulate these drives, to give up some quantum of immediate gratification in order to comply with external necessity. Freud terms this internal limiting principle, the "reality principle" or *Ananke*.[2] The reality principle asserts itself most forcefully in the compulsion to work; one must undertake painful or dissatisfying labor in order to satisfy oneself consistently in the long-term. Repression and sublimation, then, are basic features of human life since human beings must contend with external necessity and the requirement of productive labor.

In revising Freud's framework, Marcuse notes that the reality principle is viciously ahistorical. From a Marxist perspective, the compulsion to work is not a universal, natural condition, but is rather socially imposed. Through time, society has been organized into distinct historical modes of production within which labor and its fruits are unequally distributed according to class divisions. In contrast to the reality principle, then, Marcuse presents a "performance principle," which he defines as the "prevailing historical form of the *reality principle*."[3] In Freud's work, the development of the reality principle presupposes conditions of relative scarcity. In a world of abundance (whether natural or produced), necessary work is minimal. But as with labor, Marcuse suggests, scarcity is unequally socially distributed on the basis of class and is, in that sense, likewise socially imposed and historical. Scarcity, according to Marcuse, and with it the compulsion to work are thus historical conditions inasmuch as the distribution of social wealth is determined, not according to need, but according to one's position in a social hierarchy that has evolved through time with the struggle between contending social classes. Whereas this order was brutally, violently imposed in previous eras, the modern distribution of scarcity is the result of "a more rational utilization of power."[4] Nonetheless, scarcity remains historically and socially variable, resting to one degree or another on forms of social domination and oppression. The external necessity of work arises first and foremost, then, as a matter of social inequality, rather than as a matter of the natural insufficiency of the individual contending with a cruel Malthusian nature.

As with the reality principle, the performance principle is an internal regulator that commands one to forgo instant gratification in return for self-preservation and long-term satisfaction, a bifurcation of the psyche in which the pursuit of pleasure is stymied by the confrontation with necessity. The important difference is that the performance principle acknowledges that socially imposed scarcity compels one into a functional role within a historically given social organization of labor that is divided according to a social hierarchy and driven by the demand for profit. "Reality" is not a barren and stingy wild, but rather a highly integrated and advanced economic-technological system that stands before workers as something akin to an external force.

When Marcuse speaks of "rationalized domination," it is this system he has in mind. He elaborates,

> For the vast majority of the population, the scope and mode of satisfaction are determined by their own labor; but their labor is for an apparatus which they do not control, which operates as an independent power to which individuals must submit if they want to live. And it becomes the more alien the more specialized the division of labor becomes. Men do not live their own lives but perform pre-established functions.[5]

In order to survive and meet their needs, workers must transform their labor(-power) into a commodity and submit themselves to the vagaries of the labor market which is itself governed by the demands of the economic-technological system. Workers therefore internalize the command to perform within the system.

On the basis of these premises, Marcuse develops a concept of "surplus repression," thereby connecting Freudian psychoanalysis to a Marxist conception of alienation. He defines surplus repression as the "restrictions necessitated by social domination."[6] "Basic repression" amounts to the constraint placed on libidinal satisfaction that is required for the preservation of the social totality and its reproduction into the future within a given mode of production. Surplus repression, by contrast, is the constraint that results from domination within a historically specific class hierarchy.[7] While necessary work and accompanying repression can be distributed more or less equally within a given social organization of labor, they cannot be eliminated entirely barring the full automation of all necessary labor. Surplus repression is therefore the result of unnecessary domination. It has no basis other than the social hierarchy that allows some people to benefit through the domination and exploitation of others. Clearly, the relative mix of basic and surplus repression in a given society depends on a host of factors, including natural wealth, social productivity, and the degree of domination and exploitation.

In this way, surplus repression can be seen as the correlate of profit, which Marx conceives as "surplus value." Both are the result of work beyond what is necessary for the reproduction of society. Following Marx, profit may be viewed as the surplus value generated by labor beyond what is returned in the form of a wage, with the value of labor(-power) set by the bare minimum labor socially necessary to reproduce it.[8] The profit of the few is the result of the painful and dissatisfying labor of the many in excess of what is necessary to meet their basic needs. Surplus repression in the form of production for profit is the "reality" to which workers must adjust themselves—a point expressed in popular references to "going out into the real world" as a way of describing employment after the time of schooling. As Marx detailed already in 1844, workers become estranged from themselves, other people, and the objects they produce in this process—transformed, as Marx and Engels would write somewhat later in *The Communist Manifesto*, into "appendages of the machine."[9] For Marcuse, the self-estrangement of these "appendages" takes the form of the performance principle.

Drawing on the work of Martin Heidegger, Max Weber, and fellow theorists of the Frankfurt School, particularly Max Horkheimer and Theodor Adorno, Marcuse presents the economic-technological system, the "apparatus" (as he calls it), as governed by what he terms "technological rationality."[10] Marcelo Vieta describes technological rationality in this way:

> Under such a formally rationalized world, objects appear to be for us, and actually become in practice, detached, fungible, and orderable things that are emptied of any intrinsic meaning beyond their exchange value. At the disposal of willful subjects operating in a world mediated by technical systems without objective limits, objects now enter into the abstracted realm of equivalencies (for market exchange) and inventories of raw materials (for production).[11]

Technological rationality is built into the operations of the system independently of the desires or beliefs of any particular individual; ultimately structuring these desires and beliefs for its own purposes. Under the guidance of the performance principle, one must be "realistic"—which is to say, one must adjust oneself to the governing technological rationality of the apparatus. One must treat the world as an ensemble of "detached, fungible, and orderable things," or as Heidegger would call it "standing reserve."[12] For the individual, practical rationality is reduced to *effective thinking* within the system, the ordering of fungible means to efficiently produce economic growth.[13]

Before proceeding to a discussion of Marcuse's concept of one-dimensionality, it is important now to draw together what has been said concerning the performance principle with the discussions of performativity and human capital from the foregoing chapter. Performativity amounts to a demand for optimization, the maximization of output given some fixed input. In general, this is accomplished through investment in technologies of optimization and, with it, the production of efficiencies. As it applies to knowledge production, performativity requires the subordination of discourses oriented toward truth to economic discourses of investment and return. Performativity is insufficient unto itself, however; it must be performed and enter into the semiotic universe of economic discourse. If the logic of optimization is framed as return on investment, then, with the totalization of economic discourses, the imperative for social actors at all scales is to attract investment by showing or demonstrating return through their capacity to optimize and become more productive. Human capital theory extends this performative logic to individual workers, conceptualizing "knowledge, skills, competencies, and attributes" as capital that is utilized by the worker and can be enhanced in order to increase earnings by optimizing efficiency and maximizing productivity. Workers appear to themselves as standing reserve which can be ordered for maximal output. Each individual is therefore to act as an entrepreneur and invest in their human capital in order to increase their expected future earnings, which are taken to be tied to marginal product.

What, then, are the specific demands placed upon the worker in the new economy that constitute the "reality" to which they must adjust to in order to meet their needs within the economic-technological system? What are the forms of repression, the constraints on pleasure and satisfaction, the worker must internalize in order to function today? Importantly, the logic of performativity commands, not merely efficient utilization, but enhancement toward maximized output. That is, it is a form of economic rationality that seeks to increase productivity through investments in new technological means that further "rationalize" labor. Under the influence of human capital theory this economic rationality treats labor itself not as an inert or fixed factor of production but as a "produced means of production." The performance principle therefore commands not merely that one internalize the economic imperative to work and work efficiently, but further that one relates to oneself as a "bundle of skills" to be trained for ever-greater productivity, a technology of optimization. Michael Peters therefore describes the emergence and enforcement of what he terms "prudentialism" and "actuarial rationality." He writes, "In this novel form of governance, responsibilized individuals are called upon to apply certain managerial, economic, and actuarial techniques to themselves as citizen-consumer subjects—calculating the risks and returns on investment in such areas as education, health, employment, and retirement."[14] For these citizen-consumer subjects, scarcity is produced artificially through the invocation of "global competition" for jobs and ever-looming austerity, not to mention the perpetual threat and recurring reality of economic crisis, so that workers are aware that in order to meet their needs they must make themselves competitive through self-investment and bear the associated risks. They must, for example, take student loans, enroll in higher education for job training, and accept unpaid internships to acquire on-the-job skills. They are therefore both entrepreneurs of themselves and, as we might put it, *accountants of themselves*—at once fungible objects of self-enhancement and abstract managers of investments perpetually calculating the risk and return relating to their "portfolio."

From this perspective, we can discern an apparent compatibility or even overlap between Foucault's analysis of neoliberalism as a form of biopolitics and related forms of governmentality and Marcuse's invocation of the performance principle. Indeed, drawing on Marcuse's later lectures, Clayton

Pierce has highlighted a biopolitical dimension in Marcuse's critical theory of education. "What is important to recognize," Pierce writes,

> is that Marcuse's critical theory of education, read through a biopolitical lens, focuses on how education in advanced capitalist society links economic productive needs with the production of individuals and populations who are sensitized and habituated for "a competitive struggle for existence"—where how we invest in ourselves in economically rational ways translates directly to the degree of "freedom" that can be enjoyed in society.[15]

In the neoliberal knowledge economy, a biopolitical appropriation of Marcuse must focus on the production of workers who have internalized the demands of entrepreneurship and actuarial rationality necessary to invest prudently in themselves and create innovative knowledge commodities. Subjects who will identify freedom with precisely this ability to self-invest and enhance. Technological rationality now takes the form and is introjected as a competitive struggle in which only those who invest well and anticipate the "needs" of the market survive. Workers are produced, certainly, who have incorporated an ascetic "work ethic." This ethic, however, is dedicated, not to Puritan ideals of industry and mechanical discipline, but to calculations of risk, investment, and enhancement through "disruption." To perform their performativity, these actuarial subjects must be able to narrate and enhance their "personal brands," thereby attracting investment. In the social media and gig economy parlance of our age, everyone must become, or at least present, their "best self." Only by performing one's performativity in this way can one "be real."

ONE-DIMENSIONALITY AND THE ENTREPRENEURIAL SELF

With much of the groundwork laid in *Eros and Civilization*, Marcuse went on to write his master work *One-Dimensional Man*, a text that catapulted him to international recognition as the philosophical voice of the New Left. In *One-Dimensional Man*, Marcuse exposes the operations of what he, following economist Kenneth Galbraith, refers to as the "affluent society." In the aftermath of World War II and on the heels of the New Deal, the United States saw unprecedented economic growth which was shared between labor and capital to an extent perhaps never before experienced.[16] Without endorsing the phrase, political scientist Michael Forman discusses the period as the "golden age of capitalism" and describes the "social pact" between the state, labor, and capital at its heart. Significantly, this pact integrated labor into society as a legitimate political force while requiring it to excise radical elements in its ranks. According to Forman, the pact was able to dramatically reduce poverty and increase individual security and wages; resolve capital's crisis of accumulation and increase political stability; and spur creative destruction through the Cold War arms race and other means.[17] Perhaps unsurprisingly, this supposed "golden age of capitalism" corresponded to the period identified in chapter 1 as the "golden age of the university," which was characterized by the "public good knowledge/learning regime" and a broad commitment on the part of the state to investment in public infrastructure. This "golden age" is also, of course, the period of the rise of what McCumber calls Cold War Philosophy to hegemony in the U.S. academy and the "red scare" that he argues catapulted it to dominance—and, as will be discussed in the next chapter, the period of what Melamed calls the "racial break." Famously, Marcuse characterized the affluent society that emerged in these halcyon days as a "comfortable, smooth, democratic unfreedom."[18] Despite growing prosperity and a realistic hope that many could attain the "American Dream," Marcuse diagnosed the affluent society as one-dimensional, conformist, and pathologically content in its "golden handcuffs."

For Marcuse, the one-dimensionality of the affluent society emerged from its capacity to contain class conflict through the alignment of the interests of workers with those of the exploiting class. As long as wealth was shared, growing productivity through technological optimization allowed most workers in the United States to look forward to a future of prosperity for themselves and for their children. Hard work would, as they assured themselves, eventually pay off and they could live the "American Dream." Of course, this meant increasingly repressive work, as labor was further automated and regimented to optimize productivity. But it also meant the emergence of a consumer economy dedicated to providing workers significant leisure and material comfort outside work.

The promise of growing wealth and consumer choice gave workers an interest in their own repression, according to Marcuse. In large part, this was accomplished through the creation of false needs. False needs, in Marcuse's account, are those which are socially produced for the purpose of perpetuating a system of exploitation and surplus repression.[19] Rather than see growing productivity turned toward the elimination of poverty, disease, war, and ultimately work itself, the affluent society oriented economic activity toward the production of wasteful, unnecessary, and, in a word, cheap satisfactions. In such a situation, Marcuse notes, caustically,

> The people recognize themselves in their commodities; they find their soul in their automobile, hi-fi set, split-level home, kitchen equipment. The very

mechanism which ties the individual to his society has changed, and social control is anchored in the new needs which it has produced.[20]

Identifying themselves with various consumable commodities and enjoying themselves in consumption, workers voluntarily submitted to the domination of the technological-economic system and its governing rationality. Even so, for Marcuse, they did not act autonomously—their needs and desires were externally programmed for the sake of ensuring the continued functioning of the system.

This condition was made possible by what Marcuse calls "repressive desublimation."[21] Repressive desublimation works to reconcile the individual psyche to the repressive reality within which it finds itself and within which it is commanded to perform. Marcuse explains primarily with reference to art and literature. In the premodern world, art and literature served as refusals of the status quo, rebellions against the repressive features of the given society. Those desires and libidinal drives that could not find satisfaction in the real world, that were repressed due to the compulsion to work, found expression in works of art and literature that stood off at an alienated distance from the prevailing social order. Such works were not absorbed into everyday life, but instead offered a negation—a counter-image—that revealed the painful truth of work-a-day existence even as it offered consolation in the form of substitute pleasures. Marcuse writes of such art, "It can speak its own language only as long as the images are alive which refuse and refute the established order."[22] Within one-dimensional culture, however, all the values and works of traditional higher culture are transformed into instruments of the system, their content now presented as an affirmation rather than negation of everyday experience through mass consumption as orchestrated by the culture industry.

The technological-economic system of the affluent society is thus able to offer satisfaction on a mass scale, including access to all the works of traditional higher culture that were previously reserved for the few. The system then functions to "desublimate" libidinal drives, directing them toward the immediate gratification provided by the wares available on the market. "The organism," as Marcuse puts it, "is thus preconditioned for the spontaneous acceptance of what is on offer."[23] One need no longer search for satisfaction outside or against the status quo, a transcendent reality, truth, or justice beyond the given social order that would reveal it as false. Gratification can now be obtained in the immediately present environment. Art becomes advertising and advertising becomes art.

But if the truth of the artwork is its capacity to reveal the falsehood of the dominant order—exploitation and surplus repression—then the incorporation of the artwork into the system serves only to falsify. Consider the person out for a morning jog, earbuds plugged in, absorbed in the latest pop hit. This is a pleasurable leisure activity, a momentary break from the work demands of the real world. It is, nonetheless, a form of repressive desublimation insofar as the enjoyment of the song streaming in via the smartphone binds the person to a cruel and ugly social order in which the precondition for consumption of the pleasurable tune is the enslavement of children.[24] Removed from the aural sensation of the surrounding world, itself now reconstituted by urbanization and industrialization, and identifying with the fetishized cultural commodity, the jogger is aesthetically disconnected from and inured to the violence and brutality of the system which delivers the song. Rather than a counterimage of beauty, pacification, and reconciliation, art is a marketable commodity and along with each art-object it sells the system as a whole. Repressive desublimation falsifies and flattens experience, and one can hardly imagine a better example of a false need than a smartphone. Revolt against the system as a whole, the desire for something beyond or against it, now appears an irrational aberration against a world of relative ease and pleasure. Are you really going to give up your phone?

In an allusion to Hegel, Marcuse describes the individual who has adjusted to the system in this way as a "Happy Consciousness." The Happy Consciousness is a self-deluding inversion of the form of consciousness that Hegel describes as the "Unhappy Consciousness."[25] The Unhappy Consciousness views itself as separated from its own essence and from the truth, which it locates in a transcendent realm beyond the world in which it lives and acts. In Marcuse's account, by contrast, one is presented with the image of a form of consciousness that finds its essence and truth given directly and immediately within its mundane social environment. This form of consciousness, then, identifies with and locates its freedom in the types of repression and enjoyment that are on hand within the prevailing order. In contrast to the interiority and asceticism of the Unhappy Consciousness, Happy Consciousness affirms itself as it appears and takes pleasure in the status quo. Thus, the culture produced by the Happy Consciousness of the affluent society represents contentment in subjection. As Marcuse quips, "It reflects the belief that the real is rational, and that the established system, in spite of everything, delivers the goods."[26] The one-dimensionality of Happy Consciousness, its desublimated enjoyment of consumer goods and inability to separate itself from its performance in the economic system, is reflected in all aspects of culture, including in philosophy.

With the account of the one-dimensional society and Happy Consciousness in hand, we can now return to Pierce's invocation of a "biopolitical Marcuse" to develop an understanding of neoliberal one-dimensionality. For human capital theory, earnings are the return on prudent self-investment and the goal in any given period of investment is to maximize the return. One is not to challenge the system but to produce more within it so as to increase one's "earnings." In order to receive the satisfactions of a high-tech consumer culture and continued economic growth, one must invest well. Consistent with Marcuse's analysis of Happy Consciousness, then, the entrepreneurial subject of neoliberalism not only submits to self-optimization, but actively *wants and even enjoys it*. Such subjects "do what they love" and "love what they do."[27] Identifying themselves with their performance, they demand a future of asymptotic growth in productivity (i.e., ever greater and more deeply internalized performativity). Even as debt and poverty are pervasive, inequality unparalleled, and life-expectancy declining, the internalized ideology of the one-dimensional society requires that one perpetually "hustle" in order to "get ahead." Becker himself will come to consider even consumption a form of production that can be optimized, referring to the domestic home as a "factory" for the production of useful commodities.[28] Thus, another neoliberal mantra: Work hard, play hard. For one-dimensional neoliberalism, "prosumption" erases the line between leisure and work; to do either well, to maximize the payoff, one must invest wisely. Work can be pleasurable, perhaps, but pleasure is hard work.

MANAGING ACADEMIC CAPITALISM IN THE KNOWLEDGE ECONOMY

My argument throughout this chapter is that Neoliberal Philosophy is one-dimensional insofar as it serves to adjust individual philosophers and students to the prevailing social order. This occurs particularly through the feedback effects of strategic marketing in which individual philosophers and philosophy departments attempt to survive and advance their position by attracting investment. In the second chapter, I showed that Neoliberal Philosophy advertises philosophical education as training in critical thinking skills for the knowledge economy. It produces technologies of optimization that will be profitable in an era of rapid change, technological innovation, and information saturation. This one-dimensionality affects not only pedagogy and curriculum, however, but also philosophical research.

Lyotard already presaged the coming of the knowledge economy in *The Postmodern Condition*, at the time hypothesizing and predicting what are by now commonplace aspects of life in the twenty-first century. Most important for this discussion, he envisioned that rapid growth in information and communications technologies coupled with the expanding role of the technosciences in the economy would result in what he termed the "mercantilization of knowledge."[29] That is, knowledge would be produced for exchange as a commodity. Whether in the global competition between nation-states for geopolitical dominance or through its role in creating technologies of optimization for the capitalist production process, knowledge emerged in the course of the twentieth century as a major factor in social life and one which gave its possessor an advantage over competitors—with social life in general imagined as an only slightly circumscribed war of all against all. Rapid advancements in information and computing technologies have of course deepened this trend.

Importantly, with the obsolescence of the metanarratives that characterized modernity and the growing importance of the technosciences in a wide range of social activities, the site of knowledge production has shifted since mid-century. This shift is marked by Michael Gibbons et al., in their characterization of a new "Mode 2" form of knowledge production. Within Mode 2, knowledge is no longer bound by the spatial confines of the university or the professional contours of academic disciplines. It is instead distributed across social space, produced by transdisciplinary teams in many heterogeneous contexts of application and without appeal to any universal standard or framework of justification, accountable instead to its users in their varied contexts.[30] Thus, for example, we see the rise of think tanks, research and development departments, consultancies, institutes, freelance experts, and so on. In the time since the writings of Lyotard or Gibbons et al., one might also point to the establishment of various new sites of knowledge production scattered across the internet.

Even as knowledge has penetrated and transformed the market, pervading production, exchange, and consumption in a multitude of ways—take, for instance, the algorithms that guide Netflix or Spotify recommendations— there has also been a reverse trend through which the market has penetrated and transformed knowledge production as it is undertaken within the confines of the university. As discussed in chapter 1, Slaughter and Rhoades characterize this transformation as a shift from a "public good knowledge/ learning regime" to an "academic capitalist knowledge/learning regime."[31] Importantly, the public good knowledge/learning regime was not immune to market or state pressures, though it was supposed to function with relative autonomy and in service to the commonweal.[32] The central idea animating it was that the state would fund basic science, which would then function relatively free from intrusion to ensure objectivity—though, as McCumber's work highlights, academic autonomy always had limits and objectivity was not, as it claimed to be, apolitical. In any case, basic scientific research, it was thought, would produce new discoveries and technologies that would in turn benefit the public through their application in diverse spheres outside the academy. Slaughter and Rhoades associate the public good knowledge/learning regime that characterized the post-WWII period with Vannevar Bush's report to President Franklin D. Roosevelt, *Science: The Endless Frontier.* As Bush described,

The publicly and privately supported colleges, universities, and research institutes are the centers of basic research. They are the wellsprings of knowledge and understanding. As long as they are vigorous and healthy and their scientists are free to pursue the truth wherever it may lead, there will be a flow of new scientific knowledge to those who can apply it to practical problems in Government [sic], in industry, or elsewhere.[33]

Bush argued that government funding of basic scientific research would serve the public good through eventual application in the "war against disease," the production of new weapons for "national security," and the creation of jobs through the invention of new consumer goods. This vision characterized to a great extent the ideal and organization of the university prior to the emergence of the Neoliberal University and is the crucible from which Cold War Philosophy came into being. Perhaps one could point to creation of NASA and the space race as the preeminent example of the public good knowledge/learning regime at work.

To conceptualize the academic capitalist knowledge/learning regime and the Neoliberal University within which it dominates, it is important to recall that neoliberalism is characterized by a reconfiguration of the state's role in relationship to other social actors, rather than a withdrawal. The role of the state vis-à-vis the economy is not simply to let nature take its course in a laissez-faire free for all, red in tooth and claw. It is instead to establish markets, ensure competition, and guarantee transparency. Following Henry Etzkowitz and Loet Leydesdorff, sociologist Gerard Delanty therefore views the shift in terms of a complex entwinement of the relationships between the state, higher education, and the market. He elucidates this shift as follows: "What were once bilateral relations between government and university and between industry and university are now evolving into a triple set of links."[34] Rather than a series of two-way relationships between the state, industry, and the university, there emerges an interlacing in which the three are linked by strands forming a "triple helix." For example, Slaughter and Rhoades focus on changes in U.S. patent law and the legal frameworks governing intellectual property as significant in the establishment of academic capitalism, as for example with the passage of the Bayh-Dole Act of 1980.[35] Thus, the penetration of higher education by economic imperatives was facilitated through legislative efforts by the state with the more or less express purpose of producing markets in now privately held knowledge commodities. These efforts allowed universities and faculty to materially profit through partnerships with external funders and research directly undertaken for application in industry. In this context, as Slaughter and Rhoades write, "Discovery is valued because it leads to high-technology products for a knowledge economy."[36]

Importantly, the major differences between the two knowledge/learning regimes have not so much to do with the involvement of the state or the focus on national economic growth through innovation. Instead, it is the means by which these goals are undertaken. The public good knowledge/learning regime sought to fund basic science through large government outlays funneled directly into institutions of higher education with the thought that the advancement of science would in turn produce public benefits in the form of advanced weapons, new cures and medicines, as well as new commercial possibilities. We see then that the public good knowledge/learning regime was shaped by what Marcuse refers to as a "productive union" of the "features of the Welfare State and the Warfare State."[37] In contrast, the academic capitalist knowledge/learning regime seeks more or less the same ends through the imposition of competitive markets or market-like behaviors on and within the university. It seeks to direct research away from basic science and more directly toward profitable applications through entrepreneurial competition and market discipline. Competition, it is believed, will inculcate in the university and its constituencies the forms of efficiency and productivity found in the "real world" and direct research toward the efficient realization of socially useful ends as directed by the market.

Ward explains that the resulting economization of academic life has produced a massive transformation in the culture of knowledge production. Within the new culture, knowledge production is decentralized, its producers act as entrepreneurs, and they are assessed on their capacity to attract grant funding and create directly applicable knowledge.[38] Ward refers to the "end of the age of the professor" and the rise of the "knowledge worker." In order to create efficiencies in knowledge production and optimize return on investment, the new knowledge worker is increasingly managed according to "best practices" drawn from the corporate world. As already discussed in the first chapter, the Neoliberal University witnesses a significant rise in the number and power of administrators who are more and more drawn from outside the academy, with many trained specifically for academic administration. Much like the central processing unit of an MP3 player in Sennett's metaphor, administrations are able to control faculty through immediate communication and pervasive surveillance systems.[39] A new managerial ethos dedicated to the production of efficiencies and accountability through the use of performance metrics is now ubiquitous in higher education. Thus, we see the casualization and managerialism characteristic of the Neoliberal University.[40]

In chapter 1, I mentioned the work of anthropologists Shore and Wright, who note the appearance of an all-pervasive "audit culture," which they define as the "widespread proliferation" of the "calculative rationalities of modern financial accounting and their effects on individuals and organizations."[41] Incorporating elements of the "new public management," "total quality management," and a long history of disciplinary mechanisms designed to "govern by numbers," these calculative rationalities rate and rank performance on the basis of output metrics. Academic production is quantified, measured, and evaluated on the basis of such measures as full-time equivalents (FTE), student satisfaction surveys, student outcomes assessment, citation metrics, department rankings, university and college rankings, graduation rates, time to degree, number of publications, impact factor, and so on. Describing their own experience of being subjected to redundancy in the name of efficiency, Leo McCann et al. write, "Collegiality, professionalism, workplace democracy and academic expertise appear to be no match for strategies driven by metrics, rankings, and league tables."[42] Far from neutral indicators of performance and guides to improvement, these metrics operate as a form of power to create academic entrepreneurs who rely on actuarial forms of rationality in order to compete for survival and to punish those who fail to perform.

Communications scholars Marco Briziarelli and Joseph Flores emphasize that the knowledge worker in the academy therefore occupies a contradictory and conflicted class position. Much like managers, Briziarelli and Flores argue, academics are both employed and nonetheless exercise a significant amount of control at work, both over their own labor and that of others (e.g., graduate students or postdoctoral researchers). In the first instance, their work appears vocational and voluntary, a form of self-actualizing or self-fashioning activity. Yet they are constrained and rendered precarious by a number of other external factors that condition their employment, including large amounts of student debt. In general, they must struggle to become and maintain themselves as "employable." Briziarelli and Flores explain, "Those concepts clustered around employability synthesize the peculiar dialectical combination between the vocational, creative and flexibility aspects, and the level of pressure that the political economy of intellectual labour exerts on its agents that is internalized in terms of self-responsibilization, self-motivation and both exploitation and self-exploitation."[43] They follow Tiziana Terranova in articulating the contradictory meanings of "free labor" that are implied in contemporary academic knowledge production.[44] Knowledge workers in the academy are "free labor"; first, because their labor is flexible, they exercise considerably more control over their time than other workers, and their work is largely self-directed. But second, they are "free labor" in the sense that much of their work is unpaid and there is a general erosion of any distinction between "identity" and "occupation," "work" and "leisure," "private space" and "public space." For example, any coffee shop in an urban center of the United States is apt to be patronized at all hours of operation by academics writing, grading, meeting with students, and updating CVs even as they also enjoy music or chat with friends between papers. These considerations only apply for those on the tenure track, sadly. Adjuncts and other precariously employed academics face incredible erosion of autonomy in the workplace and control over their lives, so that their labor is "free" almost exclusively in the second sense.

In his discussion of "semiocapitalism," Franco "Bifo" Berardi refers to the expanding class of knowledge workers as the "cognitariat." Semiocapitalism, he explains, "takes the mind, language and creativity as its primary tools for the production of value."[45] Relatedly, Jodi Dean identifies a form of "communicative capitalism" which operates through, as she puts it, "the materialization of ideas of inclusion and participation in information, entertainment, and communication technologies in ways that capture resistance and intensify global capitalism."[46] Within this form of capitalism, value is increasingly produced and realized through "immaterial" and even leisure activities like playing games or creating social media profiles, with many cognitive and affective products "peer produced" and "crowd sourced." At the same time, one is supposed to realize oneself as a human being and as a citizen in the free activity of communication—making one's voice heard by tweeting, creating and sharing content with friends, building networks, and so on. The illusion of virtual democracy and effective political participation through online speech is harnessed to the cold reality of data harvesting, digital electioneering, and targeted social media advertising. Thus, of the Internet, Terranova writes, "[It] is always and simultaneously a gift economy and an advanced capitalist economy."[47] In this environment, academic knowledge workers join the broader cognitariat to compete for clicks in the "attention economy," increasingly rendered into self-branded "content mills" chasing "likes" and "shares." This activity is then itself imagined as self-fashioning or self-actualizing through intellectual activity and political participation.

Returning to Marcuse, the academic performance principle is internalized in the form of anxious concerns for "employability." The academic knowledge worker is an entrepreneur of themselves who, just like their students, must cultivate their human capital through self-investment in order to receive greater returns. They must perform their performativity through various means of self-marketing, aimed at demonstrating the effectiveness of their human capital—their capacity to produce profitable knowledge. Thus, we see the emergence of websites like academia.edu, the proliferation of personal webpages, and the development of research analytics dashboards like those offered by Plum Analytics or Google Scholar. All of these web-based applications feature or feed into self-narratives tailored to the academic job market and other potential consumers of or investors in academic labor. The repression entailed in the process of skills-cultivation and self-branding, referred to by Briziarelli and Flores as "self-exploitation," is also connected, however, to forms of desublimation and gratification.[48] The academic knowledge worker is "doing what they love" and, through this, achieving forms of self-fashioning and self-actualization. Their work is intellectual and creative, they have a "voice," for a few there is still the promise of tenure and the associated job security and life stability, and many receive the satisfactions of status and salary in a world where both are in desperately short supply.

Unfortunately, the self-fashioning and self-actualization that occurs is repressive inasmuch as it constitutes a kind of pathological narcissism in which the academic knowledge worker fetishizes their own commodified performance as a desirable technology of optimization and producer of knowledge commodities, their "brand." Indeed, terms like "knowledge worker," "knowledge economy," and "academic capitalism" already signify one-dimensionality to the extent that they frame knowledge as a commodity produced within and for the market rather than as a state or quality of the subject that would position them against and outside the economic sphere entirely. Where once it was believed that knowledge must transcend the everyday world of sensuous experience and the demands of appetitive satisfaction, rising above vulgar commerce in base goods and the common opinions of lesser minds, knowledge is now supposed to be integrated into and serve the purposes of economic growth and wasteful consumption. The good knowledge worker is one who optimizes their contribution to these ends. Recalling Marcuse, the manifest irrationality of this totalizing economic "rationality" becomes palpable when one realizes that voluntarily contributing to economic growth now more and more resembles agreeing to a global warming-induced suicide pact.

REORIENTING PHILOSOPHICAL DESIRE

Knowledge work within academic capitalism is one-dimensional in the sense that it collapses the traditional higher culture of the academy into the broader knowledge economy—transforming knowledge from an oppositional state of the subject into human capital, cognitive and other skills that are supposed to function as important factors of production and consumption. Much as art, according to Marcuse, traditionally represented sublimated desire and revolt against the ugliness of the established social order—taking its satisfaction by transcending the world through the production and enjoyment of counter-images—so, too, knowledge in its traditional form appealed to transcendent values and eternal verities against the way of the world.[49] Indeed, under the heading of "negative thinking," Marcuse discusses the manner in which traditional metaphysics comprehended reality dialectically as an "antagonistic unity." "In the equation Reason = Truth = Reality, which joins the subjective and the objective world into one antagonistic unity,"

Marcuse writes, "Reason is the subversive power, the 'power of the negative' that establishes, as theoretical and practical Reason, the truth for men and things—that is, the conditions in which men and things become what they really are."[50] Such thinking saw the phenomenal world not merely as false but the false appearance of Truth, as striving to realize its authentic nature and fulfill its immanent essence in a movement of actualization. Consciousness itself, in this traditional view, was to participate in the movement by seeking wisdom and virtue through the comprehension of the essential and the universal, an intellectual discovery through which the knower would participate in the being of the known object. In contrast, Marcuse viewed what he characterized as the "one-dimensional thinking" of his own time not as a revolt against the established order but as an effort to correspond, conform, and adjust to prevailing "reality."

The traditional philosophical image of knowledge is captured classically in Plato's Cave Allegory. The prisoners' bondage corresponds to the primitive condition of ignorance; it is a condition in which one is immersed in the sensory given, unable to distinguish between the phenomenal image of a thing and the thing itself. The discovery of the thing itself, depicted by Plato as a prisoner suddenly unshackled and able to turn away from the shadows, simultaneously reveals the ignorance characteristic of the primitive condition and the falsehood of the objects that appear within it, their ontological dependence and incompleteness. Each new step to a higher order of reality is accompanied by a similar revelation, an apprehension that both the standpoint and the objects that came before were false or merely partial. The prisoner's advance to the light is conceived by Plato as progressive emancipation through participation in the Truth, a journey of enlightenment in which the Sun both provides the power to see and illuminates higher objects of vision.

The prisoner's emancipatory sojourn of enlightenment, however, is not merely a matter of coming to know a higher reality, it is also a transformation of the subject through the redirection of desire. The erotic element is captured, of course, in the very name "philosophy"—*love* of wisdom—and presented most forcefully perhaps in Plato's *Symposium*. It is as evident, however, in St. Augustine's "restless hearts" as it is in the erotic striving of all beings for the Highest, the "unmoved mover," in Aristotle. The philosophical pursuit of wisdom manifests the desire to know and, through this, the desire to realize and express one's nature as a rational being. Marcuse summarizes the central points of this traditional view as follows:

> The philosophic quest proceeds from the finite world to the construction of a reality which is not subject to the painful difference between potentiality and actuality, which has mastered its negativity and is complete and independent in itself—*free*.[51]

The traditional figure of knowledge, according to Marcuse, is therefore two-dimensional, dynamic, erotic, internally antagonistic, and teleologically bound to libidinal striving for self-actualization. The central premise of all such thought is, perhaps, "Nothing is as it seems." Or "Everything is other than itself."

Marcuse's discussion of one-dimensional thinking and one-dimensional philosophy reveals the extent of the shift away from such traditional two-dimensional thinking. The dominant trends of philosophy in the twentieth century—positivism, behaviorism, operationalism, logical and linguistic analysis—were decidedly anti-metaphysical in their orientation. He refers to these trends as an "empiricist onslaught," which, "in its denial of the transcending elements of Reason, forms the academic counterpart of the socially required behavior."[52] The Happy Consciousness of the affluent society comes to expression in this triumphant empiricism. Its language, Marcuse contends, amounts to a "closing of the universe of discourse" so that those elements that might appear as transcending or negating the present order are instead systematically occluded and assimilated to it. This impoverishment of language serves to erase the internal contradictions and antagonism characteristic of negative thinking by collapsing any transcending or oppositional aspect of reason into the technological rationality of the given social order. He writes,

> The concepts which comprehend the facts and thereby transcend the facts are losing their authentic linguistic representation. Without these mediations, language tends to express and promote the immediate identification of reason and fact, truth and established truth, essence and existence, the thing and its function.[53]

For this thinking, appearance is reality and the real is the rational. Things are reduced to their functional role within a system that orders the world for quantification, measurement, effective administration, and productivity. Everything is in its right place.

One-dimensional thinking and its discourses are characterized particularly by two central operations: (1) isolation and atomization of facts and (2) mobilization of criteria drawn from the prevailing order. By isolating and atomizing facts, one-dimensional thinking is able to sever them from the broader social world within which they appear. Take, for example, contemporary discussions of unemployment and the recurrent announcement of "jobs numbers" or stock valuations. Such facts are taken to stand alone and speak for themselves, mobilized uncritically as indicators of the state of "the economy." Rather than reflect on the essence, value, or history of the economic or the nature of labor as such and its contemporary social organization, rather than question whether and why work is necessary or who it benefits and how, lower unemployment numbers are "good" and higher employment numbers are "bad." Similar remarks apply to other indicators such as GDP and stock market indices. The criteria for a well-functioning economic and social system are dictated in advance according to the terms of the system, in which it must be taken for granted that the labor of the many can and should be employed for the profit of the few. Concepts like reality, truth, and justice are similarly calibrated to fit and indeed to serve the system, rather than transcend or negate it. As Marcuse writes of such thinking, "Its very empiricism is ideological."[54] By the twenty-first century, such ideological empiricism has become self-parody as figures like Sam Harris and Richard Dawkins promote anti-Islamic bigotry as "science," presidential advisors opine concerning "alternative facts," and psychologists and philosophers alike search fMRI images for freedom of the will.

With respect to philosophy, Marcuse turns his attention especially to the Oxford ordinary language school and Wittgenstein's later work, presenting scathing criticisms. Marcuse reads this philosophical standpoint, and with it all of mid-century analytic philosophy, as fundamentally therapeutic in orientation. The intention, he thinks, is to demystify philosophical thought through the infusion of logical clarity and rigor, thereby disabusing the wayward mind of its obscure and unscientific metaphysical pretensions. If in ordinary language philosophy the aim is to return philosophical thought to everyday speech rather than logical or mathematical axioms, this represents a shift, not in the fundamental standpoint, but only in the relevant conception of philosophical indiscretion and muddle-headedness. In either case, much as Immanuel Kant sought to lay bare the bounds of reason and to expose the illusions and paralogisms that emerge when those bounds are transgressed, so, too, in Marcuse's reading, analytic philosophy set out to call reason back from its speculative misadventures to a properly scientific attitude. For such thinking, Marcuse writes, "Thought is on the level with reality when it is cured from transgression beyond a framework which is either purely axiomatic (logic, mathematics) or co-extensive with the established universe of discourse and behavior."[55] Philosophy in this paradigm is a matter of lowering the sights and adjusting the mind so that one learns to accept that the world is in order just as it is.[56]

Though Marcuse did not do so, one may look to Reichenbach's already-mentioned work, *The Rise of Scientific Philosophy*, to substantiate Marcuse's claims.[57] While certainly not a defender of ordinary language philosophy or an enthusiast of Wittgenstein's later works, Reichenbach promoted a "scientific philosophy" that, he held, requires a "reorientation of philosophic desires"—very much in accord with Marcuse's discussion of one-dimensional philosophy.[58] The scientific philosopher must renounce the desires of the speculative philosopher for absolute certainty, moral knowledge, and so on. Only then can one possess a secure method and produce truly scientific results. Once the transition is made, Reichenbach writes,

> Philosophy is no longer the story of men who attempted in vain to "say the unsayable" in pictures or verbose constructions of pseudological form. Philosophy is logical analysis of all forms of human thought; what it has to say can be stated in comprehensible terms, and there is nothing "unsayable" to which it must capitulate.[59]

Here, Reichenbach announces and enacts the very constriction of speech and impoverishment of the transcending features of language derided by Marcuse. What can be said at all can be said clearly, and there is nothing that cannot be said in the terms already at one's disposal.

For Reichenbach, scientific philosophy must give up its desire for anything unconditional, transcendent, or absolute in favor of submission to the facts as they present themselves. He expostulates,

> Truth comes from without: the observation of physical objects tells us what is true. But ethics comes from within: it expresses an "I will," not a "there is." Such is the reorientation of philosophic desires required of the scientific philosopher. Those who are able to control their desires will discover that they gain much more than they lose.[60]

The philosophical erotics advocated by Reichenbach, the therapy he advances, is formally identical to the repressive desublimation identified by Marcuse as characteristic of the Happy Consciousness. For Marcuse, therapeutic adjustment to the prevailing order is the essence of what McCumber will later come to understand as Cold War Philosophy. Unlike Marcuse, McCumber advances an explanation of the rise of this paradigm that goes beyond noting its formal unity with broader social and cultural transformations produced by the affluent society. In particular, such a philosophical perspective could claim to be objective and apolitical, thereby avoiding the scrutiny of McCarthyist censors and adjusting itself to the demands of the affluent society.

NEOLIBERAL PHILOSOPHY AS ONE-DIMENSIONAL

In contrast to the era of Cold War Philosophy and its scientistic bent, much of what is today called analytic philosophy is happily speculative and more than willing to discuss normative ethics and political philosophy. As an indication of the shift, one may note that no less than twenty-three philosophers at New York (NYU) and Rutgers Universities, the top two rated departments in the United States according to the *Philosophical Gourmet Report* (PGR), list metaphysics as an area of specialization.[61] Of course, precisely metaphysics was to have been abandoned as meaningless within Cold War Philosophy. In their recent *Metaphysics: An Introduction to Contemporary Debates and Their History*, Anna Marmodoro and Erasmus Mayr describe contemporary metaphysics in strikingly traditional ways: it is a science of the fundamental makeup of reality, being as such, distinguished from other sciences by its fundamentality and generality.[62] If at mid-century Reichenbach was happy to write what might be appropriately termed a "manifesto" purporting to answer every major philosophical question while demolishing metaphysics, no similar grand gesture is conceivable in the present day. Cold War Philosophy was to have mobilized the corrosive acid of logical or conceptual analysis to dissolve the metaphysical and ethical propositions of previous philosophy, showing them, once and for all, for what they truly were: poetry at best, pseudological bullshit at worst. This is a far cry from Neoliberal Philosophy.

One would search in vain among the practitioners of Neoliberal Philosophy for a singular method or conception of *prima philosophia*, despite the resurgence of metaphysics. Instead, the discipline is marked by hyperspecialization and, while certain methodological tools or approaches may be common (e.g., thought experiments), there is no single methodological approach that would, for instance, encompass work in mathematical logic, philosophy of mind, feminist philosophy, and, say, philosophy of law. The PGR ranks departments in more than thirty specialty areas, most of which could easily be subdivided; linkages between them are complex and, in the language of Gilles Deleuze and Felix Guattari, rhizomatic.[63] Rather than a hierarchical organization of knowledge in which some specializations would take ontological, epistemological, or practical precedence over others, the "roots" of which other specializations are "branches," communication proceeds along a network of links connecting one specialization to the next. Arguments or theses developed in one specialization are can be brought to bear on new questions in new areas, but few contemporary philosophers would assert the unqualified primacy of philosophy of language over metaphysics or normative ethics, for example. Even fields such as applied ethics and moral psychology function relatively autonomously with respect to what may seem to be their "root" subdiscipline, normative ethics. In fact, the organization or structure of contemporary philosophical knowledge is so flattened and fragmented that even "metaphilosophy" is merely one subdiscipline among others with no particular claim to govern or subordinate them. Without a metanarrative or governing logic, fields blossom as the occasion demands.

Reinvigoration of previously moribund questions, proliferation of subdisciplines, continual narrowing of fields of specialization, horizontal, networked organization of the epistemic terrain—these features occur within a competitive, stratified, entrepreneurial market with an accompanying system of philosophical celebrities. Perhaps the most well-known and easily identifiable indicator of the competition for funding and prestige is the PGR itself. Much as in a game show, departments are rated by expert celebrity judges as to their quality—dubiously considered a function of the ratings of the celebrity judges. While such ratings are officially disavowed by the APA, they nonetheless play a role in faculty hiring and funding decisions both on campus and off as they provide administrators and grantors a quantitative measure by which to compare the performance of departments and the individuals within them.[64] The highest rated departments at the top of the ranking system function like professional sports teams, poaching talent from around the country and even the world to pad their roster with superstars. In the game-show world of Neoliberal Philosophy, there are winners and losers, the losers very often limited in their audience, overworked with previously unimaginable teaching loads, insecure in their employment and prospects, and generally erased as legitimate interlocutors or contributors to the broad philosophical conversation. Adjuncts in philosophy, as elsewhere, form a precarious underclass within the cognitariat, denied even the most basic forms of voice or security.

As it flattens the field, narrows and subdivides endlessly, and is infused with competition and accompanying stratification of status, Neoliberal Philosophy takes on the characteristics of Mode 2 knowledge production. Whereas scientific research has been historically divided between "basic" and "applied" science, philosophers now, particularly since the 1970s, draw a distinction between "pure" and "applied" philosophy.[65] As mentioned above, according to Gibbons et al., knowledge production takes place more and more in the context of application, so that the distinction between basic and applied science is no longer as relevant. They mention such disciplines as aeronautical engineering and computer science as examples in which the barrier between basic and applied science breaks down in such a way that the discipline in question is already both and neither.[66] It is worth noting Lyotard's vision of the technosciences in their plurality here—not only the products but even the processes of the technosciences are integrated into and pervade social relations of all kinds.

The related phenomena in contemporary philosophy center on the production of "applied philosophy" and "public philosophy." Applied philosophy began to take shape in the 1970s due to the perceived need—emerging, we must speculate, out of the political involvements of many young philosophers—for philosophy to address the political and social problems of the time as they were raised both by social movements and by massive technological change. Indeed, in describing its founding, the Society for Applied Philosophy says that it "arose from the awareness that many topics of public debate—in law, politics, economics, science, technology, medicine and more—can be illuminated by critical analysis, philosophical questioning, and reflection of questions of value."[67] There is considerable discussion about what it means to do applied philosophy, but David Archard helpfully distinguishes what he calls "Top-Down Models" from "Bottom-Up Models."[68] In the Top-Down view, there is a strong distinction between pure philosophy, which is taken to be general, abstract, theoretical, and written strictly for an expert audience, and applied philosophy. Applied philosophy occurs when one discusses specific contemporary issues in light of general philosophical principles or methods already developed within "pure philosophy," perhaps especially when addressed to a public audience. By contrast, in "Bottom-Up Models," "the philosopher starts from a specific domain, or set of circumstances, or case; she acquires a proper and informed appreciation of it, and develops the relevant philosophical judgment, understanding, or evaluation."[69] For advocates of a Bottom-Up Model, a useful analogy may be drawn between casuistry or jurisprudential reasoning on the basis of case law and applied philosophy—the main focus is on paradigm cases and one may permissibly reason on the basis of analogy. As discussed by Archard, there are important objections to either conception. It cannot be disputed, however, that applied philosophy has grown immensely in influence in the discipline.

For Robert Frodeman and Adam Briggle, the changes have not been sufficient. They argue for a new form of "Mode 2 philosophy" that they also call "field philosophy," in which, they write, "philosophers work in real time with a variety of audiences and stakeholders."[70] There is a case to be made, however, that there are many philosophers already at work "in the field"—even beyond Frodeman and Briggle themselves. A good example comes from the *Pacific Standard* magazine, which chronicles the work of philosopher of information Luciano Floridi, there dubbed "Google's Philosopher," who worked with a panel of experts assembled to address privacy concerns in response to rulings of the European Union's Court of Justice.[71] Indeed, work on and in the context of application and, with it, transdisciplinarity are now basic features of the philosophical landscape. Consider the following areas of specialty that have featured in recent job appointments as cataloged by philjobs.org: applied ethics, business ethics, philosophy of cognitive science, philosophy of psychology, philosophy of biology, philosophy of medicine, bioethics, environmental philosophy, philosophy of artificial intelligence, medical ethics, philosophy of social sciences, philosophy of gender and race, and so on.[72] Note also the homes of some of the appointments: School of Life Sciences (Arizona State University), McCoy Family Center for Ethics in Society, Surrey School of Law, National Institutes of Health, Taipei Medical University, Philosophy/Neuroscience/Psychology Program, Center for Bioethics, University Center for Human Values and Woodrow Wilson School of Public and International Affairs—the list goes on. It may be that philosophy has not changed to the extent that some might wish, but it is hard to deny the changes.

Indeed, while Frodeman and Briggle may argue that philosophy has remained unreasonably insular due to its professionalization and institutionalization, philosophers in the United States have in fact produced an unprecedented amount of work with and for public audiences in recent years. Take the "Popular Culture and Philosophy Series" published by Open Court. Since 2000, they have published more than 130 titles on everything from *The Sopranos* to the Atkins Diet.[73] Notably, this is only one such series. Popular works such as *Plato at the Googleplex* or *Hiking with Nietzsche* or *At the Existentialist Cafe* illustrate another brand of public-oriented philosophizing. These print publications are complemented by online magazines such as *Aeon*, dedicated to the popularization of "big ideas." Similarly, the *New York Times* hosts *The Stone* blog where, according to the website, "contemporary philosophers and other thinkers" address "issues both timely and timeless."[74] With the emergence of dailynous.com, there is also now a major public forum for news and views related to academic philosophy that is more or less open to a broad non-philosophical readership. There are, further, innumerable blogs, podcasts, YouTube videos and channels, Wikipedia entries, Reddit threads, and other less formal forums in which academic philosophers are engaged in public work. Finally, while philosophical ideas and theories have played roles in film and television since the inception of the media, one must certainly remark on the recent popular success of NBC's *The Good Place*, which featured not only philosophical themes but also direct, on-screen instruction in philosophy and off-screen consultation from two professional philosophers, Todd May and Pamela Hieronymi.[75] In all these venues, we see philosophy in the context of Mode 2 knowledge production, not only making exoteric the wisdom of the inner circle but in fact doing philosophy in public in the context of its "use."

Indeed, Frodeman and Briggle themselves observe the emergence of what they term a "modern day 'Republic of Letters,'" in which philosophical questions are discussed in public forums by non-philosophers—or, at a minimum, non-academic philosophers. Of such philosophers, they write,

> Sometimes they work on the margins of the academy in units like Oxford's Future of Humanity Institute. But more often they are located in non-academic locations like the Center for Applied Rationality, Google, and the Breakthrough Institute—or at magazines (e.g. *Wired*), blogs large and small, YouTube channels, and other social media. These are the modern day salons—though they make up a decidedly uneven landscape, in some cases backed by enormous amounts of capital that are able to turn ideas into realities, with all the profits and problems that follow.[76]

Unsurprisingly, the list of venues and knowledge workers mentioned is closely associated with Silicon Valley and its brand of technophiliac futurology, an aesthetic most fully on display in the TED brand and associated spinoffs. From the standpoint of Frodeman and Briggle, philosophers remain aloof of the conversations fostered in these "salons" at their peril—possibly at society's. It is hardly the case, however, that academic philosophers have been missing from such outlets. Rebecca Newberger Goldstein, David Chalmers, Ruth Chang, Michael Lynch, Daniel Cohen, and Peter Singer are just a few among the many academic philosophers who have appeared on the TED stage to address the "Republic."[77] All of the named philosophers above and others besides are engaged in projects that are thought relevant to the prognostications of the futurologists. Further, philosophers are contributing to public discussion beyond such high-tech venues, dripping as they are with capital and the aura of science fiction. There are also projects like the Socrates Café or Philosophy for Children, in my estimation considerably more worthwhile. In contrast to the image of philosophy as a stale, Mode 1 dinosaur, then, philosophy is already adapting well to Mode 2 conditions. Possibly more like the rest of the humanities than many are wont to admit, philosophy is not a recalcitrant holdout against the imperatives of the postmodern knowledge economy but an "early adopter."[78]

Much lamentation about the ineffectual nature of academic philosophy, participates, even when its barbs are on the mark and deserved, in a well-established form of scientistic anti-intellectualism. It draws on the anti-metaphysical ethos characteristic of Cold War Philosophy as well as the rhetorical bravado of philosophical modernizers of all ages. Even as it condemns pretensions to the status of science and the attempt to remain indifferent to political and social concerns, the newest iteration of this anti-intellectualism demands real-world results. Frodeman and Briggle, for instance, decry the inability of philosophers to produce work that is appropriately impactful, writing, "Philosophy needs to demonstrate its bona fides by showing how it can make timely and effective contributions to contemporary discussions."[79] They do not adopt this position lightly. Rather, they see it as the only strategic response to the demands of neoliberal culture. But Marcuse had already in the 1960s attacked what he perceived then as the "academic sadomasochism, self-humiliation, and self-denunciation of the intellectual whose labor does not issue in scientific, technical or like achievements."[80] The chief charge against philosophy remains that it is unproductive, useless in the real world—a sentiment unfortunately shared by the ideologues of empiricism, like science-popularizer Neil deGrasse Tyson.[81]

Whereas the academic sadomasochism of the anti-metaphysical philosophy of the Cold War period consisted in a reorientation of desire toward the project of inoculating reason against its own speculative excesses, attacks on philosophy as Mode 1 take a perverse pleasure in the self-castigating command to "make a difference." In this, they seem to agree with Marx's famous Eleventh Thesis: "The philosophers have only interpreted the world, but the point is to change it."[82] The cathecting of philosophical desire into a critique of philosophy aimed at "changing the world," however, remains trapped by its antecedent acceptance of the world as it is—that is, by its general inability to desire beyond or against neoliberalism and the knowledge economy. Much like the pedagogy of critical thinking, philosophical knowledge production is harnessed in advance to the values of performativity and entrepreneurship even, and perhaps especially, when it is practiced as critique or critical thinking. In contrast to Marx's demand that philosophy negated through its realization in revolutionary praxis, we have an annihilation of philosophy realized as a demand for measurable amelioration. Rather than the sadomasochistic self-discipline of science, one is instead to accept the disciplining anxieties of the market and "change the world by investing well." "Effective altruism" supplants the desire for transcendence. Much as with the APA's discussion of the value of philosophy, the strategic imperative of marketing requires that the individual philosopher or department internalize the demand to perform their performativity.

NOTES

1. See especially Sigmund Freud, *Beyond the Pleasure Principle*, trans. James Strachey (New York: W.W. Norton, 1961). From the very first page, Freud will describe his approach to psychology as "economic." For a succinct summation of Freud's early theory, see Sigmund Freud, "Formulations on the Two Principles of Mental Functioning," in *The Standard Edition of the Complete Psychological Works of Sigmund Freud, Volume XII (1911–1913): The Case of Schreber, Papers on Technique and Other Works*, trans. and ed., James Strachey (London, Hogarth Press, 1958), pp. 213–226.

2. See Sigmund Freud, *Civilization and Its Discontents*, trans. and ed. James Strachey (New York: W.W. Norton & Company, 1961), 34.

3. Herbert Marcuse, *Eros and Civilization: A Philosophical Inquiry into Freud* (Boston, MA: Beacon Press, 1966), 35. Emphasis in original.

4. Ibid., 36. Emphasis in original.

5. Ibid., 45.

6. Ibid., 35.

7. Ibid.

8. Karl Marx, *Capital* in *Karl Marx: Selected Writings, Second Edition*, ed. David McLellan (New York: Oxford University Press, 2000), 490–491.

9. Karl Marx and Friedrich Engels, *The Communist Manifest* in *Karl Marx: Selected Writings, Second Edition*, ed. David McLellan (New York: Oxford University Press,

2000), 251. See also Karl Marx, *Economic and Philosophical Manuscripts* in *Karl Marx: Selected Writings, Second Edition*, ed. David McLellan (New York: Oxford University Press, 2000): 83–121.

10. Herbert Marcuse, *One-Dimensional Man: Studies in the Ideology of Advanced Industrial Society* (Boston: Beacon Press, 1964), 11ff.

11. Marcelo Vieta, "Marcuse's 'Transcendent Project' at 50: 'Post-Technological Rationality' for Our Times," *Radical Philosophy Review* 19, no. 1 (2016), 151–152.

12. See Martin Heidegger, "The Question Concerning Technology," in *The Question Concerning Technology and Other Essays*, trans. William Lovitt (New York: Harper & Row Publishers, 1977): 3–35.

13. See Marianna Papastephanou and Charoula Angeli, "Critical Thinking Beyond Skill," *Educational Philosophy and Theory* 39, no. 6 (2007), 610ff. They write, "Effective thinking as proneness to find the optimal means for achieving the desired ends is an important element of human existence (and in no way peculiar to the West, for sure). But the exaggeration and hegemony of effectiveness constitutes an absolutization and universalization of the specific western context and an effacement of complementary or alternative spaces" (613).

14. Michael Peters, "The New Prudentialism in Education: Actuarial Rationality and the Entrepreneurial Self," *Educational Theory* 55, no. 2 (2005), 134.

15. Clayton Pierce, "Education for Life and Death: Marcuse's Critical Theory of Education in the Neoliberal Era," *Radical Philosophy Review* 16, no. 2 (2013), 613. See also Andrew Lyndon Knighton, "Beyond 'Education in Sickness': A Biopolitical Marcuse and Some Prospects for University Self-Administration," *Theory & Event* 20, no. 2 (2017): 769–787. Knighton writes, "For Marcuse, the case of higher education poses a somatic, affective, and even instinctual problem of capitalist corporeality and the management of aggregated forces of human creative power" (770). Likewise, see Tyson Lewis, "Biopower, Play, and Experience in Education," in *Marcuse's Challenge to Education*, eds. Douglass Kellner, Tyson Lewis, Clayton Pierce, and K. Daniel Cho (Lanham, MD: Rowman & Littlefield, 2009), 45–57. Lewis is more interested in a reading that draws a link between Giorgio Agamben's theorization of biopower and a biopolitical reading of Marcuse.

16. See Thomas Piketty, *Capital in the Twenty-First Century*, trans. Arthur Goldhammer (Cambridge, MA: Harvard University Press, 2017). In particular, Piketty writes, "Briefly, the shocks that buffeted the economy in the period 1914–1945—World War I, the Bolshevik Revolution of 1917, the Great Depression, World War II, and the consequent advent of new regulatory and tax policies along with controls on capital—reduced capital's share of income to historically low levels in the 1950s. Very soon, however, capital began to reconstitute itself" (53). He documents elsewhere that at a low point in the 1950s the top decile of income earners commanded less than 35 percent of national income—by the 2000s that number would soar to nearly 50 percent (31).

17. Michael Forman, "One-Dimensional Man and the Crisis of Neoliberal Capitalism: Revisiting Marcuse in the Occupation," *Radical Philosophy Review* 16, no 2. (2013), 510.

18. *One-Dimensional Man*, 1.

19. Ibid., 4–5.
20. Ibid., 9.
21. Ibid., 71ff.
22. Ibid., 62.
23. Ibid., 74.
24. For more on this subject, see Siddhartha Kara, "Is Your Phone Tainted by the Misery of the 35,000 Children in Congo's Mines?" Modern Day Slavery in Focus, *The Guardian*, October 12, 2018, https://www.theguardian.com/global-development/2018/oct/12/phone-misery-children-congo-cobalt-mines-drc.
25. See G.W.F. Hegel, *The Phenomenology of Spirit*, trans. A.V. Miller (New York: Oxford University Press, 1977), §207ff.
26. *One-Dimensional Man*, 79.
27. For more on this neoliberal mantra, see Miya Tokumitsu, *Do What You Love: And Other Lies about Success and Happiness* (New York: Regan Arts, 2015). As well as "In the Name of Love," *Jacobin*, January 12, 2014.
28. See Gary Becker, "A Theory of the Allocation of Time," *The Economic Journal* 75, no. 299 (September 1965), 493–517. Becker considers the home a "small factory" because "it combines capital goods, raw materials and labour to clean, feed, procreate and otherwise produce useful commodities" (496).
29. Jean-François Lyotard, *The Postmodern Condition*, trans. Geoff Bennington and Brian Massumi (Minneapolis: University of Minnesota Press, 1984), 4–5.
30. See Michael Gibbons, Camille Limoges, Helga Nowotny, Simon Schwartzman, Peter Scott, and Martin Trow, *The New Knowledge Production: The Dynamics of Science and Research in Contemporary Societies* (Los Angeles: Sage, 1994), 3–8.
31. See Sheila Slaughter and Gary Rhoades, *Academic Capitalism and the New Economy: Markets, State, and Higher Education* (Baltimore: Johns Hopkins University Press, 2010), 28ff.
32. Ibid., 33.
33. Vannevar Bush, "Science: The Endless Frontier," *Transactions of the Kansas Academy of Science (1903-)* 48, no. 3 (December 1945), 234.
34. Gerard Delanty, *Challenging Knowledge: The University in the Knowledge Society* (Philadelphia, PA: Open University Press, 2001), 120. See also Henry Etzkowitz and Loet Leydesdorff, "The Dynamics of Innovation: From National Systems and 'Mode 2' to a Triple Helix of University—Industry—Government Relations," *Research Policy* 29, no. 2 (2000), 109–123.
35. *Academic Capitalism*, 51.
36. Ibid., 29.
37. *One-Dimensional Man*, 19.
38. Steven C. Ward, *Neoliberalism and the Global Restructuring of Knowledge and Education* (New York: Routledge, 2012), 106–114.
39. Richard Sennett, *The Culture of the New Capitalism* (New Haven, CT: Yale UP, 2006), 47–58.
40. *Neoliberalism and the Global Restructuring of Knowledge and Education*, 115.
41. Cris Shore and Susan Wright, "Audit Culture Revisited: Rankings, Ratings, and the Reassembling of Society," *Current Anthropology* 56, no. 3 (June 2015), 421.

42. Leo McCann, Edward Granter, Paula Hyde, and Jeremy Aroles, "'Upon the Gears and Upon the Wheels': Terror Convergence and Total Administration in the Neoliberal University," *Management Learning* 51, no. 4 (2020), 11.

43. Marco Briziarelli and Joseph L. Flores, "Professing Contradictions: Knowledge Work and the Neoliberal Condition of Academic Workers," *TripleC* 16, no. 1 (2018), 121.

44. See Tiziana Terranova, "Free Labor: Producing Culture for the Digital Economy," *Social Text* 18, no. 2 (2000): 33–58.

45. Franco "Bifo" Berardi, *The Soul at Work: From Alienation to Autonomy*, trans. Francesca Cadel and Giuseppina Mecchia (Los Angeles, CA: Semiotext(e), 2009), 21. Interestingly, much of Berardi's text is directed toward a critique of theories of alienation and a critique of Marcuse in particular. Strangely, Berardi misses the important feature of refusal that is fundamental to Marcuse's conception of revolutionary subjectivity. For further discussion, see Michael Gardiner, "An Autonomist Marcuse?" *Rethinking Marxism: A Journal of Economics, Culture, and Society* 30, no. 2 (2018): 232–255.

46. Jodi Dean, *Democracy and Other Illusions: Communicative Capitalism and Left Politics* (Durham, NC: Duke University Press, 2009), 2.

47. "Free Labor," 51. Relatedly, Justin Pack cites George Gilder's *Wealth and Poverty*, a favorite of Ronald Reagan, as arguing that capitalism is itself a gift economy reliant on the generosity of entrepreneurs. See *How the Neoliberalization of Academia Leads to Thoughtlessness: Arendt and the Modern University* (Lanham, MD: Lexington Books, 2018), 130.

48. "Professing Contradictions," 119–121.

49. For a rewarding and rigorous discussion of Marcuse's aesthetics in relation to the theory of alienation, see Charles Reitz, *Art, Alienation, and the Humanities: A Critical Engagement with Herbert Marcuse* (Albany, NY: SUNY Press, 2000). Reitz notes a shift in Marcuse's thinking toward an increasing emphasis on the importance of artistic estrangement and distance in the later works, culminating in Marcuse's *The Aesthetic Dimension: Toward a Critique of Marxist Aesthetics* (Boston, MA: Beacon Press, 1978).

50. *One-Dimensional Man*, 123.

51. Ibid., 127.

52. Ibid., 13.

53. Ibid., 85.

54. Ibid., 117.

55. Ibid., 170.

56. Cf. Ibid., 170–173. Marcuse particularly references Wittgenstein's dictum that "[Philosophy] leaves everything as it is." See Ludwig Wittgenstein, *Philosophical Investigations, 3rd Ed.*, trans. and ed. G.E.M. Anscombe (Malden, MA: Blackwell, 2001), §124. Marcuse's interpretation of Wittgenstein operates in broad strokes and, it seems to me, misses much of the nuance of the text.

57. Marcuse does refer to Reichenbach once in *One-Dimensional Man*. See *One-Dimensional Man*, 149.

58. Hans Reichenbach, *The Rise of Scientific Philosophy* (Berkeley, CA: University of California Press, 1951), 305.

59. Ibid., 308.

60. Ibid., 306.

61. See "Faculty," Department of Philosophy, New York University, accessed September 28, 2020. https://as.nyu.edu/content/nyu-as/as/departments/philosophy/directory/faculty.html. As well as "Faculty," Department of Philosophy, Rutgers University, accessed September 28, 2020. https://philosophy.rutgers.edu/people/faculty.

62. Anna Marmadoro and Erasmus Mayr, *Metaphysics: An Introduction to Contemporary Debates and Their History* (New York: Oxford University Press, 2019), 1–9.

63. Gilles Deleuze and Felix Guattari, *A Thousand Plateaus: Capitalism and Schizophrenia*, trans. Brian Massumi (Minneapolis, MN: University of Minnesota Press, 1987).

64. See "Statement on Rankings of Departments," American Philosophical Association, accessed September 28, 2020. https://www.apaonline.org/page/rankings. For an important discussion of flaws in the methodology used by the *Philosophical Gourmet Report*, see Bryan Bruya, "Appearance and Reality in *The Philosophical Gourmet Report*: Why the Discrepancy Matters to the Profession of Philosophy," *Metaphilosophy* 46, nos. 4–5 (October 2015): 657–690. For a discussion of how these flaws relate to continuing forms of identity-based oppression in Neoliberal Philosophy, see chapter 4.

65. For a very useful treatment dealing with much the same history in much the same context, see Robert Frodeman, Adam Briggle, and J. Britt Holbrook, "Philosophy in the Age of Neoliberalism," *Social Epistemology: A Journal of Knowledge, Culture, and Policy* 26, nos. 3–4 (2012): 1–20.

66. *The New Production of Knowledge*, 4. As the authors point out, however, these disciplines nonetheless retain many aspects of Mode 1, despite their hybrid nature, due to their being housed in relatively traditional Mode 1 institutional settings.

67. "About Us," *The Society for Applied Philosophy*, accessed September 28, 2020. https://www.appliedphil.org.

68. David Archard, "The Methodology of Applied Philosophy," in *A Companion to Applied Philosophy*, eds. Kasper Lippert-Rasmussen, Kimberley Brownlee, and David Coady (Hoboken, NJ: Wiley Blackwell, 2017): 18–33.

69. Ibid., 24.

70. Robert Frodeman and Adam Briggle, *Socrates Tenured: The Institutions of 21st-Century Philosophy* (New York: Rowman & Littlefield, 2016), Kindle, 25.

71. Robert Herritt, "Google's Philosopher," *Pacific Standard*, December 30, 2014 (Updated: Jun 14, 2017). https://psmag.com/environment/googles-philosopher-technology-nature-identity-court-legal-policy-95456.

72. See "Data Feed," *PhilJobs: Jobs for Philosophers*, accessed September 28, 2020. https://philjobs.org/appointments/dataFeed. The data is available via a downloadable spreadsheet.

73. See "Philosophy and Popular Culture Series," *Open Court Publishing Company*, accessed September 28, 2020. http://www.opencourtbooks.com/categories/pcp.htm.

74. "The Stone," Opinion, *The New York Times*, accessed September 28, 2020. https://www.nytimes.com/column/the-stone.

75. Chris Quintana, "Meet the Philosophers Who Give 'The Good Place' Its Scholarly Bona Fides," *The Chronicle of Higher Education*, February 6, 2018, https://www.chronicle.com/article/Meet-the-Philosophers-Who-Give/242462.

76. *Socrates Tenured*, 122.

77. "TED Speakers," *TED: Ideas Worth Spreading*, accessed September 28, 2020. https://www.ted.com/speakers.

78. In *The New Knowledge Production*, Gibbons et al. argue that "reflexivity" is a central feature of Mode 2 knowledge production. As they frame it, precisely this reflexivity creates increased demand for humanistic forms of inquiry, as the public looks for guidance on the ethical and practical issues they encounter (7–8). Indeed, Gibbons et al. write that "In terms of other closely related Mode 2 characteristics [beyond rapid expansion, heterogeneity, and contextualization]—the generation of knowledge within a context of application, greater social accountability, and quality control no longer determined by scientific quality alone but including wider criteria—the humanities have always been forerunners" (99).

79. *Socrates Tenured*, 23–24.

80. *One-Dimensional Man*, 173.

81. See Massimo Piggliuci's presentation of Tyson's comments and criticisms of them in "Neil deGrasse Tyson and the Value of Philosophy," *The Huffington Post*, May 16, 2014 (Updated: July 16, 2014). https://www.huffpost.com/entry/neil-degrasse-tyson-and-the-value-of-philosophy_b_5330216.

82. Karl Marx, *Theses on Feuerbach* in *Karl Marx: Selected Writings*, Second Edition, ed. David McLellan (New York: Oxford University Press, 2000), 173.

Chapter 4

Diversity and Neoliberal Philosophy

My analysis of the Neoliberal University thus far has highlighted four central trends: (1) defunding higher education and reframing it as a private consumer good, (2) reconceiving the purpose of higher education as training rather than education, (3) the instrumentalization and commodification of knowledge, and (4) the centralization and bureaucratization of administration. In response to these trends, I have argued, the discipline of philosophy has been reconfigured. The imperative within the Neoliberal University is to perform and indeed to demonstrate that one performs well. Strategically, the discipline has acted to market itself, to show that it can provide return on investment in the form of critical thinking skills. Such skills are taken to be part of a broader "bundle of skills" that allow a person to function as what I have termed a technology of optimization. Through investment in these skills, one is thought to maximize productivity and thereby contribute to national economic growth, provide advantages in global economic competition, and increase one's own earnings. Claiming to produce such technologies of optimization, Neoliberal Philosophy presents itself as a good investment, it performs its performativity.

Further, as I showed in the previous chapter, Neoliberal Philosophy is increasingly integrated into the broader knowledge economy. Alongside other knowledge workers, philosophers compete on the market to ensure their employability utilizing an actuarial form of rationality. Much as the discipline markets itself to stakeholders, individual philosophers and departments must market themselves, creating a consumable brand that demonstrates their capacity to produce profitable goods for exchange. Within this environment, philosophers are rated according to a variety of metrics and compete amongst themselves for funding and favor. Each must show optimal productivity in order to attract investment in the form of employment. If the desire of the philosopher in centuries past was to rise above the established order to understand eternal verities, this is no longer the case. As Marcuse argued, such desire was masochistically reoriented toward adjustment to reality during the heyday of Cold War Philosophy; hence we encounter the anti-metaphysical ethos of its dominant schools. Unlike its predecessor, Neoliberal Philosophy rejects this anti-metaphysical ethos even while it flattens the epistemic field, philosophical specialties proliferate, and philosophical questions abandoned by Cold War Philosophy are resuscitated and interrogated with new vigor and urgency. The strategic imperative, indeed the animating desire, is to show measurable results. Neoliberal Philosophy is one-dimensional, I have therefore argued, in that it internalizes economic standards of evaluation, treating philosophical knowledge as an alienable commodity that can be exchanged and measured to determine its "impact."

For the most part, I have analyzed the Neoliberal University, indeed neoliberalism itself, as if it were neutral with respect to identity-based forms of oppression. In fact, according to its own self-presentation, neoliberalism is "blind" to questions of race, gender, sexuality, and so on.[1] *Homo economicus* has neither race nor religion, neither sexual identity nor preferred pronouns. Market rationality does not care for these categories or practices, except insofar as they may contribute in some way to productivity or function as commodities themselves. In fact, neoliberal economization may at times represent itself as actively hostile to identity-based oppression inasmuch as such oppression is thought to irrationally hamper and intervene in the market's dynamics of competition and optimization. In what respect and to what extent, then, are the processes unleashed by neoliberalism, as these affect and structure the Neoliberal University and within it Neoliberal Philosophy, imbricated with identity-based oppressions?

To begin to answer this question, I draw on Melamed's work *Represent and Destroy: Rationalizing Violence in the New Racial Capitalism*. Following the work of sociologist Howard Winant, Melamed theorizes a post-war "racial break" in which White supremacy, both within the United States and globally, was defeated as a formal program of governance. A number of factors played a role in producing the racial break, among many others the discrediting of biological racism globally with the revelation of the horrors of the Holocaust.[2] According to Melamed's telling, the racial break resulted in the emergence of "official antiracisms" that served to legitimate capitalism and the dominant position of the United States globally. These official antiracisms, however, were not mere ideological window-dressing. They functioned rather as racializing technologies themselves, sorting people as valued citizens or disposable surplus populations according to newly articulated "cultural" criteria. Through this process, antiracism was incorporated into the machinations of capital and state in such a way that it could function to render populations disposable and to normalize their oppression through discourses of meritocracy and cultural pathology.

For Melamed, neoliberal multiculturalism represents the apotheosis of this process, simultaneously obfuscating the operations of global capitalism and transforming antiracism into a subjective disposition marked by "openness to diversity." The Neoliberal University is far from a bystander in this process but is instead the primary institution responsible for creating the cosmopolitan subjects required for the production and consumption of the new cultural commodities of the knowledge economy, including multicultural diversity itself. While different forms of identity-based oppression are irreducible to one another, it is important to acknowledge that the strategies for their incorporation into neoliberalism have been broadly similar. Thus, terms like "equity," "diversity," and "inclusion," now unmoored from discourses related to race and racism (especially anti-Black racism) or policies designed to redress racial injustice, function indiscriminately with vague reference to all forms of "difference" whatever they may be and however they may be related.

A GENEALOGY OF NEOLIBERAL MULTICULTURALISM

Melamed divides the post-war history of the United States in the aftermath of the "racial break" into three periods, each characterized by a dominant form of official antiracism. The three periods she identifies are characterized by the dominance of: (1) race liberalism, (2) liberal multiculturalism, and (3) neoliberal multiculturalism. These successive forms of dominant antiracist thought incorporated and co-opted antiracist categories into projects of U.S. imperialism and neocolonialism and the expanding prerogatives of global capitalism.

Melamed follows numerous critical race theorists in suggesting that the success of the civil rights movement in the United States corresponded to the larger geopolitical interests of the state and White elites in the post-war period.[3] "In order to successfully define the terms of global governance after World War II," she explains,

> U.S. bourgeoisie classes had to manage the racial contradictions that antiracist and anticolonial movements exposed. As racial liberalism provided the logic and idiom of such management, it became an essential organizing discourse and force for U.S. postwar society and global power.[4]

Locked in the Cold War with the Soviet Union, facing increasing political pressure domestically, and struggling to win the allegiance of the "wretched of the earth" around the world, the United States transformed its dominant narrative to position itself as a progressive purveyor of liberty and equality. Capitalist modernity, of the kind the United States claimed to offer, was not essentially bound up with racial oppression but was, on the contrary, a vehicle for its elimination. Through the adoption of race liberalism as a dominant discursive formation, long-held narratives of Manifest Destiny and American Exceptionalism could now be rearticulated in terms of racial equality.

Analyzing particularly Gunnar Myrdal's massive and influential 1944 study, *An American Dilemma*, Melamed identifies three important features of the race liberalism that came to dominate in the post-war period.[5] Firstly, race liberalism sutured antiracism to American nationalism. Racial progress could therefore be seen as taking place not in spite of or against American culture and its institutions, but because of them. Secondly, race liberalism conceived racism as a problem of individual White prejudice and ignorance, so that it was able to center White people and tell the story of race in America as one of gradual White enlightenment. Hence, antiracist activism, in this frame, took the form of educating Whites. Finally, race liberalism rejected biological conceptions of race in favor of a cultural conception. The cultural conception of race combined with the antecedent embrace of American nationalism to produce a viewpoint in which Americans of all skin colors and geographical backgrounds could be seen as united in their inheritance of American culture. To the extent that Black people differed from dominant Whites, this was only a pathological distortion produced by White prejudice and ignorance, itself sustained by conditions of segregation. Writing in the *New Republic* as late as 1962, Myrdal would express his hope for the future in this way,

> Increasingly, the false and derogatory beliefs about Negroes, which have filled the function of rationalizing prejudices, can be expressed only by those willing to betray their own lack of culture. As the white and Negro people are increasingly mingling in work and pleasure, all are discovering that they are the same sort of people with the same cultural moorings, the same likes and dislikes, and the same aspirations and ambitions for themselves and for America.[6]

Such race liberalism effectively decoupled antiracism from critique of American imperialism and expanding global capitalism, as Melamed makes clear. For race liberals, antiracism would involve less of a transformation of material realities and social relations than a therapeutic adjustment of personal psychologies through the education of White people.

According to Melamed, this race liberal consensus faced sustained pressure in the late 1960s and 1970s as social movements evolved to challenge its basic framework. They contested the continued subordination of Black, Indigenous, and other people of color in the United States as well as the war in Vietnam. These movements further manifested an internationalist solidarity with national independence struggles throughout the Third World, whether in South America or Southeast Asia. Arising in the post–civil rights era, they broke with American nationalism, consumerism, and the centrality of formal legal equality.[7] Cultural and epistemic demands were central to the new social movements, even as they were connected to a real focus on material social change. Such demands were crucially aimed at universities, where students and community members organized to force the creation of Black and Africana studies, Native American studies, women and gender studies, ethnic studies, and other programs. In all these cases, knowledge production through the creation of visual and performance art, literature, history, and theory was viewed as deeply entwined with radical activism and the envisioning of a social world beyond exploitation and oppression. The labor of cultural expression could and should be liberating.

In contrast to the social movements' vision of culture as a material force emerging out of collective liberatory praxis, liberal multiculturalism acted, in the words of Melamed, as a "counterinsurgency" to recalibrate race liberalism in response to the new demands.[8] Rather than the social transformations called for by insurgent social movements, liberal multiculturalism offered, "respect for multiple identities conceived as cultural property."[9] Thus, cultural representation was to act as an ameliorating alternative to deep change of the underlying racialized social structure. Melamed identifies the canon wars of the 1980s and 1990s as symptomatic of the recalibration in question. Whereas the previously dominant race liberalism assumed a single American culture held in common, both sides in the debate, she argues, shared an unacknowledged assumption of cultural pluralism.

The goal of conservatives was assimilation to dominant White culture and its values, which were presumed to be objective and universal. Thus, those on the "Great Books" side of the canon wars debate defended a Western canon which they thought revealed universal truth, or minimally a rich cultural heritage. All would benefit from the truths or cultural values expressed in the "Great Books," even those unenlightened souls whose backwardness had rendered them provincial and unduly particular in their interests and outlook. Melamed refers to this position as "assimilative pluralism."[10] There are many cultures in the United States, according to this view, but the dominant White culture should function as the universal normative standard in relation to which all others must be deemed inferior and into which all should seek to assimilate. In contrast, the liberal position sought integration through cultural representation. It endorsed a "positive pluralism" in which the many cultures of the United States deserved equal respect and representation in the cultural sphere. Melamed observes, "On one side was a vision of assimilative pluralism that represented the Western tradition as the common culture of the nation; on the other side was a positive pluralism that portrayed America's common culture as a uniquely multicultural one."[11] In either case, culture was imagined as separate from economics and global U.S. dominance, so that it could fulfill the aims of integration without fundamentally challenging the material social order.[12]

Overall, liberal multiculturalism abstracted cultural creation and identity from history and treated them as inert entities existing outside or beyond economic and social relations. For Melamed, such pluralism obscured and even entrenched social inequalities. Of this pluralism, she writes, it

> restricts permissible antiracism to forms that assent to U.S. nationalism and normal politics and prioritize individualism and property rights over collective social goods. It reduces culture to aesthetics and then overvalorizes aesthetic culture by ascribing an agency to it separable from and superior to social, political, and economic forces.[13]

Within the canon wars debates, this meant that inclusion of works written by Black or queer authors on syllabi, for example, could function as the achievement of justice in knowledge production, and thereby in society broadly. The proof of social transformation with respect to questions of race would come with the appearance of cultural diversity in the curriculum and, eventually, in positions of economic and political power. The defeat of racism would require only that people who check the right boxes be represented in the right cultural venues, most importantly on syllabi. It would not require a major social transformation or even minor adjustments such as hiring and supporting faculty members of color.

Of course, the canon wars themselves coincided with the consolidation of neoliberalism as a governing rationality globally and within the United States. Central to this process was a rhetoric of "globalization" in which, as Thomas Friedman had it, the world was "flattening."[14] The increasing mobility of capital and goods meant a decline of the power and significance of the nation-state. Or, so it was thought. In any case, in the context of globalization, economic discourse could, and many believed should, subsume discourses of national pride and unity; a convenient shift given the crimes of transnational corporations and their willingness to abandon the public good in the pursuit of private profit. Nation-states would compete with one another for investment and jobs in a world where capital was mobile, fluid, and lacking allegiance or subservience to any national government.

How would official antiracism fare in an environment of obsolescent nationalism? Race liberalism had yoked antiracism to the triumph of the United States as a global superpower. An enlightened end to White prejudice and the triumph of formal equality would demonstrate the world-historical mission of the United States and the realization of the "American Creed," the common culture of all Americans. Liberal multiculturalism recalibrated this narrative in response to the challenges of the social movements of the 1960s and 1970s. Rather than a common culture already shared by all, pluralism was the unacknowledged presupposition of all parties to the canon wars. Conservatives argued that the United States should hold out the promise of assimilation into the superior lifeways of dominant White culture. Those willing to adopt these "universal" norms of modernity could be rewarded with the American Dream. Liberal multiculturalism, in opposition, asserted a "positive pluralism" in which difference would be valued for its own sake and the contributions of the many cultures coloring the American landscape would be celebrated. In both cases, the prior commitment to American nationalism and exceptionalism was taken for granted. To survive in the post-national context of neoliberal globalization, the underlying narrative would again have to change.

The new narrative, according to Melamed, reimagined multiculturalism as an attribute of neoliberal governance itself. Through a series of symbolic substitutions and material transformations, neoliberal market reforms have come to stand in for the hegemony of the United States on the world stage, which, in turn, has come to stand in for cosmopolitan diversity. For Melamed, this neoliberal multiculturalism is inherently tied to what she terms "neoliberal sovereignty."[15] With this term, she highlights the fact that neoliberalism is not merely an autonomous operation of the market but instead a form of biopolitics that configures biological and social life according to economic imperatives. With the discussion of a "biopolitical Marcuse" in the previous chapter, we are in a better position to appreciate the ways that the configuration of bodies and populations is connected to a similar molding of instincts and rationality. In any case, in previous iterations, official antiracisms positioned the dominant White culture as either the shared property of all Americans or one among many in the pluralistic American tapestry. By contrast, neoliberal multiculturalism depicts liberal multiculturalism itself as a feature of both globally dominant Western or American culture and the neoliberal sovereignty imposed through (neo-)imperialism. Melamed explains, "Whereas in the previous two phases official antiracisms were sutured to U.S. governmentality and leadership for global capitalism, in this third phase official antiracism has attached to neoliberal sovereignty, which increasingly incorporates segments of U.S. governmentality and economic activity."[16] What emerges is a decidedly one-dimensional vision in which U.S. institutions and so-called free markets are, as if by definition, multicultural. Competition for survival in a winner-takes-all world of investment and return is, in this view, inherently antiracist.

Take, for example, former President Obama's first inaugural address. There, he echoed his predecessor's message that the attacks of September 11,

2001, were attacks on "freedom itself."[17] In response to the threat of terrorism, Obama proclaimed that the United States would not waver in defense of its "way of life." "For we know," he said, "that our patchwork heritage is a strength, not a weakness."[18] Obama's narrative, much as that of George W. Bush before him, held that the United States was under attack by Islamic extremists who resented the supposed liberal tolerance of American society and its pluralistic cultural heritage. "Defense" of the American way of life (which took the form during Obama's administration of ramped-up drone strikes in countries throughout the Middle East and Africa, among other things) meant affirming a purportedly secular government in which people of all faiths might participate on equal footing—in contrast to the barbarous and premodern theocratic visions of individuals like Osama bin Laden. Obama therefore continued, "We are a nation of Christians and Muslims, Jews and Hindus, and non-believers."[19] This message of a tolerant multicultural polity distinguished by its embrace of liberal freedoms acknowledged a "dark" past in which the United States had "tasted the bitter swill of civil war and segregation"—mention of the Civil War apparently serving as a sanitized allusion to slavery. Nonetheless, it called forth a utopian image of the United States in which, as part of its narrative of exceptionalism, "America must play its role in ushering in a new era of peace."[20] This time of peace would emerge with the revealing of common humanity as the "lines of tribe" dissolved, presumably through the corrosive effects of neoliberal globalization and American rule. The use of "tribe" as an alternative for "race" here suggesting that the residual irrational bonds of identity are premodern and uncivilized, belonging to a bygone world of savages now surpassed by capitalist modernity that is posited as de-racialized and non-tribal.[21] All that is solid, as we know, tends to melt into air.

Prior to President Obama's election, neoconservatives had mobilized the American public and its huge military apparatus to deliver "freedom" to the peoples of Afghanistan and Iraq. Much like three decades before in Chile, neoliberal policies were foisted on unwilling populations at gunpoint under the banner of liberty by a nation that was at the time accelerating the project of imprisoning large segments of its own citizenry. While Obama promised to extricate the United States from these imperial misadventures (more easily said than done it turns out), he nonetheless retained the core message of the neoconservatives: In the aftermath of the Cold War, with the United States in a position of uncontested geopolitical supremacy, the nation would spread freedom throughout the world in "defense" of its "way of life." Of course, the "freedom" in question was largely a matter of enforcing neoliberal sovereignty and "defense" was an Orwellian euphemism for conquest. Yet, through its entanglement in narratives of civilizational conflict, modernity, progress, secularism, and, most significantly, neoliberal multiculturalism, U.S. imperial power was made to appear just and even humanitarian. After all, as Melamed summarizes, "Neoliberal multiculturalism represents multiculturalism to be the spirit of neoliberalism. It represents the access of producers and investors to diverse markets and the access of consumers to diverse goods to be emblematic of multicultural values and required for global antiracist justice."[22] What might otherwise appear to be the murderous pillage of one nation by another and the imposition of foreign control through violent military occupation was instead viewed as a liberation in which Iraqis were freed to experience cultural diversity and liberal tolerance through integration into the circuits of the global market economy and subjection to U.S.-style structures of governance.

NEOLIBERAL MULTICULTURALISM AS RACIALIZING TECHNOLOGY

Despite its obvious ascendancy, race liberalism did not combat racism. Indeed, for Melamed, it served both as an ideology to conceal the racial structure of society and as a racializing technology itself. To see how this is so, it is useful to note that Melamed follows geographer Ruth Wilson Gilmore in defining racism in materialist terms. As Gilmore defines racism, it is "state-sanctioned or extra-legal production and exploitation of group-differentiated vulnerability to premature death."[23] Race must therefore be viewed through the prism of the concrete social relationships through which social groups are differentially marked for violence, exploitation, or death. Melamed further continues a long tradition of antiracism that views the emergence of White supremacy as a global phenomenon associated with the transition to modernity.[24] Connecting White supremacy to the emerging needs of capitalism, she writes,

> By representing and assigning meaning to human identities, white supremacy made it possible to locate all human individuals and collectives within an emerging world social order. White supremacy also allowed for an overarching and unequal system of capital accumulation by inscribing race on bodies as a marker of their relative value or valuelessness.[25]

The post-war racial break through which White supremacy was defeated as a formal program of governance did not signal the end of racism or of the global dominance of the imperial European states and their colonies; rather, it refracted those relationships through the prism of race liberalism. Value and valuelessness, the difference between those people worth saving and those who could legitimately be left to die or even killed, could now be reinterpreted on the basis of cultural or individual "pathologies." The system of racialized group differentiation could be made to seem natural and just, much as it had before.

Take the debate about affirmative action as it played out over several decades in the United States. Philosopher Iris Marion Young notes that affirmative action was generally supposed to be a response to and reparative for past discrimination.[26] In this way, the issue was framed in terms of whether current discriminatory group-based remedies were fair as a form of reparation for past injustice. If the initial wrong was itself past group-based discrimination, then, conservative critics argued, further group-based discrimination (i.e., affirmative action) could only compound injustice through "reverse racism." As we know, two wrongs don't make a right. Justice therefore required policies and practices that were neutral with respect to group identity. It was argued that group-neutral policies for admissions, hiring, promotion, and similar social benefits ought to rely on an honest assessment of ability so that those who justly deserved them would be rewarded. Through this subterfuge, however, racial differences were merely reinscribed into metrics said to measure "qualifications." Such measures achieved racializing ends without reference to natural biological differences, pointing instead to "merit." In the name of "meritocracy," only the best would be rewarded. As Christopher Newfield sardonically describes the vision, "If a society is roughly equal, it is not meritocratic. The reverse is equally true: if a society is meritocratic, it cannot possibly be egalitarian."[27] Thus, with the defeat of affirmative action as a policy, inequalities endured and expanded in basically all aspects of life in the United States as they were adjusted to refer to supposed merit rather than biology. Racism was and continues to be—even in the Trump era—publicly disavowed by the majority and there are constitutional bans on intentionally discriminatory laws, yet racializing effects persist and, in many cases, grow. Here we have the phenomenon described by Eduardo Bonilla-Silva as "racism without racists."[28]

To use language reminiscent of Young, race liberalism decoupled discrimination and the individual psychological characteristics thought to motivate it from social structures of oppression. For race liberals, the end of racism was to come in a color-blind world where White people no longer discriminated on the basis of race and instead learned to sympathize with and understand "minority groups." As Melamed shows, however, the United States was able to portray itself as a land of racial equality despite persistent and widening racial gaps and entrenched, though informal, segregation by adopting the framework of race liberalism. Newfield therefore describes a period of "pseudointegration" beginning in the 1980s.[29] As Newfield further argues, pseudointegration has not opposed but has ultimately thrived on discourses of diversity, which emerged into cultural dominance just as the United States began its long plunge into renewed segregation and what Bonilla-Silva calls the "New Racism."[30]

As with previous forms of dominant antiracist discourse, neoliberal multiculturalism serves less to end racism than to dissimulate and reinstate it through supposedly group-neutral metrics of ability and performance. To demonstrate this, Melamed turns to the work of anthropologist Aihwa Ong and the concept of differentiated forms of global citizenship.[31] Some of the cosmopolitan subjects of neoliberalism are highly mobile and are able to exercise citizenship rights in a variety of spaces globally. Others, in contrast, are utterly dispossessed, prohibited from free movement, and broadly subject to extreme forms of social exclusion, deprivation, and death. As Ong puts it, "We are beginning to see a detachment of entitlements from political membership and national territory, as certain rights and benefits are distributed to bearers of marketable talents and denied to those who are judged to lack such capacity or potential."[32] Within this division, human capital becomes a significant measure by which some are included and others are excluded from rights, which are unevenly distributed across social and even global space. As an example, it is useful here to consider the asylum claims of children and others from Central America seeking refugee status in the United States. Arguments about whether the state should be allowed to separate children from their families and incarcerate them for crossing the border ultimately hinge on the question of what rights immigrating children have that are bound to be respected by the U.S government. One can compare this debate to another, similar debate occasioned by the draconian and racist policies of the administration of then-President Trump as it sought to overturn the Obama administration's Deferred Action for Childhood Arrivals (DACA) policy. While it is certainly a matter of degree, what one may notice is that those multicultural subjects with a college education and the tolerant openness to difference and diversity that it supposedly inculcates are fit for life as globe-trotting consumers and producers in the multicultural knowledge economy. Those who remain "monocultural" and "intolerant" lack the requisite "intercultural understanding" to succeed and are therefore rightly punished. One defends DACA recipients—if at all—because they are well-educated, hard-working, productive members of society who, despite their lack of legal status, entered the country through no fault of their own. One way or another, the state utilizes calculations regarding human capital and population management to situate people—citizens and non-citizens—on an uneven spectrum of rights and entitlements ostensibly designed to maximize productivity and growth.

Philosopher Milton Fisk draws upon the example of Guatemala and the concept of *el indio permitido* to make a similar point. As he recounts, Óscar Berger's rise to the presidency of Guatemala in 2004 resulted in the naming of Rigoberta Menchu as a goodwill ambassador and the establishment of an Academy for Mayan Languages. At the same time, Berger ruthlessly evicted Indigenous landless peasants who were occupying farm lands. Within Berger's platform, neoliberal multicultural respect for difference sat comfortably alongside the armed removal and dispossession of destitute Indigenous peasants.[33] The racialized global poor, regardless of the languages they speak or the ethnic and cultural backgrounds with which they are familiar, are debarred from full citizenship rights and subjected to variegated regimes of rights on the basis of their supposed lack of human capital. The global racial order is thereby reproduced by these differential forms of citizenship through which human capital is valorized and made to circulate in the global knowledge economy. White supremacy remains intact as a global system despite its formal disavowal through the mechanism of neoliberal multiculturalism, which at once dissimulates, reproduces, and recalibrates the racial order to serve the needs of U.S.-led global capitalism.

Within this racial order, performativity and the *homo economicus* it calls forth can both be seen as racializing technologies of neoliberal multiculturalism. As I showed in chapter 1, neoliberalism involves a subordination of all other discourses to economic discourse. Individuals, institutions, and governments at all scales are judged according to their capacity to produce return on investment. They are thus called upon to self-enhance for optimization by attracting investment in their human capital. In the third chapter, I analyzed how the resulting demand to perform one's performativity is internalized in the form of the "performance principle." Exposed to potential joblessness and the ravages of unregulated markets, neoliberal subjects introject this demand to compete in an environment of artificial scarcity for limited social resources through self-enhancement and self-branding. More deeply, induced into a form of Happy Consciousness, they come to identify with and take pleasure in performative self-narratives, with those on top viewing themselves as successful "hustlers" who have mastered the "game" and those on bottom rendered into disposable surplus populations.

With Melamed's account of neoliberal multiculturalism, one can now discern the manner in which these economic and calculative discourses recode rather than supplant modes of governance based on biological notions of race. Take, for example, the use of standardized test scores as performance metrics that determine educational funding at state and federal levels since the passage of the No Child Left Behind Act by former President George W. Bush. Social investment is predicated on performance which functions to punish poor school districts of color and reward wealthy White school districts, redistributing social wealth away from broadly egalitarian ends toward "meritocracy." Similar developments in higher education involve, for example, the use of selective admissions criteria to manipulate *U.S. News*

& *World Report* rankings, thereby decreasing educational access for poor students and students of color from high schools that have already been punished through the competitive system of funding based on performance. State funding is thus used to subsidize the education of those who are already the beneficiaries of immense social and racial privilege while punishing those in the greatest need. As indicated in my previous discussion of Brown's critique of Foucault as overlooking the importance of gender, the supposed neutrality of *homo economicus* is itself a means of concealing and reproducing such identity-based oppressions, as members of oppressed groups are made responsible for impossible "investment choices."

SELLING DIVERSITY IN THE NEOLIBERAL UNIVERSITY

In previous chapters, I showed how higher education is transformed within the Neoliberal University. Students are conceived at once as consumers of educational commodities, as human capital to be enhanced, and as entrepreneurs investing in themselves in hopes of future return in the form of higher earnings. The educational commodities on offer are knowledge and skills that will optimize productivity in the knowledge economy. Neoliberal multiculturalism produces a number of effects in the Neoliberal University. Understood as a kind of factory for the production of human capital, the Neoliberal University is tasked with creating subjects suitable for the globalized knowledge economy. This involves more than training for the "twenty-first century skills" of critical thinking, problem solving, and communication. It includes further developing the cosmopolitan dispositions of openness toward cultural difference characteristic of neoliberal multiculturalism and along with them the capacity to work toward common ends in multicultural workplaces. Diversity itself also functions as a kind of cultural commodity, an attribute of corporations and organizations which is part of the sought-after consumer experience. Diversity is now read not as an antiracist ideal that institutions of higher education should aspire to or strive for but as a feature which they already embody to one extent or another and which students might consume. Through participation in or exposure to this diversity one can oneself become an enlightened cosmopolitan, achieving a self-actualizing sense of virtue. Within this framework, diversity also serves as a technology of racialization. On the one hand, there are people who *are* the diversity of the institution: relatively small numbers of faculty, students, and administrators through whose presence the Neoliberal University performs its diversity. On the other hand, there is the segregation of institutions of higher education and the construction of such spaces as White, so that diverse others are contingently "included" by enlightened Whites so long as they demonstrate merit and comply with the dictates of the Neoliberal University. This vision applies both within the Neoliberal University and across the spheres of global capitalism.

Among their list of necessary skills for the twenty-first century, Trilling and Fadel, whom I discussed in chapter 2, name not only critical thinking and creative problem-solving but also "social and cross-cultural skills." These skills are taken to belong to a larger category of "life and career skills." As they write, "Understanding and accommodating cultural and social differences, and using these to come up with even more creative ideas and solutions to problems, will be increasingly important throughout our century."[34] The thought is commonplace: globalization and technological change mean that the workforce of the knowledge economy must be able to interact across cultures. Diversity is not only necessary due to changing circumstances, it is also supposed to be desirable since it enhances productivity through greater innovation and creativity. All individuals are now thought to contribute to diversity in various ways since we are all different, as understood within the frame of neoliberal multiculturalism. Indeed, Trilling and Fadel use a commonly quoted *bon mot* as the epigraph for their section on the importance of "Social and Cross-Cultural Interaction": "Diversity is the one thing we all have in common."[35] Cleansed almost entirely of its prior connection to antiracism, diversity here functions as an attribute of individuals that indexes abstract differences that contribute to the productivity and innovation of a "team" by adding to its diversity.[36] As Melamed observes, this broad situation allows, even incentivizes, Walmart to refer to itself as "the world's most multicultural employer."[37] Whether understood as belonging to individuals, so-called teams, institutions, or even nations, diversity is considered human capital, a technology of optimization.

The changed conception of diversity is evident in the surveys of business executives and hiring managers conducted by the Association of American Colleges and Universities (AAC&U), as well. Here, diversity is conceived entirely in terms of skills that enable one to "analyze and solve problems with people from different backgrounds and cultures."[38] The report notes a marked increase in employers' rating of the importance of this skill between the 2014 survey and the 2018 iteration. In its Valid Assessment of Learning in Undergraduate Education or "VALUE" rubric for "Intercultural Knowledge and Competence," the AAC&U relies on Janet M. Bennett's definition of such competence as "a set of cognitive, affective, and behavioral skills and characteristics that support effective and appropriate interaction in a variety of cultural contexts."[39] Bennett's cited work opens with a narrative in which skeptical engineers sneer at intercultural competence training because "electrons don't have culture."[40] However, she makes the case that such training is important in an increasingly global work environment because it involves, "recognizing [differences in cultural patterns] as contributions to the productivity of the organization."[41] Diversity and the "cultural competence" necessary to "manage difference" are matters of performativity. After all, as Bennett explains, "The interculturally skilled organization becomes the employer of choice for the best and brightest applicants, avoids rapid employee turnover, and presents a welcoming face to clients and vendors."[42]

It is for this reason that, in her complex ethnography of "diversity workers" in universities in the United Kingdom, Sara Ahmed observes that within the context of the dominance of performativity, work on diversity is closely connected to public relations and the management of organizational brands.[43] Similarly, according to linguist Bonnie Uriciuoli, the shift in the use of diversity to become a form of public relations or marketing aligns it with a host of other terms taken up from the corporate world. Uriciuoli explains, "Its migration into promotional discourse is easy to understand; such uses are presuppositionally coherent with already-sedimented terms like *skills*, and *leadership* and with the rhetorical rise of *excellence* in conjunction with *assessment*."[44] As a form of human capital, diversity is also a part of the marketing and promotional discourse through which universities present and create their brand. It functions, that is, as a performance of performativity. Diversity must also then be measured or documented in its effects. Yet this performance of performativity emerges as a way of not talking about or indeed silencing claims that might identify the racism of institutions. As Ahmed writes, "To argue that diversity is exercised as a form of public relations is to suggest that diversity is mobilized in response or as a response to a problem."[45] Because the Neoliberal University is definitionally diverse (or, minimally, "committed to diversity") it cannot be racist. The "real racists" are those "essentialists" who cling to outdated discourses of equality and social justice through reparative action and intentional efforts to genuinely integrate institutions and dismantle systems of oppression.

Through its association with virtue and self-actualization, diversity is also a valuable cultural commodity; the cosmopolitan subject is one who embodies, purchases and enjoys diversity. To unpack this, Melamed provides a useful reading of the UPS slogan, "What can Brown do for you?" As she explains, the term "Brown" emerged in the antiracist discourse of the 1960s and 1970s as a way to break the hold of the Black-White binary that often circumscribes questions of race in the United States. It therefore developed positive connotations of racial affirmation. The UPS slogan, Melamed argues, draws on these connotations even as it erases the reference to race or antiracism. "'What can Brown do for you?'" she writes, "thus took a watchword of progressive 1970s antiracism and turned it into a slogan of happy subservience that promised efficient access to the networks of the global economy."[46] A similar act of rebranding occurs with the word "diversity" and its associated terms. Drawing on Žižek, sociologist Arthur Scarritt therefore differentiates the forms of cultural knowledge associated with selling diversity from those of a genuine knowledge of others. Within the context of a cultural capitalism in which self-actualization and creativity are absorbed into both production and consumption, the Neoliberal University advertises diversity to students as a form of self-fashioning through which, on the one hand, they may take pleasure in becoming better people and, on the other hand, establish a diverse, global brand for themselves. He laments, "Because we are told we can better develop our humanity simply through product selection, or more accurately, selecting all the right kinds of products we can skip the messy intermediating processes and go right to possessing a fulfilling experience available right at the food court."[47] In promotional discourse, universities and colleges represent themselves as spaces of multicultural interaction and racial diversity in order to brand themselves as offering the human capital required to participate in the globalized knowledge economy through a kind of cultural tourism which will allow students to actualize their humanity by becoming enlightened, virtuous cosmopolitans. Cosmopolitanism apparently thrives on campus at the same time as colleges and universities have cut, as I mentioned in chapter 1, over six hundred languages departments in recent years.[48]

Now reframed as a cultural commodity, diversity as abstract difference is not only unmoored from race but enables active hostility toward racialized others. Hence, Scarritt documents the racist views of students in relation to diversity, marking their deliberate divestment of antiracist meanings from diversity and the association of ideas of social justice with "reverse racism." For the students, he explains,

> Diversity is the inherent state we find ourselves in at any given time. It is merely the way we are, it is not something to try and achieve. Race comprises only one potential choice. And giving it more weight unjustly undermines the other choices individuals might make.[49]

In this way, as Ahmed describes, diversity can function as a kind of "happy talk" in which the students or the university depict themselves as having accomplished diversity and thereby recast those who claim otherwise as "the problem."[50] As she puts, it in a reference to Betty Friedan, "The smile of diversity stops a 'rotten core' from surfacing."[51] Diversity is performed in marketing literature to sell the Neoliberal University as a "happy place" where one can pursue authenticity, manifold consumer pleasures, and self-actualization.

This performance of diversity, however, serves to conceal and reproduce racism by casting institutions of higher education as already diverse—after all, "diversity is the one thing we all have in common." By situating diversity as an individual choice, something one may choose to consume or not, individuals and institutions are able to depict genuine efforts to redress racism through affirmative action or other policies as discriminatory and authoritarian. For this reason, Newfield connects the power of diversity discourse to the rise of pseudointegration. "Diversity," he concludes, "was the pivotal concept through which the college-educated middle classes could officially reject racism and yet tolerate, even perpetuate, racism's traditional symptom, racial inequality."[52] When it comes to true integration, Newfield shows that the Neoliberal University has limited results at best.[53] Indeed, the Association for the Study of Higher Education (ASHE) documented in 2013 that there remained deep inequalities in educational attainment by race, with, for example, about 29 percent of White people holding a bachelor's degree or higher while only 20 percent of their Black counterparts held similar degrees.[54] Even this data, of course, overlooks the depth of the already mentioned stratification of higher education, important gender differences in attainment, and disparities in quality.

Finally, as per Melamed's genealogy, diversity functions in the Neoliberal University as a kind of racializing technology. In its alignment with "merit," the diversity of the Neoliberal University serves to separate those who deserve reward and protection from those who may be exposed to neglect and punishment. The deserving few may participate in the diversity of the Neoliberal University and develop the required intercultural understanding to manage difference in the global workplace of the knowledge economy—notwithstanding their monolingual condition. The undeserving many, however, are systematically locked out and subjected to the privations and brutalities of an economy in which the campaign for higher minimum wages for food service workers, to take only one example, is met with derision and animosity by many. Mass incarceration, rampant foreclosures, widespread houselessness, inadequate healthcare, overexposure to disease—these and other punishments await the racialized poor and others who do not merit social investment. As colleges and universities in the United States compete with one another to attract students from around the globe who are willing to pay an incredible sticker price—thereby augmenting the diversity and brand of the college or university—poor students and students of color are systematically removed from the opportunities that higher education is supposed to promise as they are priced out and unable to meet selective admissions criteria.

Ahmed further notes that the very logic of "inclusion" through which the Neoliberal University achieves its supposed diversity often serves to ratify the Whiteness of institutions. Faculty or students of color who are "included" in an effort to augment diversity are positioned as visiting guests welcomed by hosts. Inclusion functions as a kind of hospitality. In this way, dominant White culture is positioned implicitly as belonging in higher education or higher education is viewed as its property, so that inclusion of diverse others amounts to welcoming in those who do not belong or have no right to be there.[55] Diversity images and discourses thus confirm the enlightened cosmopolitan status of the "hosts" even as they position others as dependent on the hosts' virtuous inclinations. Ahmed explains,

> People of color in white organizations are treated as guests, temporary residents in someone else's home. People of color are welcomed *on condition* they return that hospitality by integrating into a common organizational culture, or by "being" diverse, and allowing institutions to celebrate their diversity.[56]

For those few who are allowed to *be* the diversity of the institution, to add "color," the hosts have made an exception. They have opened their doors and recognized the merit of their guests. Yet the White hosts retain the position of racialized power and privilege inasmuch as the institution—even the nation—is conceived in advance as their rightful property and as a sphere in which their body is at home. Those who are welcomed in may be just as easily shown the door if they fail to perform according to the expectations of the White institution; inclusion is always conditional.

Importantly, these processes affect both pedagogy and scholarship. Critical pedagogue Antonia Darder describes the effects of neoliberal multiculturalism within higher education by focusing on faculty working in what she terms the "academic borderlands." As Darder details, the borderlands of academe emerged largely through the social movements of the 1960s and 1970s described by Melamed. These movements sought to challenge the structure of knowledge production by radically democratizing the university, demanding the inclusion of oppressed peoples, subordinated knowledges, and neglected cultural formations. Within these borderlands, systemic inequalities and collective liberatory praxis were the subject of scholarly and pedagogical focus from the beginning. Darder also mentions that the research practices of the borderlands have tended to utilize transdisciplinary or interdisciplinary methodologies and occupy or give voice to multiple identities or subject positions. As a field of study, for example, queer studies emerged on the borderlands as a trans- or interdisciplinary form of research and teaching intrinsically connected to the liberation of LGBTQ+ people.[57] In contrast, the "neoliberal diversity regime," to use a phrase borrowed from Sirma Bilge, works to discipline scholars and approaches connected to the borderlands, providing convenient financial justification for the closure of departments and meritocratic rhetoric to impugn and delegitimize borderlands scholarship.[58]

Would-be scholars of the academic borderlands therefore find themselves disciplined to the market and its ideological empiricism, scrambling for grants and other means of career advancement. The contributions and concepts of the borderlands are then co-opted and transformed to fit the needs of the neoliberal order. Thus, for instance, Bilge observes the emergence of an "ornamental intersectionality." As she writes, "Recast in depoliticized terms, intersectionality becomes a tool that certain feminist scholars can invoke to demonstrate 'marketable expertise' in managing particularly problematic kinds of diversity."[59] Much like "diversity" or "multiculturalism" before it, "intersectionality" is captured and transformed so that it can be disconnected from antiracist politics and made to perform. Nonconforming academics who are unable or unwilling to get with the program, insisting on the necessarily political and antiracist status of such terms or concepts, can be relegated to perpetual adjunct status or pushed out of the academy entirely.

THE WHITENESS OF NEOLIBERAL PHILOSOPHY

How does the account of multiculturalism and diversity as it operates in the Neoliberal University relate to philosophy? Much as with the Neoliberal University broadly, Neoliberal Philosophy markets itself as providing the diversity skills that are necessary for careers in the global knowledge economy. Likewise, it positions the discipline of philosophy as already possessing diversity, suggesting that students who study philosophy will develop intercultural understanding and cosmopolitan openness to difference. Even as it appeals to diversity as a kind of "happy talk" in its promotional discourse, Neoliberal Philosophy is deeply segregated and generally hostile toward initiatives that would integrate the discipline and transform its practices. Instead, it utilizes forms of meritocratic discipline policing to marginalize and frequently exclude philosophers on the academic borderlands, particularly women and philosophers of color. Thus, while advancing an "official epistemology" according to which bodies and social identities are irrelevant, the paradigm actively reproduces identity-based oppressions through circular appeals to "quality."

In a section of the American Philosophical Association's (APA) already-discussed "Department Advocacy Toolkit" devoted to diversity, one finds that courses with a focus on "equity, diversity, and inclusion," given the acronym "EDI," have "broad appeal and assist students in professional programs who need intercultural understanding in order to be successful in their fields."[60] The existence of coursework that explores "EDI" is taken as a given, such that philosophy as a discipline may be promoted on the basis of such courses. The value of the courses is immediately attached to the value of philosophy as such. The operation is complete when this value is finally explained in terms of the contribution that philosophy with an "EDI" focus might make in terms of its performativity. Rather than insist that equity, diversity, and inclusion are important for a more just or democratic society, these attributes of a philosophy curriculum are marketed on the basis of their ability to produce human capital. It is noteworthy here that, as presented, Neoliberal Philosophy performs its diversity through the content of courses, rather than through the demographics of faculty or students. It is only in this way that a discipline that remains deeply segregated and hostile to philosophers of color and women is able to brand itself as adding diversity. In broad alignment with the multiculturalism practiced throughout the Neoliberal University, Neoliberal Philosophy offers the intercultural understanding necessary for productivity within the global knowledge economy.

The subsequent section of the "Toolkit" concerns marketing philosophy to students as a double major. In the section, the authors discuss the "added value" that philosophy might offer to one's course of study. Predictably, one finds an emphasis on the twenty-first-century skills that philosophy provides: "important transferable skills such as critical thinking, clear writing, and ethical reasoning about important societal issues such as justice and equality."[61] The text goes further, however, to encourage departments to teach students how to brand themselves, though they do not use this language, by highlighting the human capital provided by their philosophical education. "For example," they write,

> aspiring medical students who have also thought about diverse metaphysical, social, political, and religious worldviews can present themselves as intellectually flexible, attentive to the whole patient, and cognizant of the demands of the medical profession.[62]

In this piece of advice, diversity is now presented as an attribute of "worldviews" and the philosophy classroom is imagined as the place where one might think about such worldviews in order to become "intellectually flexible." Though worldviews are divided into various kinds, it is unclear what constitutes a worldview or to whom they are considered to belong. It is noteworthy here that in its "Statement on the Role of Philosophy in Higher Education," the APA lists the transmission of "cultural heritages" as one of the fundamental ways that academic philosophy contributes to education. Implicitly, the pluralization of "heritage" suggests that Neoliberal Philosophy is but one among a number of "cultural heritages" that might be transmitted to a student of philosophy. A short while later, however, the plural is dropped. Now, one reads that "The history of philosophy is virtually the history of our intellectual heritage."[63] It is unclear to whom it is exactly that this cultural or intellectual inheritance is supposed to belong, but the subsequent mention of a "plurality of intellectual traditions" that includes Asian philosophy, Latin American philosophy, African philosophy, and African American philosophy would seem to suggest that the reader is positioned as an inheritor of the "Western tradition" and, therefore, as White.

In Neoliberal Philosophy, diversity now appears as abstract difference of opinion and as cultural inheritance, recast as worldview, and of course similarly situated cisgendered bourgeois White men born and raised in the same country, even the same region, may have different worldviews. Intellectual diversity therefore demands that a variety of such opinions be represented so that students may "hear both sides" and develop tolerance, updated into the corporate newspeak of "flexibility" in order to align with the broader ethos of compliance and precarity required of knowledge workers. To be flexible, one must be an inheritor of the Western tradition alongside the plurality of other intellectual traditions that philosophy is purported to engage. This invocation of a "Western cultural inheritance" and various associated worldviews should not be overlooked in an environment in which conservatives, fascists, and White supremacists now routinely demand representation on college campuses as a matter of promoting "intellectual diversity." Of this trend, Dotson explains further,

> This move, to identify diversity among people racialized as white and label that a kind of "diversity" is not a particularly new phenomenon. It is not unusual to encounter all white (and mostly cis-gendered male) philosophy departments citing their "diversity," by highlighting differences of opinion among the, otherwise, similarly situated faculty.[64]

It is a matter of great irony that a discipline would market itself as a torchbearer of such "intellectual pluralism," "flexibility," and "hearing both sides" when many of its most significant scholars tout their commitment to the pretense of rigor and vehemently reject alternative methods.

Bonnie Mann has provided a taxonomy of forms of philosophical pluralism that illuminates this irony further. The first form of pluralism identified by Mann is one she finds expressed in Brian Leiter's denunciation of an alternative ranking system for philosophy departments called *The Pluralist's Guide*, developed by Linda Martín Alcoff, William Wilkerson, and Paul Taylor.[65] According to this first form of pluralism, it amounts to a matter of philosophical taste. Pluralism is an attribute that attaches to the individual and has to do with the kinds of philosophy one enjoys reading and thinking about. This is pluralism understood as a consumer practice of "intellectual flexibility." Mann looks to Alcoff's defense of *The Pluralist's Guide* for an alternative view. According to the vision presented by Alcoff, the exclusions historically practiced by philosophers are an "intrinsic philosophical concern" because they have significant epistemic effects.[66] As Mann describes, for Alcoff, the issue of pluralism is a matter of "who one's living, breathing interlocutors are."[67] In this case, the exclusion of people of color, women, LGBTQ+ people, and others is an, if not *the*, issue that must be discussed under the heading of pluralism. Summarizing, Mann asks, "In other words, is pluralism more about who your interlocutors are, or more about having a flexible philosophical appetite, which you can satisfy all by yourself?"[68] Finally, Mann identifies a third kind of philosophical pluralism, which is perhaps the dominant conception in the discipline. As she writes, "This is the pluralism that first comes on the scene historically when tolerance first emerges as a virtue between analytic, continental and pragmatist philosophers and their practices."[69] This "methodological pluralism," as I have called it, is perhaps best understood as the result of the "pluralist rebellion" breathlessly chronicled by Bruce Wilshire.[70] Regardless, a person or department might be pluralistic in this way, even as the Whiteness and maleness of philosophy go unchallenged or unremarked. As Mann notes, however, this "pluralism" only looks pluralistic from a certain internal viewpoint; from outside looking in, it is just "three White men at a bar." What we have seen over time, according to Mann, is a relatively successful strategic attempt on the part of those excluded from the conversation to identify demographic diversity with methodological pluralism, as with Alcoff. Similar to the situation described by Ahmed, however, the process of inclusion within philosophy has been conditional—departments may make "diversity hires," but those allowed in are expected to "know their place."

The "place" of such philosophers and their work is illustrated well by the *Philosophical Gourmet Report* (PGR). As is well known, PGR has long been criticized for its obvious slant. Indeed, Brian Bruya has recently provided a statistical demonstration of five serious flaws in the methodology, such as it is: (1) selection bias based on a nonrepresentative sample, (2) lack of expertise among evaluators, (3) unstated assumptions driving the selection, (4) underrepresentation for areas listed under "history," and (5) underrepresentation for areas listed under "other."[71] Bruya's statistical demonstrations are relatively complex, and I will not present them here. What is worth mentioning, however, is the depth of the bias present in the report against the subfields listed under "other." The most evident prejudice is the very category of "other" itself, in which are seemingly haphazardly listed feminist philosophy, philosophy of race, and Chinese philosophy. As Bruya shows, in the schema created by PGR, faculty with an area of expertise in "other" would account for only 9 percent of a department's overall ranking in an "ideally balanced program."[72] What is perhaps even more disturbing is that the actual rankings discount such subfields even further. Bruya shows, for example, that in 2011 the top-rated department at New York University (NYU) scored a 0 in the category. One can see manifest here the depth of the ideological empiricism embedded in the practice of Neoliberal Philosophy. What presents itself as a rating of departmental quality functions in fact as a form of discipline policing that obscures the racism and sexism of the discipline even as it reinscribes it in seemingly neutral metrics. Similar points can be made regarding the use of related metrics such as number of citations, impact factor, student evaluation scores, and so on. Casting a numerical spell, some of the wealthiest, Whitest, least diverse departments in the country are made to appear as the "best," indeed even as "pluralistic."[73]

Again, much like the Neoliberal University as a whole, Neoliberal Philosophy also utilizes representations of diversity to advertise itself to students and others as a kind of cultural commodity. This is demonstrated in a genre of webpage focused on answering the question "Who Studies Philosophy?" connected to the "Why Study Philosophy?" (WSP) pages discussed in chapter 2. The APA itself offers a webpage and produces a series of posters dedicated to providing potential students with an image of the philosophy graduate.[74] There are many things worth noting about the page and accompanying posters. The careers of the people depicted are obviously not representative of the types of careers that philosophy graduates will go on to have; after all, there are very few Supreme Court justices. In fact, Payscale.com, often cited uncritically as a source of information on the salaries of philosophy graduates, lists such relatively probable options as attorney, software engineer, project manager, and software developer.[75] Of course, no one depicted in the posters is a professional project manager. Instead, the page and posters portray the "best and the brightest" in the form of famous actors, politicians, business leaders, and so on.[76] In doing so, they assume and reproduce a dominant cultural value system; these are the "success" stories. It should be said that the careers here coded as "success" are themselves deeply segregated.

Presenting only such "success" stories, the posters collapse the distinction between the aspirational and the factual. The inclusion of Stephen Colbert on the poster, for example, would seem to suggest to prospective students that they might also use their philosophy degree to become late-night television hosts. The individuals depicted are not, therefore, demographically representative—they are not really an answer to the question "Who studies philosophy?"—so much as they are selected for their power to elicit imaginative identification with aspirational stories of career achievement. Of the 112 individuals listed on the "Who Studies Philosophy?" downloadable poster, then, it warrants observation that eight are Black, amounting to roughly 7 percent of the list.[77] For comparison, according to its own demographic report, only about 127 members of the APA listed themselves as Black/African

American in 2018 on their demographic questionnaire, amounting to less than 3 percent of those who provided racial data.[78] While the limited number of Black people appearing on the poster still intimates their underrepresentation in philosophy compared to the general population, it nonetheless also over-represents their number in philosophy compared to, among other data, those who presently teach and produce scholarship in the discipline. That is to say, it presents Neoliberal Philosophy as being more diverse than it actually is just as it simultaneously confounds the aspirational and the factual.

Other subtleties in the posters serve to reify an obviously prejudicial notion of what it means to "do philosophy." A disproportionate number of the people of color (in fact, nearly all of the Black people) listed on the poster appear in the "Activism" section. Of those, Angela Davis is listed as a "social activist," while Grace Lee Boggs is listed as a "social activist and philosopher." Oddly, while Davis, initially employed as a philosopher at the University of California–Los Angeles, has had a long and distinguished academic career and continues to do so, Boggs was never employed as an academic.[79] Similar inconsistencies in the deployment of the term "philosopher" are found throughout the poster: Beauvoir, for example, is a "writer, philosopher, and political activist," while Iris Murdoch is merely an "author." One apparent suggestion of the poster is that there are many things that one may go on to do with a philosophy degree that may not include work in professional philosophy. Yet this impression is disrupted by the use of the term "philosopher" in the poster itself and by the highlighting of figures like Beauvoir and Davis. While it is clear that women and people of color who do or did philosophy in a professional capacity may appear on the poster under one or another of its headings, the relative absence of White men who are presently or were at some point professionals in the discipline is a powerful contrast.[80] Does inclusion on the poster mean that Davis is not a philosopher? Why would one list Beauvoir while excluding Jean-Paul Sartre or Albert Camus? Broadly, it seems to me that the poster unwittingly reproduces the "culture of legitimation" described by Dotson.[81] It subtly excludes those individuals who are not perceived as doing "real philosophy" from the title of "philosopher" (which is admittedly distributed somewhat randomly in the poster itself) while it also invites students to imaginatively identify with the figures presented as part of an aspirational story about the kind of success they may have with a philosophy degree. The overrepresentation of Black people and their association with radical activism and the civil rights movement serves to lend philosophy a certain commodifiable cachet through its suggested affiliation with rebellion and nonconformity—something like a Che Guevara coffee mug. This supposed affiliation is patently out of tune with the composition of most philosophy departments.

The poster series aside, Neoliberal Philosophy is not welcoming to radical Black scholar-activists, nor is it a multicultural hotbed. So much is this the case that Jay L. Garfield and Bryan W. Van Norden created a bit of an online firestorm with their recent suggestion that philosophy departments in the United States change their titles to "Department of European and American Philosophy."[82] Adopting the Confucian practice of "rectification of names," Garfield and Van Norden sought to provoke a reconsideration of the lack of curricular and demographic diversity in contemporary philosophy departments in the United States by demanding they describe themselves accurately. The subsequent debate exemplified a long-theorized aspect of racial and cultural dominance as practiced in the aftermath of Western colonization in its entanglement with the Enlightenment. Namely, Neoliberal Philosophy was depicted by its defenders as the universal, so that all philosophy is Neoliberal Philosophy and vice versa. Ancient or contemporary Chinese philosophy, as defended by Van Norden, for example, is *not really* philosophy from this point of view but a particular deviation or inadequate instantiation. Notably, despite its own obvious provincialism and cultural chauvinism, Neoliberal Philosophy is able therefore to refuse any engagement with an outside Other. For Neoliberal Philosophy, there is no outside, no Other. Whatever is not Neoliberal Philosophy simply is not (philosophy). Thus, insofar as Neoliberal Philosophy recognizes any pluralism regarding philosophy it must take the form of what Melamed earlier theorized as "assimilative pluralism"; to be taken seriously or treated as legitimate interlocutors, the Others of Neoliberal Philosophy must transform themselves to contribute to its debates, reason according to its norms, and speak in its language. Asian philosophy, Africana philosophy, and so on are deviant subfields which can be included only on condition that they concede their own irrelevance. As Mann explains, the power of judgment regarding what or who counts as (good) philosophy remains invested in only a few White male hands and the attempt to wrest this power away will not be taken lightly.[83] Thus, tellingly, in her presidential address given to the APA in December 2012, Linda Martín Alcoff quoted Colin McGinn as having written that "feminism now has a place in many philosophy departments, for good or ill, but it has not made any impact on the core areas of the subject."[84] Anything but an expert on the matter, McGinn arrogated to himself the power to judge the value and contribution of feminist philosophy while suggesting that it could only be a legitimate form of philosophy if it contributed to the "core areas," an impossibility in any case since the largely White male group of philosophers comprising the "core" would not stoop to reading something with such a low impact as feminist philosophy.[85]

In chapter 2, I argued that, in broad conformity to the postmodern culture of Mode 2 knowledge production, Neoliberal Philosophy exhibits a horizontal and rhizomatic structure. In contrast, to the hierarchical ordering of knowledge and arborescent division into "roots" and "branches" characteristic of modernity, we find a flattened terrain in which subspecialties within the discipline form a nonhierarchical network of relationships to other subfields. This flattening, however, clearly does not mean that all specialties function on equal footing or are treated as equally part of the discipline. Rather, as McGinn's comment suggests, the discipline divides itself into "core" and "periphery" subdisciplines. Metaphysics, logic, and epistemology are taken to be core areas. And, as indicated by their much lower weighting in the PGR or disappearance from the report altogether, other disciplinary areas are marginalized, such as feminism or philosophy of race. This marginalization and demotion to the periphery can be conceptualized in terms of the power (or lack thereof) that individual philosophers are granted to judge departmental quality, the role various subfields play in such judgment, as well as the directionality of flow regarding readership, citation, and prestige. One gains readership, citations, and prestige by proximity to the core and quality faculty are those who publish in the journals of the core. Those in the core have the power to judge who or what is consequential and what ultimately counts as (good) philosophy. It is useful here to think of Neoliberal Philosophy in terms of social networks and the exercise of power in the discipline as operating in accordance with the logics of such networks.[86] To be central and therefore powerful is to accrue links in the professional network but also to have the capacity to structure flows. Thus, power works through the marginalization of individuals and subfields even as it is made to disappear through the invocation of quality and the "happy talk" of diversity and inclusion. Much like social media influencers, those positioned at the core set the trends and determine the philosophical fashion. It should come as no shock that the work of academics teaching and writing on what Darder refers to as the borderlands are precisely those who are silenced in the process and whose judgments of quality are derided.

No doubt, there is a kind of progress in the claims of Neoliberal Philosophy to identify philosophers whose works are focused on "equity, diversity, and inclusion," to promote their work as part of the value of a degree in philosophy, and to present an image of the philosophy graduate that includes women and people of color. As Melamed points out, many scholars who were more committed to critical understandings of multiculturalism during the canon wars were strategic defenders of liberal multiculturalism out of necessity. They faced severe conservative attacks in the public sphere and only adopted liberal rhetoric when more radical alternatives were foreclosed.[87] In similar fashion, the diversity regime adopted by Neoliberal Philosophy is almost certainly a compromise position in which the dominant paradigm has offered representation as a "moderate" compromise in cases where more substantive changes were politically impossible. Ahmed, however, points toward the dangers associated with this "middle ground" that emerges to co-opt or redirect antiracist struggle. In a discussion of "institutional whiteness" in relation to image management, she highlights that in such cases, "Diversity becomes about *changing perceptions of whiteness rather than changing the whiteness of organizations*."[88] Neoliberal Philosophy certainly would like to be perceived as diverse and therefore produces an externally directed marketing discourse related to its supposed diversity. Yet it remains a basically White male enterprise.

NOTES

1. As discussed in chapter 1, Brown has nicely criticized this purported neutrality from a feminist perspective. See Wendy Brown, *Undoing the Demos: Neoliberalism's Stealth Revolution* (New York: Zone Books, 2015), 99–107.

2. See Howard Winant, *The New Politics of Race: Globalism, Difference, Justice* (Minneapolis, MN: University of Minnesota Press, 2004). Thanks to Rachel Walsh for bringing to my attention the necessity of mentioning the role of the Holocaust in discrediting biological racism in the United States and globally.

3. See, for example, Derek Bell, "Brown v. Board of Education and the Interest-Convergence Dilemma," *Harvard Law Review* 93, no. 3 (January, 1980), 524–525. As James Baldwin writes concerning the 1954 *Brown v Board of Education* decision, "Most of the Negroes I know do not believe that this immense concession would ever have been made if it had not been for the competition of the Cold War, and the fact that Africa was clearly liberating herself and therefore had, for political reasons, to be wooed by the descendants of her former masters." See "Down at the Cross: Letter from a Region in My Mind," in *The Fire Next Time* (New York: Vintage International Books, 1962), 86–87.

4. Jodi Melamed, *Represent and Destroy: Rationalizing Violence in the New Racial Capitalism* (Minneapolis, Minnesota University Press, 2011), 53.

5. Ibid., 20ff, 56ff.

6. Gunnar Myrdal, "The Negro Problem: A Prognosis," *New Republic* 147, no. 2 (July 9, 1962), 12.

7. *Represent and Destroy*, 26.

8. On this point, compare Herbert Marcuse, *Counterrevolution and Revolt* (Boston, MA: Beacon Press, 1972). Marcuse diagnoses an unfolding preventative counterrevolution aimed at stifling the demands of the insurgent movements.

9. *Represent and Destroy*, 108.

10. Ibid., 109.

11. Ibid.

12. For a helpful and deeply sympathetic account from the period of the culture wars, see Peter McClaren, "Chapter III: White Terror and Oppositional Agency: Towards a Critical Multiculturalism," *Counterpoints* 4 (1995): 87–124.

13. *Represent and Destroy*, 96.

14. See Thomas Friedman, *The World Is Flat: A Brief History of the Twenty-First Century* (New York: Farrar, Straus, and Giroux, 2005).

15. *Represent and Destroy*, 39.

16. Ibid., 41.

17. "President Bush Addresses the Nation," *The Washington Post*, September 20, 2001, accessed December 20, 2021, https://www.washingtonpost.com/wp-srv/nation/specials/attacked/transcripts/bushaddress_092001.html.

18. Barack Obama, "President Barack Obama's Inaugural Address," accessed December 20, 2021, https://obamawhitehouse.archives.gov/blog/2009/01/21/president-barack-obamas-inaugural-address.

19. Ibid.

20. Ibid.

21. Indeed, a whole discourse of "tribalism" now exists in various quarters to describe any form of identity or community that resists incorporation into U.S.-led global capitalism and its supposed "universalism."

22. *Represent and Destroy*, 183.

23. See Ruth Wilson Gilmore, *Golden Gulag: Prisons, Surplus, Crisis, and Opposition in Globalizing California* (Berkeley, CA: University of California Press, 2007), 28. See also *Represent and Destroy*, 247 n1.

24. As Charles Mills puts it in his discussion of the "racial contract," "The modern world was thus expressly created as a *racially hierarchical* polity, globally dominated by Europeans." See *The Racial Contract* (Ithaca, NY: Cornell University Press, 1997), 27. Emphasis in original.

25. *Represent and Destroy*, 7.

26. Iris Marion Young, *Justice and the Politics of Difference* (Princeton, NJ: Princeton University Press, 2011), 193–198.

27. Christopher Newfield, *Unmaking the Public University: The Forty Year Assault on the Middle Class* (Cambridge, MA: Harvard University Press, 2008), 97. Newfield actually distinguishes two competing forms of "meritocracy." The first requires the kind of sorting described above, whereas the second emphasizes the widespread possession of native intelligence and the importance of development through education.

28. See Eduardo Bonilla-Silva, *Racism Without Racists: Colorblind Racism and the Persistence of Racial Inequality in America* (Lanham, MD: Rowman & Littlefield, 2014). In the Trump era, however, one might feel more inclined to say that we have "racism with a pretty decent number of racists."

29. *Unmaking the Public University*, 121.

30. *Racism without Racists*, 25ff.

31. See Aihwa Ong, *Neoliberalism as Exception: Mutations in Citizenship and Sovereignty* (Durham, NC: Duke University Press, 2006).

32. Ibid., 17.

33. Milton Fisk, "Multiculturalism and Neoliberalism," *Praxis Filosófica* 21 (2005): 21–28.

34. Bernie Trilling and Charles Fadel, *21st Century Skills: Learning for Life in Our Times* (San Francisco, CA: Jossey-Bass, 2009), 80.

35. Ibid.

36. Bonnie Uriciuoli comments on a "semantic wobble" occurring in the early 2000s which allowed diversity to be used as a "strategically shifting signifier," in some contexts carrying the pragmatic weight of antiracism and simultaneously manifesting the kind of corporate newspeak of Trilling and Fadel in others. See Bonnie Uriciuoli, "Excellence, Leadership, Skills, Diversity: Marketing Liberal Arts Education," *Language & Communication* 23 (2003), 400.

37. *Represent and Destroy*, 42.

38. Hart Research Associates, "Fulfilling the American Dream: Liberal Education and the Future of Work: Selected Findings from Online Surveys of Business Executives and Hiring Managers" (Washington, DC: Association of American Colleges and Universities, 2018), 13. https://www.aacu.org/sites/default/files/files/LEAP/2018EmployerResearchReport.pdf.

39. See Terrel Rhodes, *Assessing Outcomes and Improving Achievement: Tips and Tools for Using Rubrics* (Washington, DC: Association of American Colleges and Universities, 2010). See also Janet M. Bennett, "Transformative Training: Designing Programs for Culture Learning," in *Contemporary Leadership and Intercultural Competence: Exploring the Cross-Cultural Dynamics Within Organizations*, ed. M.A. Moodian (Thousand Oaks, CA: Sage Publishing, 2009), 97.

40. Ibid., 95.

41. Ibid., 96.

42. Ibid., 96.

43. Sara Ahmed, *On Being Included: Racism and Diversity in Institutional Life* (Durham, NC: Duke University Press, 2012), 143–152.

44. "Excellence, Leadership, Skills, Diversity," 398.

45. *On Being Included*, 143.

46. *Represent and Destroy*, 145.

47. Arthur Scarritt, "Selling Diversity, Promoting Racism: How Universities Pushing a Form of Diversity Empowers Oppression," *Journal for Critical Education Policy Studies* 17, no. 1 (2019), 201.

48. See Steven Johnson, "Colleges Lose a 'Stunning' 651 Foreign-Language Programs in 3 Years," *The Chronicle of Higher Education*, January 22, 2019, https://www.chronicle.com/article/Colleges-Lose-a-Stunning-/245526.

49. "Selling Diversity," 206.

50. *On Being Included*, 10.

51. Ibid., 72.

52. *Unmaking the Public University*, 114.

53. Ibid., 116–119.

54. Samuel D. Museus, María C. Ledesma, and Tara L. Parker, "Introduction" in "Racism and Racial Equity in Higher Education," special issue, *ASHE Higher Education Report*, 42, no. 1 (2015), 6–7.

55. *On Being Included*, 42–43.

56. Ibid., 43.

57. Antonia Darder, "Neoliberalism in the Academic Borderlands: An On-Going Struggle for Equality and Human Rights," *Educational Studies* 48, no. 5 (2012): 412–426.

58. Sirma Bilge, "Intersectionality Undone: Saving Intersectionality from Feminist Intersectionality Studies," *Du Bois Review* 10, no. 2 (2013): 405–424.

59. Ibid., 408.

60. "Department Advocacy Toolkit," American Philosophical Association, accessed September 2, 2020, 20, https://www.apaonline.org/page/deptadvocacytoolkit.

61. Ibid., 21.

62. Ibid.

63. Committee on the Status and Future of the Profession, "Statement on the Role of Philosophy in Higher Education," American Philosophical Association, accessed September 2, 2020. https://www.apaonline.org/page/role_of_phil.

64. Kristie Dotson, "On Intellectual Diversity and Differences That May Not Make a Difference," *Ethics and Education* 13, no. 1 (2018), 124.

65. Bonnie Mann, "Three White Men Walk into a Bar: Philosophy's Pluralism," *Radical Philosophy Review* 16, no. 3 (2013), 734.

66. Linda Martín Alcoff, "Pluralism and Diversity as Intrinsic Philosophical Concerns," *The Pluralist's Guide.Org: The Pluralist's Guide to Philosophy Programs*, accessed December 8, 2020, https://sites.psu.edu/pluralistsguide/2015/07/30/pluralism-and-diversity-as-intrinsic-philosophical-concerns. See also "Three White Men," 733ff.

67. Ibid., 736.

68. Ibid., 737.

69. Ibid., 738.

70. Bruce Wilshire, *Fashionable Nihilism: A Critique of Analytic Philosophy* (Albany, NY: State University of New York Press, 2002), 51ff. See the introduction for more about methodological pluralism.

71. Brian Bruya, "Appearance and Reality in *The Philosophical Gourmet Report*: Why the Discrepancy Matters to the Profession of Philosophy," *Metaphilosophy* 46, nos. 4–5 (2015), 678–679. PGR is presently under new leadership and the methodology has been revised to some extent. The effect of the changes is unclear.

72. The "ideally balanced department" is a mathematical construct which describes a scenario in which there is a faculty member in each of the areas of specialty listed by PGR and each faculty member is rated a 5. In such a scenario, out of a highest possible ranking of 165 points, the category of other would account for only 15 points.

73. Through the inclusion of Kwame Anthony Appiah on their faculty, the lone person of color in the department, NYU has managed to be ranked as one of the top ten programs in the United States for philosophy of race in the most recent PGR. See "Other Areas," *The Philosophical Gourmet Report*, accessed December 6, 2020, https://www.philosophicalgourmet.com/other-areas/.

74. "Who Studies Philosophy?" American Philosophical Association, accessed December 5, 2020, https://www.apaonline.org/page/whostudiesphilosophy.

75. "Bachelor of Arts (BA), Philosophy Degree," Payscale.com, accessed December 5, 2020, https://www.payscale.com/research/US/Degree=Bachelor_of_Arts_(BA)%2C_Philosophy/Salary.

76. See also my discussion of the profile of investor Bill Miller in chapter 2.

77. "Who Studies Philosophy?" American Philosophical Association, https://cdn.ymaws.com/www.apaonline.org/resource/resmgr/diversity/Who_Studies_Philosophy_Poste.pdf.

78. "Demographic Statistics on the APA Membership, FY 2016 to FY 2018," American Philosophical Association, https://cdn.ymaws.com/www.apaonline.org/resource/resmgr/data_on_profession/fy2018-demographic_statistic.pdf. See also Tina Fernandes Botts, Liam Kofi Bright, Myisha Cherry, Guntar Mallarangeng, and Quayshawn Spencer, "What Is the State of Blacks in Philosophy?" *Critical Philosophy of Race* 2, no. 2 (2014): 224–242. In 2014, Botts et al. identified 156 Black philosophers in the entire United States.

79. It is further notable that Grace Lee Boggs explicitly links her decision not to pursue an academic career to racial discrimination. See Grace Lee Boggs, *Living for Change: An Autobiography* (Minneapolis, MN: University of Minneapolis Press, 2016). She writes, "In June 1940, I returned to my mother's house in Jackson Heights. I had no plans for the future. It would have been a waste of time for me, a Chinese woman with a Ph.D. in philosophy, to apply to a university for a teaching job" (34).

80. To be fair, one could make a case for Noam Chomsky, Pope John Paul II, and perhaps a couple of others.

81. Kristie Dotson, "How Is This Paper Philosophy?" *Comparative Philosophy* 3, no. 1 (2012). See also introduction.

82. Jay L. Garfield and Bryan W. Van Norden, "If Philosophy Won't Diversify, Let's Call It What It Really Is," *The Stone, New York Times*, May 11, 2016, https://www.nytimes.com/2016/05/11/opinion/if-philosophy-wont-diversify-lets-call-it-what-it-really-is.html. For a snapshot of some of the ensuing vitriol, see Jay L. Garfield, foreword to *Taking Back Philosophy: A Multicultural Manifesto* by Bryan W. Van Norden (New York: Columbia University Press, 2017).

83. "Three White Men," 741ff.

84. Linda Martín Alcoff, "Philosophy's Civil Wars," *Proceedings and Addresses of the American Philosophical Association* 87 (November 2013): 16–43.

85. See also Sally Haslanger, "Changing the Culture and Ideology of Philosophy: Not By Reason (Alone)," *Hypatia* 23, no. 2 (2008): 210–223. Haslanger documents both personal harassment and institutional discrimination as operating throughout the field.

86. For more on this, see Manuel Castells, *Communication Power* (New York: Oxford University Press, 2009).

87. *Represent and Destroy*, 111.

88. *On Being Included*, 34. Emphasis in the original.

Chapter 5

Toward a New Paradigm

The picture of philosophy within the Neoliberal University has now come into sharper focus. Following McCumber's methodology, I have shown that, with the discipline shaped by its own strategic marketing and the demand to perform its performativity, a new paradigm of philosophy has emerged: Neoliberal Philosophy. Neoliberal Philosophy sells itself as a purveyor of human capital in the form of critical thinking skills. As I argued in chapter 2, however, this critical thinking pedagogy is submitted in advance to the motivating desires and values of the social world within which it operates. Above all, performativity itself is posited beforehand as a value. Furthermore, Neoliberal Philosophy is integrated into the broader knowledge economy, where it treats knowledge as an alienable commodity. Struggling to maintain their employability, philosophers compete in the "marketplace of ideas" to demonstrate their capacity to produce profitable knowledge. Individual philosophers and departments thus brand themselves in a variety of ways to show their return on investment. In an act of narcissistic Happy Consciousness, they ultimately come to consume and take pleasure in their own marketed performance as a measure of status and self-worth. According to the neoliberal vision, competition supposedly works to separate the wheat from the chaff; only the strong survive and success is a reward for merit. The market is the measure of truth and value. As I showed in the previous chapter, however, this meritocratic ideal is fundamentally anti-egalitarian and works to reinscribe officially disavowed White supremacy and other oppressive systems in supposedly neutral performance metrics. In this way, Neoliberal Philosophy reproduces and normalizes the forms of inequality and oppression characteristic of the broader society, internalizing them as natural and just.

In comparison to its predecessor, Cold War Philosophy, there are many remarkable aspects of Neoliberal Philosophy. It has seemingly renounced the positivism, operationalism, and behaviorism of Cold War Philosophy along with the project of installing linguistic or logical analysis as the heir to metaphysics. Indeed, rather than a hierarchical ordering of knowledge in which philosophy of language or logic is positioned as first philosophy, one finds an intricately woven web of specializations and subspecializations in which none occupies widely agreed upon primacy. Metaphysics, ethics, and political philosophy are revived as substantive philosophical fields alongside logic, philosophy of language, and epistemology. On this flattened terrain, some areas are considered "core," while others are peripheral. The core continues to feature a cluster of subdisciplines previously understood as occupying the position of first philosophy: logic, language, epistemology, philosophy of science, and metaphysics. From the standpoint of Neoliberal Philosophy, issues, ideas, works, or philosophers not discussed at the core are not (good or real) philosophy and are only included, when they are, as an afterthought for the sake of "diversity" or "pluralism." Organized and understood in this way, Neoliberal Philosophy positions itself as the universal, philosophy as such.

Can we envision a future for philosophy in the United States beyond the paradigm of Neoliberal Philosophy? No doubt, this is something of a politically awkward question in our moment. As I have argued throughout this book, Neoliberal Philosophy emerges as a strategic response to macrosocial phenomena that have affected and transformed higher education in the United States and globally over the course of decades. In the process, the anti-intellectual attacks of culture warriors have weakened the public perception of university education even as they have sought to reframe its value in terms of training.[1] Unlike the sciences, philosophy has little to offer in the way of directly profitable knowledge and the fact that philosophy has promised to produce coveted human capital has failed to save the jobs of many philosophers, with departments struggling to secure funding and stay afloat. The impulse of the moment is certainly not one of revolutionary transformation; most seem inclined to a defensive posture of self-preservation. Furthermore, Neoliberal Philosophy and its associated intellectual culture and power hierarchies are deeply entrenched in the U.S. academy. Those who would seek change face an uphill battle. Indeed, much as the political Left has retreated in recent decades from radical demands and futuristic dreams to the defense of policies that were once viewed as compromising half-measures, so, too, have philosophers found themselves strangely embroiled in rearguard actions in the academy and unable to envision intellectual horizons that might exceed those produced by the Neoliberal University and its dominant philosophical paradigm. Perhaps, however, as others have argued, it is the exhaustion of the Left's utopian energy and its self-effacement that has created the political space for the ascendancy of neoliberalism, at least insofar as it required popular ideological buy-in. Similarly, perhaps it is the inability of philosophers, indeed of the academy more broadly, to imagine institutions and organizations of knowledge beyond those that are presently dominant that has allowed right-wing culture warriors to prevail in their efforts to diminish the life of the mind in popular consciousness and to carry out the broad program of austerity as it has applied to higher education.

BEYOND DISCIPLINARY DECADENCE

As I argued in chapter 2, the position of philosophy in the academy has been transformed in the postmodern landscape. Whereas philosophy previously functioned as a legitimating discourse for empirical science, this is no longer possible or necessary in a culture skeptical of metanarratives. The sciences are instead provided their social legitimacy by appealing to economic discourses through which they promise return on investment in the form of technologies of optimization. No longer in a position of preeminence, philosophy finds itself situated alongside the sciences in the order of knowledge and subject to the same economic demands. It is worth being clear here about the kind of one-dimensional reversal that this demotion entails. Namely, within this framework, it is no longer the case that the economy or economic discourse can be submitted to external criteria of truth or justice. Instead, these concepts, articulated and refined in the philosophical workshop, so to speak, must be recalibrated to fit and serve the economy or economic discourse—which, under neoliberalism, functions as the a priori conceptual and value framework guiding all social decision-making, the governing rationality. If, for instance, addressing climate change requires curtailing economic growth, well, so much the worse for the planet.

Neoliberal Philosophy has an answer to the question of why one ought to study philosophy. Its answer is premised on the antecedent acceptance of this a priori framework. One ought to study philosophy in order to enhance one's human capital, thereby optimizing productivity in the twenty-first-century knowledge economy. In particular, philosophy can offer the critical thinking, communication skills, and intercultural understanding required to be a competitive knowledge worker. Again, a form of one-dimensionality is central to this rhetoric. Critical thinking skills in this pedagogy accept in advance and uncritically the values of the prevailing social system and its governing rationality so that they may be put to productive use. This is the "pedagogical logic of late capitalism," as described by McMillan.[2] According to this pedagogical logic, critical thinking is repackaged as a form of human capital and as a cultural commodity—it can thus, for example, be attached to the techno-utopian aesthetic of the TED Talk. But if not critical thinking, what should philosophy teach and why? What might an alternative philosophical paradigm be and what might it offer to the public as its educational value?

Before proceeding to any definite answer, it should be clear that these questions are already philosophical. It should also therefore be apparent that, under the guise of a self-sufficient economics discourse, neoliberalism is premised on philosophical theses concerning human nature, reason, value, and so on. With this realization, we confront a phenomenon which philosopher Lewis Gordon has termed, "disciplinary decadence." Disciplinary decadence involves the deadening of a discipline in such a way that its methodology and basic assumptions come to dominate reality and foreclose thought. As he writes,

> Disciplinary decadence is the ontologizing or reification of a discipline. In such an attitude, we treat our discipline as though it was never born and has always existed and will never change or, in some cases, die. More than immortal, it is eternal.[3]

The trick of neoliberalism is to fetishize economic methods, concepts, and assumptions as if they were simply identical to reality; that which does not exist within its frame *does not exist*. Recall that, as I discussed in chapter 2, neoliberalism develops a conception of economic rationality and *homo economicus* that is, all at once, supposed to be descriptive, explanatory, and normative. To the extent that there "is" economic irrationality, for example, this is conceived as a lack or disorder, as a normative failure or sin. Economic rationality is both natural and good. Indeed, Gordon is explicit in connecting his theory of disciplinary decadence to the need for theodicical narratives that are able to absorb the discipline's contradictions or encounters with countervailing evidence as these emerge in the discourse of "economic development."[4] In short, neoliberalism is at least in part the result of the hegemony of a decadent disciplinary framework.

To move beyond neoliberalism, we must question its assumptions and the conceptions of human nature, rationality, value, and so on embedded within them. Through such questioning, one can expose the limits of neoliberalism. We must, then, engage in what Gordon calls a "teleological suspension of the disciplinary." Such a suspension occurs "when a discipline suspends its own centering because of a commitment to questions greater than the discipline itself."[5] Economic orthodoxy is quite powerful in the United States and globally and has endured as a framework even in the wake of escalating global catastrophes which it has been unable to address and has in some cases caused. Those of us who are not yet inured to reality entirely, however, must look beyond neoliberal thinking and its brand of rationality. In the case of philosophy, such a teleological suspension requires that one recognize that any dogmatic valuation of philosophy based on neoliberal assumptions helps itself to a philosophy of value that it has not justified and indeed has sought to impose monologically. Neoliberal assumptions and values are ontologized, treated as coterminous with reality itself.

One can see this ontologizing of neoliberalism in the public performances within which philosophy (and the other humanities disciplines) are brought to trial and denounced. One could and should question the assumptions that underlie the kind of statements made by Marco Rubio that there are too many philosophers and too few welders.[6] Who is a philosopher? Are there not philosophers who are welders and welders who are philosophers? How many philosophers or welders should there be and by what measure would we know that there were enough? In general, what principle underlies our own social division between manual and intellectual labor and the attendant status hierarchies? We see a number of philosophical theses assumed and imposed as natural, merely "the way things are." Reflecting on recent conservative demands for "ideological diversity," Gordon thus refers to the current social climate as an anti-political market totalitarianism.[7] He writes, "What is the political threat posed by contemporary educational institutions? Philosophy, at a time when it wasn't ashamed of itself, had a name for it. It is called *thinking*."[8] The thoughtlessness of the demands that knowledge submit to performativity and the vacuity of the rhetoric that mobilizes them becomes relatively patent when one reflects on the denial of reality at their heart. No evidence or explanation is necessary to justify them because there is no reality outside their deductive mathematical machinations. No failure is sufficient to refute them because there is simply nothing beyond them. The principle that emerges from this consideration of the decadence of neoliberalism and its assessment of philosophy is one already well known by Plato.[9] Namely, there is an opposition between monological power, which must always at some point declare that might makes right, and dialogical reason, which is ever-exposed to the demand to justify itself by standards acceptable to all parties and open to the reality that presents itself beyond reason's own methods or assumptions. One might say that this opposition is "transcendental" in the sense that it precedes any subsequent division of knowledge or choice of method or measure; it is excessive with respect to any paradigm and becomes evident in the "teleological suspension of the disciplinary."

It is useful here to turn briefly to the example of Socrates and his trial and defense. As we know, Socrates was accused (at least proximately) and brought to trial by Meletus on charges of impiety and corrupting the youth. Regarding the latter accusation, Socrates engages in a somewhat comical series of arguments, trotting out seemingly well-worn themes and exposing his accuser Meletus for what he no doubt was—an ignorant opportunist and charlatan acting on behalf of the Athenian elite. Underlying the exchange, I think, is a significant point for the discussion of the educational value of philosophy and its importance to the public. From one point of view, it is virtually undeniable that Socrates had corrupted the youth. As he himself explains,

> [T]he young men who follow me around of their own free will, those who have most leisure, the sons of the very rich, take pleasure in hearing people questioned; they themselves often imitate me and try to question others. I think they find an abundance of men who believe they have some knowledge but know little or nothing. The result is that those whom they question are angry, not with themselves, but with me.[10]

One might first note that, despite their own inability to explain or justify themselves, the "problem" for the gentlemen of Athens was not their own lack of knowledge, but instead those who exposed it. In what sense were the youth of Athens "corrupted" by Socrates? Clearly, they failed to know their place in the social order and impertinently questioned people whom Socrates describes as "ambitious, violent, and numerous."[11] From another point of view, of course, the actions of the Athenian youth who emulated Socrates were evidence of virtue rather than corruption. After all, they sought to submit social authority to the standard of evidence and rational explanation. Could those who claimed such authority offer a legitimating account of themselves? Could the social order on the whole provide a rationale for its structure and existence? The Athenians' failure to explain themselves was, of course, corrosive for a decadent social system that, as demonstrated in any number of Plato's dialogues and other sources, extolled the dubious "virtues" of strategic obedience, gladhanding, and conquest fueled by demagoguery.[12]

The monological imposition of a governing rationality through violence and silencing is also theorized to a great extent by Lyotard. In *The Postmodern Condition*, he highlights and denounces what he there calls "terror." He writes,

> By terror I mean the efficiency gained by eliminating, or threatening to eliminate, a player from the language game one shares with him. He is silenced or consents, not because he has been refuted, but because his ability to participate has been threatened (there are many ways to prevent someone from playing).[13]

In defending the governing rationality or the dominant paradigm, whether in society in general or within some particular domain of knowledge, one cannot appeal to the rules established by that form of rationality or paradigm. Issued presumably from outside the dominant discourse, a challenge cannot be met from within that paradigm unless one submits the challenge to a form of monological "terrorism"—the challenge is silenced inasmuch as it is forced to speak according to the rules or rationality whose legitimacy it has attempted to question. For example, the discipline policing identified by Dotson in her discussion of the "culture of legitimation" in philosophy, it seems to me, works through the kind of "terror" identified by Lyotard. Either explain how you are following the norms of Neoliberal Philosophy or be removed from the discourse entirely. This is the (anti-)politics of disciplinary decadence. Of course, one will no doubt rejoin that both challenge and defense must make appeal to higher order concepts or values that transcend the discipline, such as truth or justice. Certainly. But even such higher order concepts and values are always contestable and cannot be reduced to any particular conception or discursive articulation. They are always at issue themselves in any disagreement.

To summarize, the neoliberal determination of the value of philosophy presupposes a philosophy of value. In a performance of bad faith, however, the philosophy of value underlying the neoliberal valuation of philosophy, and with it Neoliberal Philosophy, is disavowed as such and ossified as "the way things are." To this extent, Neoliberal Philosophy therefore participates in what Gordon calls disciplinary decadence. The refusal of thought implied in the subsequent assignment of value is a form of what Lyotard calls "terror," since it monologically submits heterogeneous discourses to its own law. Unable to legitimate itself in terms acceptable to all parties and sealed off from evidence that might contradict its basic methods or assumptions, it resorts to the reason of force: might makes right. The (anti-)politics of preemptive exclusion is carried out through the tautological invocation of definitions and hypnotic repetition of fetishized formulas. The economization of society and the totalization of economic discourse—the "stealth revolution" described by Brown[14]—is an exercise of such "terror." It functions by silencing or otherwise erasing anything that refuses or is not easily submitted to its own logic. Whatever we might say about the value of philosophy and what it teaches should come through a teleological suspension of neoliberalism.

But, of course, with this suspension we are already *doing philosophy*. Philosophy is here practiced as a teleological suspension of the disciplinary and a living form of resistance to the "terror" of forms of rationality that attempt to totalize themselves and foreclose alternatives. What does this philosophy teach? It would not seem to inculcate skills that take for granted the dominant social order with its values and governing rationality. Instead, philosophy of this sort would seem to teach the insubordination of the Socratic operation in which the dominant rationality along with the values and people it authorizes are called to account and submitted to a questioning regarding their legitimacy. Perhaps it is *this* concept of "critical thinking" that Urciuoli has in mind when she writes ironically, "Actual critical and precise thinking can get people fired pretty damn fast, and is unlikely to count as a skill."[15] Indeed, Socrates is only one in a long line of people to be imprisoned and even killed for speaking out of turn and posing inconvenient questions; that is, for *doing philosophy*.

TOWARD AN ALTERNATIVE PHILOSOPHICAL EROTICS

These considerations point us back to the question of philosophical desire, the will to know. What would drive someone to such a form of questioning? Neoliberal Philosophy involves an orientation of philosophical desire in which it is adjusted to and aligned with the broader economic order and its governing rationality. In chapter 3, I discussed this orientation of philosophical desire in terms of the demand for measurable impact. Neoliberal Philosophy wants to know in order to produce results, ultimately to optimize productivity, ensure employment, and increase earnings. Just as for Marx, the point of Neoliberal Philosophy is to change the world. Yet, in stark opposition to Marx, the change in question involves ameliorating improvements according to the values dictated a priori by the neoliberal knowledge economy (i.e., "impact"). Why should one study philosophy? In order to enhance one's critical thinking skills and become a more productive member of the cognitariat. Why should one produce philosophical scholarship? In order to get and retain one of the few stable academic jobs available and make a measurable contribution through cutting edge research. Why should individuals or society invest in philosophy departments, whether through tuition, donations, or public outlays? In order to remain competitive in the global marketplace by developing twenty-first century skills and proprietary control over the useful applications, such as they may be, of philosophical knowledge. Philosophical desire is, in this way, deeply invested in the status quo and the decadence characteristic of the neoliberal totalization of economic discourse.

Traditional philosophical erotics stemming from the ancient Greeks, by contrast, viewed the will to know as an innate human desire for transcendence; an excessive volitional impulse to rise above the condition of partiality, incompleteness, and insufficiency characteristic of everyday sensuous life. The experience of wonder called one to take a step past the given appearance toward something more basic and general; the essence, the origin, the ground. Wisdom or knowledge was therefore a state of the subject beyond and opposed to immersion in the merely relative, accidental, probable, and ephemeral matters typical of mundane existence. It implied a unifying re-collection of oneself, a *metanoia*, which revealed the falsehood of naive consciousness. Immersed in what Husserl referred to as the "natural attitude," this naive consciousness was ignorant not only or even primarily in the sense that it held false beliefs but more deeply in the sense that it was lost to itself and bound by desires that affixed it to a world of second-rate goods and unreliable perceptions—it was unfree.[16] Following Plato, traditional philosophical erotics juxtaposed a higher order of being over against the lower realm of mere appearance. The negation of the world presented to sensation and desire achieved by positing and seeking out this transcendent Truth stood everyday consciousness on its head through what we may as well call a "teleological suspension of the everyday."

By contrast, as Marcuse's theory of Happy Consciousness demonstrates, the present order functions by reconciling reason to the given social reality. At once rationalizing the world and reifying reason, Happy Consciousness aligns desire with the demands of the system—creating what Marcuse calls a "Logos of domination" in *Eros and Civilization*.[17] Recall, this transformation is accomplished through what he terms "repressive desublimation."[18] Whereas art and higher culture traditionally represented an aesthetic revolt against the present order, according to Marcuse's analysis, this revolt is now absorbed into the status quo in the form of cheap, abundant commodities. The desublimated pleasure taken in the commodities available, however, is coupled with the repressive internalization of the performance principle and, with it, a broad de-aestheticization of the world. Within the neoliberal context, the one-dimensional person is committed to investment for optimum return. One actively desires self-enhancement for the sake of a "dream job" in which one can pursue fulfillment and self-actualization through a branded self-image. In increasingly narcissistic and sadomasochistic forms of enjoyment and consumption, the line between pain and gain becomes ever thinner.

As I argued in chapter 3, Neoliberal Philosophy is structured by the reorientation of desire characteristic of such Happy Consciousness. Within Cold War Philosophy, the reorientation took the form of scientific anti-intellectualism and ideological empiricism. The goal was to rid philosophy of its speculative pretensions and adjust it to the world of empirically verifiable facts. This adjustment took a number of forms, but in each case it sought to reduce the knowable to the sayable and the sayable to the behaviorally or operationally defined. From the perspective of this decadent, one-dimensional thinking, there is nothing outside the established "universe of discourse," the semiotic universe of late capitalism. It is only aberrant philosophical desire that leads one to attempt to exceed its bounds in metaphysical flights of fancy. Philosophy ought to be scientific, literal, factual. In order to do so, it must cure itself through, in the words of Reichenbach, a therapeutic "reorientation of philosophic desires."[19] Neoliberal Philosophy is heir to this self-denunciation and abasement of thought. As with Cold War Philosophy before, Neoliberal Philosophy strives to "get results," but in the paradigm of Neoliberal Philosophy such effective thinking is tied to employability and optimization of productivity. In the Social Darwinism characteristic of an environment in which one speaks without irony of being "on the market" and the necessity to "publish or perish," precarious philosophers compete by marketing themselves as (aspiring) academic celebrities poised to make an impact.

Neoliberal Philosophy thus participates in the neoliberal refashioning of the American work ethic through tropes of passion and love. It encourages libidinal attachment to one's work performance both as an identity and as itself a source of pleasure. There is a pervasive and subtle pedagogy of desire behind this attachment. For example, as I mentioned in chapter 2, the "Why Study Philosophy?" (WSP) page for the Philosophy Department at the University of North Carolina (UNC) opens by explaining that "the best reason to major in philosophy would be that you love it."[20] The difficulty here, of course, is not that it is wrong to be passionate about philosophy. And, clearly, the history of philosophical erotics shows the extent to which libidinal investment has been an existential and personal concern characteristic of philosophers. But when the animating desires of philosophy are tailored to the demands of performativity in accordance with the internalization of an actuarial rationality dedicated to accelerating productivity through investment in human capital, doing what you love is paradoxically alienating and repressive. As Miya Tokumitsu argues, this demand to "do what you love" serves to make devalued toil invisible, justify outrageous overwork and exploitation, promote extreme workplace stratification, and ultimately align the desires of workers with those of employers.[21] The narcissistic love in which one consumes a branded self-image connected to one's academic performance is also then a form of self-hate, the Freudian ego-ideal having now become a venomous task-master and crushing burden. With this development, one can perhaps see a reversal characteristic of the success and co-optation of the New Left and related movements of the 1960s and 1970s: critique of the stultifying boredom and mechanization of the blue-collar manual labor characteristic of Fordism is transformed into a valorization of white-collar knowledge work and an aesthetic of entrepreneurial self-realization through brand identity.[22] The late Steve Jobs, the creative iconoclast and genius tech-billionaire who lived his passion through perpetual self-reinvention, can thus be cast as a model for this neoliberal subjectivity. In comparison to this vaunted image, the actual knowledge worker is forever failing to live up to the phoenix-like market god perpetually renewed through self-destruction. After all, only a few can address the "Republic of Letters" on the TED stage and the market is the measure of success.

Paying attention to the alienation, frustration, stress, and depression of the overworked cognitarian produced by this fetish, one can perhaps envision an alternative form of philosophical desire. In this alternative erotics, philosophy would extricate knowledge from its entanglement with performativity and commodification, reconnecting it to a practice dedicated to living a good life—a life moved by a passion for thought, certainly, but emphatically *not* by a passion for work. If, as argued above, any valuation of philosophy presupposes a philosophy of value, then philosophy in its connection to the good life cannot be the heteronomous legislation of external values without repeating the form of decadent bad faith previously explained. Rather, it must be the case that the values with which one identifies are autonomously chosen through a process of creative self-discovery enabled by philosophical dialogue. In accordance with Marcuse's invocation of a "Great Refusal," this process of creative self-discovery requires an antecedent dissociation, a voluntary alienation, from the motivating values and desires of the prevailing social order capable of illuminating another dimension of life and creating what Marcuse terms a "new sensibility."[23] One must learn to be discontent with the paltry "satisfactions" of a life dedicated to performance and refuse to be seduced by the "beauty" of a world predicated on violence, brutality, exploitation, and oppression.

The development of such an attitude of discontent, was a relatively frequent theme in the speeches of Martin Luther King Jr., where he invoked the psychological concept of "adjustment." For King, much like Marcuse, psychological adjustment to the status quo entailed acceptance of conditions of injustice, war, and vast social inequality. In fact, in a speech given to the American Psychological Association in 1967, King called for the establishment of an "International Association for the Advancement of Creative Maladjustment."[24] Already a decade prior to the speech given to the American Psychological Association, in a 1957 address to the Young Men's Christian Association (YMCA) and Young Women's Christian Association (YWCA) at the University of California–Berkeley, he explained,

> Now we all should seek to live a well adjusted life in order to avoid neurotic and schizophrenic personalities. But there are some things within our social order to which I am proud to be maladjusted and to which I call upon you to be maladjusted. I never intend to adjust myself to segregation and discrimination. I never intend to adjust myself to mob rule. I never intend to adjust myself to the tragic effects of the methods of physical violence and tragic militarism. I call upon you to be maladjusted to such things.[25]

As in Marcuse's work, the creative maladjustment called for by King requires a rejection of the Logos of domination in favor of an alternative rationality. Marcuse saw this alternative rationality as a development of *Eros*, a self-unfolding of the libido that moved it beyond mere genital gratification. In such a condition, Marcuse writes, "Eros redefines reason in its own terms. Reasonable is what sustains the order of gratification."[26] Here, though on the right track, it seems to me that Marcuse is misled by his reliance on Freudian metapsychology. Following King, one can identify an "ethic of love" and a related rationality that would instead emerge out of an entirely different relation to the world and others, one in which liberation, justice, and what King termed "positive peace" would be preconditions of personal contentment or satisfaction. Drawing upon his theological background, King identifies this form of love with the Greek *agape*, which he views as an image or manifestation of God's love for humanity. As explained by King,

> *Agape* means understanding, redeeming good will for all men. It is an overflowing love which is purely spontaneous, unmotivated, groundless, and creative. It is not set in motion by any quality or function of its object. It is the love of God operating in the human heart.[27]

Creative maladjustment in King's sense is connected to the cultivation of and trust in *agape* love, a love which is dedicated to liberation, justice, and peace. We might then consider King's frequent invocation of the "beloved community" as a pedagogy of discontent, a mechanism for revealing the inadequacy and ugliness of the status quo social order.

It is useful to connect this Kingian conception of *agape* love to Paulo Freire's discussion of solidarity, love, and generosity in his famous *Pedagogy of the Oppressed*. In Freire's presentation, solidarity with the oppressed emerges out of love. It cannot, therefore, be transformed into a false form of charity or generosity which ultimately upholds the present reality. It is, after all, this reality that situates the two sides, oppressor and oppressed, in antagonistic relation to one another. Following Freire, for example, one cannot "give" freedom to another and the invocation of such a phrase already hints at the reinstatement of the oppressive relationship, since it implies, however subtly, that freedom can just as well be taken away.[28] According to Freire,

> The oppressor is solidary with the oppressed only when he stops regarding the oppressed as an abstract category and sees them as persons who have been unjustly dealt with, deprived of their voice, cheated in the sale of their labor—when he stops making pious, sentimental, and individualistic gestures and risks an act of love. True solidarity is only found in the plenitude of this act of love, in its existentiality, in its praxis.[29]

For Freire, then, a member of the oppressor group can only truly act in solidarity with the oppressed through an act of love in which they join the struggle against the oppressive social order. By contrast, Freire will argue that the revolt of the oppressed is already and in itself an expression of love, even if it is not always fully conscious of itself as such.[30] An oppressive order serves to dehumanize even those at the top as their capacities for creative self-discovery and development are thwarted by their false self-understanding and incomplete perception of social reality. In describing his own approach to the struggle against segregation, King therefore explains, "Since the white man's personality is greatly distorted by segregation, and his soul is greatly scarred, he needs the love of the Negro."[31] Likewise, James Baldwin offers a radical redefinition of integration. Addressing his young nephew, he writes, "[I]f the word *integration* means anything, this is what it means: that we, with love, shall force our brothers to see themselves as they are, to cease fleeing from reality and begin to change it."[32] In movements for liberation such love is the basis for solidarity and the motivating principle of action.

Love drives discontentment with the way things are, thereby functioning as a liberating force which calls one to live a good life through dialogue aimed at creative self-discovery and collective liberatory praxis. This kind of love does not attach one to any particular paradigm of thought or to a branded self-image. Rather, it calls us to break our attachment to performativity and join struggles for liberation and justice. Here, then, one can discern the basis for a new philosophical erotics. The love driving philosophy in this paradigm is disconnected from any need for direct personal gratification and is in that sense disinterested. It is a hard love, as both King and Baldwin, for instance, will insist—active, resistant, confrontational, and committed to authenticity and truth. As Baldwin puts it, this love is "the tough and universal sense of quest and daring and growth" which, he writes, "takes off the masks that we fear we cannot live without and know we cannot live within."[33] To take only one pertinent example, this love reveals the falsehood of the masks produced by the attachment to academic celebrity. Above all, for the one guided by this kind of love, a social order built on exploitation, violence, oppression, and waste; dedicated to the satisfaction of false needs; and blithely suicidal in its constant flirtation with nuclear annihilation and climate change–induced extinction, calls for thought and demands that the dominant Logos, the Logos of domination, be called to account.

DEMOCRATIZING PHILOSOPHY

The love described above requires that professional philosophers renounce their self-congratulatory commitment to meritocracy and recognize that their position involves in many respects the perpetuation of injustice and oppression. As I argued in chapter 4, following Melamed, the focus on performativity within Neoliberal Philosophy serves to reinscribe the same forms of oppression, exclusion, and exploitation characteristic of the broader society into the practice of philosophy using seemingly neutral evaluations of "merit." Neoliberal multiculturalism, as theorized by Melamed, is the dominant form of antiracism of our era. This antiracism fuses conceptions of tolerance, openness, diversity, and multiculturalism to neoliberal sovereignty and the corresponding geopolitical hegemony of the United States. That is, while domestically the state itself is reconstituted along neoliberal lines, the institutions and networks of global capitalism are likewise transformed through the power of American empire. As this is occurring, American empire is reimagined as a force of liberation through a discursive substitution whereby civil rights and other gains and victories for oppressed groups are absorbed into the national narrative as endogenous developments of American character or institutions—the United States is a multicultural society, after all. As Melamed explains, however, this dominant antiracism itself serves as a technology of racialization that further entrenches racial inequalities. Recalibrated to the demands of the new economy, neoliberal multiculturalism produces differential forms of global citizenship in which some people are valued as cosmopolitan subjects whose human capital may contribute to national economic growth and others are devalued as "monocultural" or "backward," lacking the necessary human capital to participate effectively in the machinery of global capitalism.

The Neoliberal University brands itself as diverse and multicultural and is one of the primary institutions through which neoliberalism, entwined with American supremacy on the world stage, is able to claim diversity and multiculturalism for itself. The Neoliberal University performs and sells diversity as one of its most important commodities and in so doing outfits the cosmopolitan global citizens of neoliberal multiculturalism with the requisite intercultural understanding for success in the global economy. In this sense, the Neoliberal University functions as a key site for the forms of racialization characteristic of the global neoliberal order. By translating White supremacy into human capital and performance metrics, the Neoliberal University both obscures and reproduces the global racial order in service to the demands of neoliberal capitalism. At the institutional level, this takes the form of increasingly abstract and de-racialized formulations of diversity and other concepts central to antiracist and feminist practice, such as intersectionality, in what Sirma Bilge has termed the neoliberal diversity regime.[34] By and large, the invocation of these concepts within the institutional sphere functions less in service to social movements dedicated to liberation and more as a form of proprietary expertise arrogated to fields and practitioners now recognized as "equity, diversity, and inclusion" workers. Neoliberal Philosophy is exemplary on this score, as it markets itself as contributing to intercultural understanding through the investigation of "diverse worldviews"—nevertheless persisting in its intolerance of and disdain for contributions from people who identify as members of oppressed and subordinated groups or who teach what Bryan Van Norden has referred to as Less Commonly Taught Philosophies (LCTPs).[35] What would an alternative philosophy guided by love for those subjected to violence, marginalization, exclusion, and brutality through this process look like?

So far, we have seen that a new philosophical paradigm would call into question decadent forms of rationality in a dialogical process of creative self-discovery. Maladjusted to and discontent with a status quo of injustice, oppression, and violence, this new paradigm would be dedicated to collective liberatory praxis that would allow everyone to participate in the process of creative self-discovery, developing new capacities and self-understanding through revolutionary processes of collective liberation. In this sense, philosophers would be "freedom-workers" as defined by Loughead. As she explains, freedom should not be understood as a given attribute of the subject, but rather as a project of self-realization. Thus, she writes, "The 'freedom-workers' of any given society are those who help to foster in others the aspirations of maturity and education."[36] Crucially, then, freedom so conceived is about dialogical forms of sociality in which each person self-consciously depends on others in order to realize themselves more fully; it is not about protection from others and the related license to do as one pleases. Philosophy in this mold would therefore be actively politically engaged in the democratization of the academy and of society more broadly. This means not only, as in the "banking model" of education criticized by Freire, that everyone would have access to "knowledge deposits."[37] Rather, it means that knowledge production itself would be an egalitarian and participatory process engaging many diverse publics and answerable to the demands of collective life and individual self-discovery. To offer an example, philosophy in this alternative paradigm would work within and as part of collective processes of learning-praxis in response to global warming and the impending climate crisis.

In chapter 3, I criticized the proposals of Frodeman and Briggle for a new form of Mode 2 "field philosophy." There, I argued that such Mode 2 philosophy remains one-dimensional to the extent that it seeks to make an ameliorating impact within the present social order through public debate and reform-oriented improvements. In the presentation of Gibbons et al., Mode 2 results in the distribution of knowledge throughout the social field, beyond the bounds of discipline or institution. They also note that within this new kind of knowledge production, there are new forms of reflexivity and accountability as knowledge producers engage different audiences in various sites of application and must evaluate themselves and their methods in ethical, political, and similar terms.[38] This may seem remarkably similar to the democratization called for by my proposed philosophical paradigm. However, it is crucially important to think about how publics are dialogically engaged and the forms of accountability and reflexivity called for in the new paradigm I am advocating. Rather than as entrepreneurs, customers, or investors acting in a competitive marketplace and seeking return on investment, the new philosophical paradigm would approach its publics as *homo politicus* in the sense identified by Brown—political subjects engaged in collective decision-making about their shared lives. Its goal would not be to produce impacts within the order of neoliberal capitalism, but rather to overturn this order in favor of an emergent democratic political vision beyond capitalism. Returning to Mann's discussion of the "power to judge," the new philosophical paradigm would be accountable to the exploited, oppressed, excluded, and marginalized—rather than the wealthiest, most powerful, and normatively secure. To see the difference, one might ask: What might "good philosophy" be as judged by those subjected to violence, marginalization, exclusion, and brutality in the global neoliberal order? How might philosophy become a vehicle both for theorizing and for achieving liberation for the most marginalized and oppressed? By posing such questions, we begin to see the possibility of a radically altered sensibility regarding what constitutes good or real philosophy and who has the power to judge.

As with society more broadly, the democratization of the discipline also requires its desegregation. Desegregating the discipline is a complex process that goes beyond, though of course would certainly include, the hiring of more philosophers of color or including authors who identify as members of oppressed or subordinated groups on syllabi or conference panels. A deeper engagement would require a transformed understanding of the history of the concept of philosophy and practices labeled as such in their relationship to patriarchy, global White supremacy, capitalism, and so on.[39] Minimally, in the United States one might start with the recognition that anything that was understood as philosophy by the dominant culture prior to 1865 took place within and as part of the (re)production of a genocidal settler colonial slave state.[40] Desegregating the discipline, then, requires confronting its implication in historical injustices and its role in obscuring and rationalizing their lingering legacies. The other side of this process, however, is to look beyond the discipline for philosophers and alternative historical antecedents for a new paradigm of philosophy. For example, in recent work, philosopher Devonya Havis has sought an alternative philosophical praxis in what she calls Ancestral Black Vernacular Discourses. As she explains, "My concern is how such practices of resistance, in the form of some people's everyday living, create tools, strategies, and tactics, that constitute a way of *doing* philosophy."[41] Desegregation and democratization of the discipline, then, would necessarily involve the recovery and explicit articulation of forms of devalued and excluded philosophical practice and philosophical voices as these appear or have appeared outside what is labeled philosophy within the dominant culture.

Obviously, the paradigm on offer would have to abandon the essentialism and pretension to universality characteristic of Neoliberal Philosophy (and, indeed, all its modern ancestors). There *are* other philosophies or philosophical practices and paradigms outside Neoliberal Philosophy and, indeed, outside any given paradigm. Here, I am only restating the ontological fact of methodological pluralism already discussed in the introduction. This methodological pluralism, however, must not be allowed to fall into the kind of abstraction or be saddled with the kinds of limitations that allows Neoliberal Philosophy to present itself as studying or teaching "diverse worldviews." Rather, what must be acknowledged with this invocation of methodological pluralism is that philosophy has always been practiced by people who were denied access to the title of philosopher due to their exclusion from the institutions or conversations through which such knowledge has been historically valorized or whose contributions were subsequently erased. Philosophy, historically and presently, has been constructed through and as part of such political processes of exclusion and erasure. To put a finer point on the matter, and to briefly return to an example from chapter 4, Grace Lee Boggs *was* a philosopher and should be studied as such; both her ideas and her revolutionary activism are illuminating in that they provide, in the language of Havis, "tools, strategies, and tactics" that might inform the alternative democratic form of philosophy I am proposing. The exclusions through which individuals like Boggs and many, many others (often lacking her credentials) were prevented from "contributing to the core areas" were a form of discipline policing that acted consciously and deliberately to ensure that philosophy was the more or less exclusive property of men of higher social class, normative sexuality, and dominant ethnoracial identity. It is useful here to recall that Cold War Philosophy was ensconced in many institutions that were or only recently had been formally segregated and in which racial and other barriers were vigorously upheld even when they were not ordained by law. In fact, as McCumber himself points out, "red hunting" was often directed against targets who were considered subversive for reasons other than potential Communist sympathies: Jewish people, Black people, LGBTQ+ people, women, and atheists.[42] The claims to essentialism and universalism characteristic of Neoliberal Philosophy, then, only serve to normalize and obscure the operations of systems of oppression within the history and construction of the discipline and its practices.

Democratizing philosophy therefore requires a robust conception of the manner in which power functions to allow paradigms to gain and exercise hegemony socially. As I have suggested throughout, this means that we must pay attention to the ways that philosophy is policed externally and internally as well as the strategies employed by actors within the discipline to maintain their autonomy and secure funding, prestige, and so forth. It further requires understanding the operations of power within communicative networks. As I articulated at the end of the previous chapter, one can think about power in the discipline of philosophy in terms of professional links, directional flows of citation and readership, and the sovereign capacity to judge and rank. Those who are "linked" to in multiple core professional networks; who must be read and cited, but need not themselves read and cite; whose judgments regarding quality and value carry the social weight of fact; and who are therefore able to position themselves as worthy of social investment to the exclusion of others—they are the people who exercise power within the discipline. Finally, this democratic project necessitates that we continue to plumb the ways that subjects are produced, the mechanisms by which desire is oriented, and the pedagogies of ignorance by which individuals are taught to identify with the prerogatives of the social status quo. Among other things this means thinking deeply about how philosophers imagine, depict, and narrate themselves and their aspirations. This new paradigm calls for processes of democratization both inside and outside the discipline, processes through which the boundary between inside and outside will have to be redrawn and made considerably more fluid. Overall, it demands that we remove the power from the few and share it among the many.

NOTES

1. See Christopher Newfield, *Unmaking the Public University: The Forty Year Assault on the Middle Class* (Cambridge, MA: Harvard University Press, 2008). Newfield's central thesis is that the attacks on higher education that characterized the culture wars were largely a reaction against the growing power of the professional middle class created by the "golden age" of the university and an attempt to contain its political demands.

2. Chris McMillan, "'I've Learned to Question Everything': Critical Thinking, or, the Pedagogical Logic of Late Capitalism," *Journal for Critical Education Policy Studies* 16, no 1. (April 2018): 1–29.

3. Lewis Gordon, *Disciplinary Decadence: Living Thought in Trying Times* (New York: Routledge, 2016), 4.

4. Ibid., 87ff.

5. Ibid., 34.

6. See chapter 1.

7. *Disciplinary Decadence*, 26–27.

8. Ibid., 26. Emphasis in original. See also Justin Pack, *How the Neoliberalization of Academia Leads to Thoughtlessness: Arendt and the Modern University* (Lanham, MD: Lexington Books, 2018), 43–46 and 70–78. Pack utilizes Hannah Arendt's work to develop a theory of "thoughtless cognition" as it occurs within the Neoliberal University. In particular, in a deep resonance with much of what I have discussed

here, he shows how thoughtless "normal science" can overlook its own basis in judgments and values and how practitioners may fail to fully develop a conscience.

9. See, for example, Plato, *Gorgias*, trans. Donald J. Zeyl, in *Complete Works*, ed. John M. Cooper (Indianapolis, IN: Hackett Publishing, 1997), 791–869 (447a-527e).

10. See Plato, *Apology*, trans. G.M.A. Grube, in *Complete Works*, ed. John M. Cooper (Indianapolis, IN: Hackett Publishing, 1997), 22–23 (23c-d).

11. Ibid., 23 (23e).

12. For more on Socrates as a *symptom* of and also, to some extent, *cure* for Athenian decadence, see Friedrich Nietzsche, *Twilight of the Idols*, trans. Richard Polt (Indianapolis, IN: Hackett Publishing, 1997), 12–17.

13. Jean-François Lyotard, *The Postmodern Condition*, trans. Geoff Bennington and Brian Massumi (Minneapolis: University of Minnesota Press, 1984), 63–64.

14. See Wendy Brown, *Undoing the Demos: Neoliberalism's Stealth Revolution* (New York: Zone Books, 2015).

15. Bonnie Urciuoli, "Excellence, Leadership, Skills, Diversity," *Language & Communication* 23 (2003), 407.

16. See Edmund Husserl, *Ideas Pertaining to a Pure Phenomenology and to a Phenomenological Philosophy, First Book*, trans. F. Kersten (Boston, MA: Kluwer Academic Publishers, 1998), 51–62.

17. Herbert Marcuse, *Eros and Civilization: A Philosophical Inquiry into Freud* (Boston, MA: Beacon Press, 1966), 111–118.

18. See Herbert Marcuse, *One-Dimensional Man: Studies in the Ideology of Advanced Industrial Society* (Boston: Beacon Press, 1964), 72–73. For a fuller discussion, see chapter 3.

19. Hans Reichenbach, *The Rise of Scientific Philosophy* (Berkeley: University of California Press, 1951), 306.

20. "Why Major in Philosophy?" Philosophy Department, University of North Carolina at Chapel Hill, accessed September 2, 2020. https://philosophy.unc.edu/undergraduate/the-major/why-major-in-philosophy. As I mentioned in chapter 2, this UNC page is part of a genre of webpages that I have dubbed "WSP" for "Why Study Philosophy?"

21. See Miya Tokumitsu, *Do What You Love: And Other Lies about Success and Happiness* (New York: Regan Arts, 2015). As well as "In the Name of Love," *Jacobin*, January 12, 2014. https://www.jacobinmag.com/2014/01/in-the-name-of-love.

22. For a fuller narrative, see Franco "Bifo" Berardi, *The Soul at Work: From Alienation to Autonomy*, trans. Francesca Cadel and Giuseppina Mecchia (Los Angeles, CA: Semiotext(e), 2009), 93–96.

23. *Eros and Civilization*, 148–151. See also Herbert Marcuse, *An Essay on Liberation* (Boston, MA: Beacon Press, 1969), 23ff.

24. Martin Luther King Jr., "The Role of the Behavioral Scientist in the Civil Rights Movement," *Journal of Social Issues: A Journal of the Society for the Psychological Study of Social Issues* 74, no. 2 (2018), 222.

25. Martin Luther King Jr., "The Power of Nonviolence," in *A Testament of Hope: The Essential Writings and Speeches* (New York: Harper One, 1986), 14.

26. *Eros and Civilization*, 224.

27. Martin Luther King Jr., "An Experiment in Love," in *A Testament of Hope: The Essential Writings and Speeches* (New York: Harper One, 1986), 19.

28. Such a "giving" of freedom operates according to a similar logic as that identified by Ahmed in her discussion of inclusion as a form of conditional hospitality. See Sara Ahmed, *On Being Included: Racism and Diversity in Institutional Life* (Durham, NC: Duke University Press, 2012), 43.

29. Paolo Freire, *Pedagogy of the Oppressed, 50th Anniversary Ed.*, trans. Myra Bergman Ramos (New York: Bloomsbury Academic, 2018), 49–50.

30. Ibid., 56.

31. "An Experiment in Love," 18.

32. James Baldwin, "My Dungeon Shook: Letter to My Nephew on the One Hundredth Anniversary of the Emancipation," in *The Fire Next Time* (New York: Vintage International, 1993), 9–10. Emphasis in original.

33. James Baldwin, "Down at the Cross: Letter from a Region in My Mind," in *The Fire Next Time* (New York: Vintage International, 1993), 95.

34. Sirma Bilge, "Intersectionality Undone: Saving Intersectionality from Feminist Intersectionality Studies," *Du Bois Review* 10, no. 2 (2013): 405–424.

35. Bryan Van Norden, *Taking Back Philosophy: A Multicultural Manifesto* (New York: Columbia University Press, 2017).

36. Tanya Loughead, *Critical University: Moving Higher Education Forward* (Lanham, MD: Lexington Books, 2015), 50.

37. *Pedagogy of the Oppressed*, 72ff.

38. See Michael Gibbons, Camille Limoges, Helga Nowotny, Simon Schwartzman, Peter Scott, and Martin Trow, *The New Knowledge Production: The Dynamics of Science and Research in Contemporary Societies* (Los Angeles: Sage, 1994).

39. For a very good discussion in relation to race, colonialism, and coloniality, see Lewis Gordon, "Decolonizing Philosophy," *The Southern Journal of Philosophy* 57, Spindel Supplement (2019), 16–36.

40. One might, however, point to such examples as Henry David Thoreau and some others traditionally identified as philosophers as engaged in resistance—particularly those few involved in abolitionism or activism in the labor, women's, civil rights, or other movements.

41. Devonya Havis, "'Now, How You Sound': Considering a Different Philosophical Praxis," *Hypatia* 29, no. 1 (Winter 2014), 239.

42. John McCumber, *The Philosophy Scare: The Politics of Reason in the Early Cold War* (Chicago: Chicago University Press, 2016), 19–20.

Conclusion

In this book, I have theorized the ascendancy of Neoliberal Philosophy. Neoliberal Philosophy, as I have interpreted it, is the successor to what McCumber theorized as Cold War Philosophy. My argument has been that this new paradigm has come to dominate academic philosophy in the United States over the last several decades in response to the strategic demands of the Neoliberal University. Philosophers and departments have found it strategically necessary to market themselves. Philosophy has therefore come to, as I have put it, perform its performativity. Put differently, Neoliberal Philosophy has sought to demonstrate that it is a good investment by advertising its contributions to productivity through the production of valuable human capital and profitable knowledge. This marketing has reshaped the pedagogy of philosophy to meet the needs of the twenty-first-century knowledge economy, particularly as these relate to the development of critical thinking skills. Furthermore, such marketing has placed the demand on philosophical knowledge production that it be impactful, primarily through the application and public practice of philosophical research. What has emerged in response to these demands is a starkly stratified discipline absorbed in the culture of academic celebrity and branded self-images. Despite its supposedly color-blind commitment to merit, the discipline remains deeply segregated and hostile to forms of knowledge that might open it up to those it excludes. From a narrow perspective, the discipline can be said to be flourishing. New subspecialties abound, and philosophers are more productive and popular and applicable than ever. From a more capacious view, however, the discipline, along with the whole of higher education, is in crisis, as departments are targeted for closure nationwide and the Neoliberal University redirects investment toward majors and fields of study that are more likely to produce a return.

Since I have sought to understand Neoliberal Philosophy in terms of the external political pressures placed upon the discipline, it surely will not have been missed by the careful reader that I have referred only sparingly to the presidency of Donald Trump and not at all to the COVID-19 pandemic in this work so far. As I am writing, it is almost a year since the first diagnosis of the virus in the United States and, while widespread vaccination appears likely in the coming months, the unfolding disaster has already claimed over 300,000 lives in the United States alone, more than 1.8 million globally. In one sense, it is not difficult to know what to say. The pandemic has revealed the devastating consequences of neoliberalism as an "art of governance," its horrifying effects as an ideology, the deadly racialized social inequalities that it has fostered and reproduced, and the sociopathic cruelty at its heart. Perhaps the difficult thing to say, because tragically, heart-breakingly incomprehensible, is that *everyone already knew all of this*. In his *The Eighteenth Brumaire of Louis Bonaparte*, Marx famously modified Hegel's claim that all events of world history occur twice; in Marx's telling, the important addition is that they occur "the first time as tragedy, the second as farce."[1] There must also be a third recurrence in which they appear as unrelenting tragedies that aremiserably farcical.

The mendacity with which former President Trump and his administration sought to unravel the social fabric, foment far-right militancy, and direct state violence against the most vulnerable over the past several years is in itself deeply disturbing. The fact that large audiences cheered the spectacle of brutality, calling out time and again with greater bloodlust while embracing the lawlessness of known murderers and war criminals, should stand as a sobering reminder of how close we now are to fascism in the United States. One must only recall the relatively underreported fact that a whistleblower recently revealed that the Trump administration was sterilizing women held in a for-profit Immigration and Customs Enforcement (ICE) prison in Georgia.[2] Such a piece of news passes from memory almost before the sentence announcing it has faded from the airwaves, replaced by yet another factoid in the ugly parade of crimes and viciousness. The unconscionable is normalized. The unthinkable grows in likelihood. One hardly remembers that then-President Trump actually dropped the "Mother of All Bombs." To refer to a "crisis" is perhaps too meek.

In the midst of this deluge of bad news, somehow, paralysis reigns. In his work *Capitalist Realism: Is There No Alternative?*, Fisher describes our present condition as characterized by, "the widespread sense that not only is capitalism the only viable political and economic system, but also that it is now impossible even to *imagine* a coherent alternative to it."[3] How is it possible to watch the world collapse without even trying to stop it? Well, most of us appear to accept that, in the infamous words of Margaret Thatcher, there is no alternative. One must accept that millions will live without healthcare in the richest country in human history even as it is ravaged by a deadly virus. There is no alternative. One must accept that runaway climate change will render the planet uninhabitable for humans and most other life forms. There is no alternative. One must accept that the world will see the rise of its first trillionaire, even as millions die in a pandemic. There is no alternative. The market has decided, and the market is the measure of truth and justice. We should all be realistic.

Fisher describes the psychological and spiritual malaise that attends the situation in terms of conditions of "reflexive impotence" and "depressive hedonia"—terms that might just as well have been coined by Marcuse. Writing of the reflexive impotence he observes in his students, Fisher writes,

> They know things are bad, but more than that, they know they can't do anything about it. But that "knowledge," that reflexivity, is not a passive observation of an already existing state of affairs. It is a self-fulfilling prophecy.[4]

Generalized inability to conjure a counter-image of a better world produces the sense that we cannot create one. Social critique is irrelevant because delusional realism assures us that the best we can do is contain the worst abuses of the system through minor regulatory schemes, new markets, and philanthropy. Consider that the Green New Deal, itself inadequate to the challenge of global warming, remains a nonstarter in the U.S. Congress even as each new report reminds us that we are perilously close to ecological apocalypse. Note further that, rather than an imagined future of ecosocialism, the rhetoric of the Left draws explicitly and deliberately on the language of social programs created nearly a century ago, proposing a "New Deal." If the recent election of Joseph Biden to the presidency were not enough to make it painfully clear, and the only real contender against him in the Democratic primary was Bernie Sanders, the more or less patent politics of the official U.S. Left is premised on nostalgia. The path out of neoliberalism from this perspective is a path back to a renewed "golden age" of capitalism. It is not difficult, of course, to sell the virtues of that era to workers and young people who are burdened with crippling debt, whose communities are racked with addiction, and who have never experienced the forms of social solidarity that were normal at the time. But in the end, such calls for a return to a more humane capitalism will not be sufficient to galvanize millions for the required transformation of the world. We must let the dead bury the dead.

Accompanying reflexive impotence, Fisher describes a depressive condition in his students that, counterintuitively, drives them to compulsively seek out pleasure and stimulation. As he explains, "There is a sense that 'something is missing'—but no appreciation that this mysterious, missing enjoyment can only be accessed *beyond* the pleasure principle."[5] It is possible that, in the midst of the carnage and the seeming helplessness that has characterized most people's experience of COVID-19, it is unnecessary to explain this condition further. One searches with urgency but in vain for a new Netflix comedy to take the edge off the harshness of the news alerts appearing every few minutes on one's smartphone, only finally to give up and turn back to

Amazon for some "retail therapy." While no one could deny the extreme loneliness that has attended the world in a period of "social distancing" and "self-isolation," another very difficult truth is that we have long been on this road—eviscerating the public and the social in favor of isolated amusement and empty pleasure on demand, our common life enclosed in social media, malls, and coffee shops.

This returns us to the theme of Happy Consciousness, as theorized by Marcuse. This form of consciousness identifies with its performance in the world, finding its freedom in the forms of satisfaction on offer in the affluent society. As we have seen, for Marcuse, the pleasure taken in the goods on offer results in what he terms repressive desublimation. Rather than a sublimated escape from the ugliness and painful toil characteristic of the given social order provided by a counter-image, the work of the culture industry in the one-dimensional society is to reconcile consciousness to the established order. Wish-fulfillment becomes material reality and vice versa. Pleasure taken in consumed objects ultimately de-aestheticizes one's sensory and sensual experience of the world, fostering an addictive relationship to cheap pleasures that simultaneously discipline one to work-performance. As I have argued, the condition described is more extreme for workers in the knowledge economy who are encouraged to take pleasure in a branded self-image which is offered all at once as a consumable item, a form of self-investment, and a performance of performativity. Yet the enjoyment of this image is also associated with a great deal of denied pain: stress, anxiety, overwork, depression. If Instagram and Facebook are to be trusted, surely we are all the happiest and most productive we have ever been. Nonetheless, long before the coronavirus, millennials expected to be worse off than their parents in material terms and rates of anxiety and depression were at epidemic levels.[6] Despite the happy images produced as part of the personal brand, depressive hedonism is our shared psychological situation.

Drawing on the work of Žižek and Jacques Lacan, Fisher argues that a significant strategy for encouraging transformation involves confronting capitalist realism with its repressed "Real"—the disavowed truth that haunts every ontologized disciplinary frame. The reality to which capitalist realism demands that one adjust is a delusion created through the disavowal of the "traumatic wounds" that are its subconscious heart. Fisher himself invokes environmental catastrophe, eroding mental health, and the rise of the Kafkaesque bureaucracy he calls "market Stalinism" as ways that one might demystify the fantasies structuring this reality.[7] Each of these phenomena has, of course, been significant in my discussion of neoliberalism and the Neoliberal University. It is important, however, to take a moment to ruminate on the extent to which COVID-19 has allowed the Real to emerge into consciousness. To start, it is apparent that the privatization and commodification of healthcare has contributed significantly to the spread and death toll of the pandemic in the United States. Worse, rejected by former President Trump as signs of weakness, the mandating of masks and the issuance of stay-at-home orders were left to cities and states with little guidance or capacity for enforcement—even as many in the far-right were actively encouraged to reject such mandates or orders. The state, especially in areas controlled by Republicans, basically abdicated any role in safeguarding public health. How could it do so in a world where, as Thatcher put it, society does not exist? With such individual "freedom," businesses, large and small, fought to be considered "essential" so that they could continue to profit even as workers were exposed to infection. Consumers were often more than willing to risk both their health or lives and those of servers or bartenders in order to eat at a restaurant or have a drink at a bar. Freedom from masks. Freedom to remain in business. Freedom to consume. These are the delusions of capitalist realism. They are symptoms of the indifference and cruelty that is willing to sacrifice more than 300,000 lives in service of the "normal." The United States, which spent more than $700 billion USD on its military in the 2019 fiscal year, now has more than one quarter of all confirmed cases of COVID-19.[8]

Of course, the Neoliberal University has not been protected from the crisis caused by the pandemic, despite its efforts to immunize itself through similarly delusional commitments to realism. Already at the beginning of the pandemic, in March 2020, Anna Kornbluh prophesied an "academic shock doctrine," relying on the work of Naomi Klein.[9] The shock doctrine, according to Klein, was initially developed by the leading light of the "Chicago School," neoliberal economist Milton Friedman. Friedman advised that advocates of neoliberalization develop ideas which they could quickly transform into policy in periods of crisis by invoking emergency powers. Markets could be imposed in the midst of disasters and the surrounding chaos so that few established institutional or organizational barriers would exist to their implementation. Klein opens her famous work with a vignette about the experience of the public school system in New Orleans in the aftermath of Hurricane Katrina, when the foremost item on the agenda of the Bush administration appeared to be privatizing the system in line with the public recommendations of Friedman. Such crises as Hurricane Katrina represent opportunities for neoliberals to inflict what Klein terms "disaster capitalism."[10]

When it comes to higher education, there have been many ideas lying around, waiting in the wings for just the right moment of crisis. And it is now unquestionable that higher education in the United States as a whole faces a budget crisis that could ultimately close a significant number of colleges and universities.[11] Writing in the *Harvard Business Review* in June 2020, business scholars Vijay Govindarajan and Anup Srivastava looked ahead to provide what they titled "A Post-Pandemic Strategy for U.S. Higher Ed." In the piece, they claim that there are three main forces acting upon higher education from outside that have created a "perfect storm": (1) high tuition costs, (2) new digital technologies, and (3) "lowered psychological barriers" to online instruction created by the pandemic.[12] They go on to argue that leaders in higher education should take lessons from the experience of the virus to deal with the structural crisis that now affects colleges and universities nationwide. They offer three possible models for the post-pandemic Neoliberal University. The first is called the "Augmented Immersive Residential Model." In explanation, they write, "Top-ranked universities with all their structural advantages—global brand recognition, access to world class scholar-teachers, prestigious employers, and influential alumni—now have the opportunity to explore how their recent experience with online learning can help strengthen their traditional model."[13] The second option, named with considerably less artistic flair, is the "Hybrid Model." As Govindarajan and Srivastava see it, while offering students residential and on-campus options, this model can lower tuition costs by shifting large aspects of the educational experience online. Information generated during the pandemic about what can and cannot be successfully taught online can be utilized, they think, to calibrate different options across instructional formats. As an example, they suggest that physics can largely be taught by a "software program." Finally, Govindarajan and Srivastava describe a self-explanatory "Fully Online Model." In a completely unsurprising note, they argue:

> Universities usually follow a vertical integration model where they do everything in house, from admitting students all the way to awarding degrees. Instead, universities must outsource areas where others possess superior core competencies at scale by orchestrating an ecosystem of partners: content creators such as Outlier.org; technology platforms such as edX; and Silicon Valley edTech startups, especially those whose lineage is in the gaming industry with expertise in artificial and augmented reality and capabilities to create immersive experiences.[14]

What is the future of higher education in the prognostications of Govindarajan and Srivastava? A largely online, automated, and "customizable" experience in which students can earn a variety of certifications at relatively low cost using gaming and other technologies—unless, of course, they are among the wealthy few who will have access to an "augmented" and "immersive" experience of a more traditional stripe. Colleges and universities are to be screen-mediated training grounds for the future labor and consumer force of the twenty-first century knowledge economy, integrated "horizontally" into the high-tech firms they dream of one day joining. Virtual reality, indeed.

So much for the future. What of the present? How are administrations nationwide dealing with precipitously declining enrollment in an era of increasing tuition dependence? Unfortunately, the answer is plain: widespread layoffs of faculty and staff, attacks on tenure, increased teaching loads, massive intensification of work, unilateral changes to curriculum, Zoom-ification of instruction, transition to so-called hy-flex and remote instructional formats, reconceptualization of teaching as "delivery of content," predatory attempts to capture the intellectual property of faculty, and normalization of the idea that one can work from home through literally any kind of disaster. To take only one painful example and well-publicized example, City University of New York (CUNY) cut 2,800 adjunct positions while dramatically increasing class sizes.[15] Such cuts are not deviations from the trend. Rather, they are expressions of long-desired "reforms" and the structural contradictions of the Neoliberal University. This is the academic shock doctrine at work.

The traumatic Real of the Neoliberal University, however, belies its happy messaging and its delusional realism. Faculty are struggling with unemployment, underemployment, loss of income, increased childcare duties and expenses, new duties to care for sick or immunocompromised family members, addiction, sleeplessness, isolation, and fatigue from long days on screen and "on stage." Not to mention the grief of losing family members, colleagues, and so many fellow human beings to the virus. Students are struggling with basically all the same problems, exacerbated by the collapse of the service industry in which many were employed and the loss of important cultural experiences marking their adolescence and transition to adulthood. Many students and faculty have difficulty with healthcare expenses during an uncontrolled pandemic because employer-provided insurance has disappeared along with their jobs. Anxiety-inducing uncertainty looms for all, as it is impossible to say what the world will look like even months from now. No one can predict what the long-term effects of the virus will be on those infected or on higher education more specifically. As in so many other aspects of life under neoliberalism, the most vulnerable have been the hardest hit. It appears, for example, that the drop in enrollment has most deeply affected community colleges, a main point of entry for working class students and students of color.[16] Meanwhile, it is an understatement of almost laughable proportions to say that the dynamic experience of learning in community with others has suffered tremendously. The few students whose faces appear on Zoom show the indelible signs of grief, stress, and fatigue; mostly one just stares at black squares while "delivering content."

Tellingly, Fisher titles one of his chapters "What If You Held a Protest and Everyone Came?" The central issue that Fisher is concerned to discuss is the anticipatory capture of resistance by neoliberal capitalism. The person suffering reflexive impotence knows that things are bad but feels unable to do anything about it. In fact, however, the established order presents many ways that you can act to "make the world a better place." You can buy organic, fair trade coffee. You can contribute to campaigns that provide microloans to farmers in developing nations. You can recycle, eat less meat, and raise awareness on social media. You can even exercise your rights and demand another "New Deal." All of which is to say that you are more than allowed, you are even encouraged, to practice the reflexive impotence of feel-good consumption and symbolic protest that leaves everything just as it is.

Fisher's analysis on this score may serve as an important reminder that activist attempts aimed at countering the Neoliberal University or the ravages of late capitalism must take care to avoid replicating their logics or further empowering the offices and institutions authorized by those logics. This point returns us to another major moment of the COVID-19 pandemic: the reemergence of what has come to be known as the Black Lives Matter (BLM) movement against state-sanctioned and vigilante murder of Black people in the United States and globally. Already in July it was estimated that the 2020 manifestation of BLM was the largest protest movement in U.S. history with possibly up to 10 percent of the total population participating in marches or other street action.[17] The power of the movement and its vibrancy should not be gainsaid. However, one must admit that it marks an unprecedented event in capitalism and perhaps in human history: an insurrection of millions overtook every major city (and many small towns) in the most powerful and wealthiest nation on Earth, uniting a multiracial working class against the most directly visible symbol of state-power and White supremacy available to them—yet there was no revolution. No doubt, a multitude of contradictory processes are unfolding in its aftermath and the ramifications and reverberations of 2020's protests will certainly bear unexpected fruits of many kinds. Nonetheless, one cannot fail to notice that the Democrats elected to lead the United States in the wake of the movement are the former attorney general for California and one of the central architects of the federal law that spurred mass incarceration.

There is another side to this contradictory moment, of course. Namely, there has been an unprecedented learning-praxis through which previously undreamed numbers of people entered into the movement, became immersed in questions of strategy and tactics, and developed analysis of White supremacy at both local and global scales. Connected to this, one saw the framework of abolitionism emerge into near-hegemony on the Left—to such an extent that former President Obama felt it necessary to condescendingly chide demands to defund the police.[18] Rather than replicating the basic structures of the carceral state and its brand of "humanist" prison reform, abolitionism has sought to connect mass incarceration to the legacies of slavery and settler colonialism in the United States and to articulate an alternative political praxis dedicated to building what Davis has called "abolition democracy."[19] For example, rather than directing municipal funds toward "reforms" that would further empower police, such as body cameras or "less lethal" weapons, thereby channeling public money away from much needed social programs, abolitionists have argued for reinvestment in communities of color and alternatives to police to ensure community safety. Here, we see an emergent strategy that has the potential to escape anticipatory capture; by proposing an alternative utopian future beyond prisons and police, abolitionists have been able to open political space beyond the dead ends of managed neoliberal "Resistance."

In like manner, those of us working within and against the Neoliberal University must pose to ourselves serious questions about the future of the institution and what we hope for from it. On this score, one might do well to heed the advice of Adam Kotsko, who argues against "making the case" for the humanities.[20] As Kotsko suggests, the assumption of those who continue to "make the case" is that the failure of politicians and business leaders who are acting to destroy liberal arts education stems from a lack of knowledge of its benefits. As Kotsko writes, however,

> They do not need to be told of the benefits of a liberal arts education. They have often benefited from such an education themselves and are happy to provide it for their own children—including at elite Ivy League schools that do not even have the kind of vocational programs that they recommend for everyone else.[21]

Kotsko's central point is that the failure to persuade those in power has arisen from this fundamental misunderstanding. Attempts to cut, change, stratify, and reorient mass higher education in the United States are not about confusions concerning its value. They are instead about power and who has it. He therefore concludes,

> Strong, fully-inclusive unions that fight for decent working conditions for the whole faculty are the only viable way to form an independent power base that gives faculty members real leverage over the administration. Given how entrenched the destructive "best practices" are at most existing institutions, though, more radical measures—such as founding new, faculty-run cooperatives—may be more effective.[22]

Following on Kotsko's argument, a movement to build faculty power in opposition to what is already unfolding is absolutely necessary. But, as with abolitionism, it must produce an analysis that will escape the governing rationality of neoliberalism. Broadly, this means decommodifying and democratizing higher education while simultaneously reconceptualizing it as, in the words of Loughead, "freedom-work."

Can we imagine a movement of faculty in solidarity with students and workers dedicated to such freedom-work? Can we imagine the new ways of being and knowing that might emerge on the other side? What could philosophy be? What might it look like? In her essay "The Abolition of Philosophy," Ladelle McWhorter documents recurring pronouncements of the "death of philosophy" going as far back as 1966. In response, she writes, "The problem is not that *philosophy* is irrelevant; the problem is either that what is happening in the profession is not philosophy, or that the way of life it exemplifies has no appeal."[23] Perhaps the paradigm that I have outlined here as an alternative to Neoliberal Philosophy could resuscitate philosophy for or as a way of life beyond the Neoliberal University, articulating a form of praxis and a mode of being with broad appeal and revolutionary consequence. Committed to the Socratic practice of insubordination and impertinence through which dominant forms of rationality and the authorities and institutions they legitimize are called to account, the alternative paradigm of philosophy that I have proposed could play an important role in the struggle to reimagine the future of higher education as freedom-work. As I outlined in chapter 5, this alternative paradigm would be guided by radical love and, through that love, solidarity with the exploited and oppressed. Radical love of this kind must breed discontentment with the present social order, which is rife with exploitation and oppression. The new paradigm would therefore emerge from and alongside collective liberatory praxis, an incubator of what King called "creative maladjustment." Thus, it would be committed to the democratization and desegregation of philosophy and society more broadly, reconceptualizing knowledge and who has it in order to learn and live freedom more fully. Above all, it would not capitulate to the delusions of realism. Another world, another university, another philosophy is possible. The question is only whether we have the will, courage, the *love* to build it.

NOTES

1. Karl Marx, *The Eighteenth Brumaire of Louis Bonaparte* in *Karl Marx: Selected Writings, Second Edition*, ed. David McLellan (New York: Oxford University Press, 2000), 329.

2. Maya Manian, "Immigration Detention and Coerced Sterilization: History Tragically Repeats Itself," *News and Commentary*, American Civil Liberties Union, September 29, 2020. https://www.aclu.org/news/immigrants-rights/immigration-detention-and-coerced-sterilization-history-tragically-repeats-itself. It is worth noting that the preceding lines were written prior to the January 6, 2021, seizure of the Capitol by supporters of President Trump in an apparent attempt to overturn the 2020 election.

3. Mark Fisher, *Capitalist Realism: Is There No Alternative?* (Winchester, UK: O Books, 2009), 2.

4. Ibid., 21.

5. Ibid., 22.

6. See Jen Wieczner, "Most Millennials Think They'll Be Worse Off Than Their Parents," *Fortune Magazine*, March 1, 2016. http://fortune.com/2016/03/01/millennials-worse-parents-retirement.

7. *Capitalist Realism*, 17ff.

8. Amanda Macias, "Trump Signs $738 Billion Defense Bill. Here's What the Pentagon Is Poised to Get," *CNBC*, December 20, 2019. https://www.cnbc.com/2019/12/21/trump-signs-738-billion-defense-bill.html.

9. Anna Kornbluh, "Academe's Coronavirus Shock Doctrine," *The Chronicle of Higher Education*, March 12, 2020. https://www.chronicle.com/article/academes-coronavirus-shock-doctrine.

10. Naomi Klein, *The Shock Doctrine: The Rise of Disaster Capitalism* (New York: Metropolitan Books, 2007), 3–6.

11. For a useful and comprehensive account of the crisis, see Jeffrey Aaron Snyder, "Higher Education in the Age of Coronavirus," *Boston Review*, April 30, 2020. http://bostonreview.net/forum/jeffrey-aaron-snyder-higher-education-age-coronavirus. See also Astra Taylor, "The End of the University: The Pandemic Should Force America to Remake Higher Education," *The New Republic*, September 8, 2020.

12. Vijay Govindarajan and Anup Srivastava, "A Post-Pandemic Strategy for U.S. Higher Ed," *The Harvard Business Review*, June 2, 2020, https://hbr.org/2020/06/a-post-pandemic-strategy-for-u-s-higher-ed.

13. Ibid.

14. Ibid.

15. For more, see R.H. Lossin, "Why CUNY Faculty and Staff May Go on Strike," *The Nation*, December 21, 2020, https://www.thenation.com/article/activism/cuny-union-strike-remote.

16. See Madeline St. Amour, "Who's Up, Who's Down, and Why," *Inside Higher Ed*, November 19, 2020, https://www.insidehighered.com/news/2020/11/19/community-college-enrollments-down-nationally-not-everywhere.

17. See Larry Buchanan, Quoctrung Bui, and Jugal K. Patel, "Black Lives Matter May Be the Largest Movement in U.S. History," *The New York Times*, July 3, 2020, https://www.nytimes.com/interactive/2020/07/03/us/george-floyd-protests-crowd-size.html.

18. See Chandelis Duster, "Obama Cautions Activists Against Using 'Defund the Police' Slogan," *CNN*, December 2, 2020. https://www.cnn.com/2020/12/02/politics/barack-obama-defund-the-police/index.html.

19. Angela Davis, *Abolition Democracy: Beyond Prison, Torture, and Empire* (New York: Seven Stories Press, 2005).

20. Adam Kotsko, "Not Persuasion, But Power: Against Making the Case," *Boston Review*, May 6, 2020. https://bostonreview.net/forum/higher-education-age-coronavirus/adam-kotsko-not-persuasion-power-against-"making-case."

21. Ibid.

22. Ibid.

23. Ladelle McWhorter, "The Abolition of Philosophy," in *Active Intolerance: Michel Foucault, The Prisons Information Group, and the Future of Abolition*, eds. Perry Zurn and Andrew Dilts (New York: Palgrave Macmillan, 2016), 36.

Bibliography

"About Us." The Society for Applied Philosophy. Accessed September 28, 2020. https://www.appliedphil.org.

"Academic Labor Force Trends, 1975–2017." American Association of University Professors (AAUP). https://www.aaup.org/sites/default/files/Academic_Labor_Force_Trends_1975-2015_0.pdf.

Agamben, Giorgio. "What Is an Apparatus?" *What Is an Apparatus and Other Essays*, 1–24. Translated by David Kishik and Stefan Pedatella. Stanford, CA: Stanford University Press, 2009.

Ahmed, Sara. *On Being Included: Racism and Diversity in Institutional Life*. Durham, NC: Duke University Press, 2012.

Alcoff, Linda Martín. "Pluralism and Diversity as Intrinsic Philosophical Concerns." *The Pluralist's Guide.Org: The Pluralist's Guide to Philosophy Programs*. Accessed December 8, 2020. https://sites.psu.edu/pluralistsguide/2015/07/30/pluralism-and-diversity-as-intrinsic-philosophical-concerns.

———. "Philosophy's Civil Wars." *Proceedings and Addresses of the American Philosophical Association* 87 (November 2013): 16–43.

Althusser, Louis. "Ideology and Ideological State Apparatuses (Notes towards an Investigation)." *Lenin and Philosophy and Other Essays*, 127–188. Translated by Ben Brewster. New York: Monthly Review Press, 1971.

Archard, David. "The Methodology of Applied Philosophy." In *A Companion to Applied Philosophy*, 18–33. Edited by Kasper Lippert-Rasmussen, Kimberley Brownlee, and David Coady. Hoboken, NJ: Wiley Blackwell, 2017.

Archibald, Robert B., and David H. Feldman. "State Higher Education Spending and the Tax Revolt." *The Journal of Higher Education* 77, no. 4 (July/August 2006): 618–644.

———. *Why Does College Cost So Much?* New York: Oxford University Press, 2011.

Armitage, David, Homi Bhabha, Emma Dench, Jeffrey Hamburger, John Hamilton, Sean Kelly, Carrie Lambert-Beatty, Christie McDonald, Anne Shreffler, and James Simpson. "The Teaching of the Arts and Humanities at Harvard College: Mapping the Future." Cambridge, MA: Harvard University, May 31, 2013. https://scholar.harvard.edu/files/jamessimpson/files/mapping_the_future.pdf.

Aronowitz, Stanley. *The Knowledge Factory: Dismantling the Corporate University and Creating True Higher Learning*. Boston, MA: Beacon Press, 2000.

"Bachelor of Arts (BA), Philosophy Degree." Payscale.com. Accessed December 5, 2020. https://www.payscale.com/research/US/Degree=Bachelor_of_Arts_(BA)%2C_Philosophy/Salary.

Baghramian, Maria and Andrew Jorgensen. "Quine, Kripke, and Putnam." In *The Oxford Handbook of the History of Analytic Philosophy*, 594–620. Edited by Michael Beaney. New York: Oxford University Press, 2013.

Baldwin, James. "Down at the Cross: Letter from a Region in My Mind." In *The Fire Next Time*, 11–106. New York: Vintage International, 1993.

———. "My Dungeon Shook: Letter to My Nephew on the One Hundredth Anniversary of the Emancipation." In *The Fire Next Time*, 1–10. New York: Vintage International, 1993.

Bartlett, Bruce. "'Starve the Beast': Origins and Development of a Budgetary Metaphor." *The Independent Review* XII, no. 1 (Summer 2007): 5–26.

Beaney, Michael. "What Is Analytic Philosophy?" In *The Oxford Handbook of the History of Analytic Philosophy*, 3–29. Edited by Michael Beaney. New York: Oxford University Press, 2013.

Beck, Molly. "Scott Walker Sought Changes to Wisconsin Idea, Emails Show After Judge Orders Release of Records." *Wisconsin State Journal*, May 28, 2016. https://madison.com/wsj/news/local/govt-and-politics/scott-walker-sought-changes-to-wisconsin-idea-emails-show-after-judge-orders-release-of-records/article_268eb62f-d548-5a2d-a2f0-ca977dac2346.html.

Becker, Gary S. "A Theory of the Allocation of Time." *The Economic Journal* 75, no. 299 (September 1965): 493–517.

———. "Introduction to the First Edition." In *Human Capital: A Theoretical and Empirical Analysis, with Special Reference to Education, Second Edition*, 9–11. Chicago: University of Chicago Press, 1975.

———. "Investment in Human Capital: Effects on Earnings." In *Human Capital: A Theoretical and Empirical Analysis, with Special Reference to Education, Second Edition*, 15–44. Chicago: University of Chicago Press, 1975.

———. "Investment in Human Capital: Rates of Return." In *Human Capital: A Theoretical and Empirical Analysis, with Special Reference to Education, Second Edition*, 45–144. Chicago: University of Chicago Press, 1975.

Bell, Derek. "Brown v. Board of Education and the Interest-Convergence Dilemma." *Harvard Law Review* 93, no. 3 (January, 1980): 518–533.

Bennett, Janet M. "Transformative Training: Designing Programs for Culture Learning." In *Contemporary Leadership and Intercultural Competence: Exploring the Cross-Cultural Dynamics Within Organizations*, 95–110. Edited by M.A. Moodian. Thousand Oaks, CA: Sage Publishing, 2009.

Berardi, Franco. *The Soul at Work: From Alienation to Autonomy*. Translated by Francesca Cadel and Giuseppina Mecchia. Los Angeles, CA: Semiotext(e), 2009.

Bérubé, Michael. "The Futility of the Humanities." *Qui Parle* 20, no.1 (Fall/Winter 2011): 95–107.

Bilge, Sirma. "Intersectionality Undone: Saving Intersectionality from Feminist Intersectionality Studies." *Du Bois Review* 10, no. 2 (2013): 405–424.

Boggs, Grace Lee. *Living for Change: An Autobiography*. Minneapolis, MN: University of Minnesota Press, 2016.

Bok, Derek. *Universities in the Marketplace: The Commercialization of Higher Education*. Princeton, NJ: Princeton University Press, 2003.

Bonilla-Silva, Eduardo. *Racism Without Racists: Colorblind Racism and the Persistence of Racial Inequality in America*. Lanham, MD: Rowman & Littlefield, 2014.

Botts, Tina Fernandes, Liam Kofi Bright, Myisha Cherry, Guntar Mallarangeng, and Quayshawn Spencer. "What Is the State of Blacks in Philosophy?" *Critical Philosophy of Race* 2, no. 2 (2014): 224–242.

Bourget, David, and David J. Chalmers. "What Do Philosophers Believe?" *Philosophical Studies: An International Journal for Philosophy in the Analytic Tradition* 170, no. 3 (2014): 465–500.

Briziarelli, Marco, and Joseph L. Flores. "Professing Contradictions: Knowledge Work and the Neoliberal Condition of Academic Workers." *TripleC* 16, no. 1 (2018): 114–128.

Brogaard, Berit, and Christopher A. Pynes, eds. "The Overall Rankings." *The Philosophical Gourmet Report*. Accessed September 2, 2020. https://www.philosophicalgourmet.com.

———. "Other Areas." *The Philosophical Gourmet Report*. Accessed September 2, 2020. https://www.philosophicalgourmet.com.

Brown, Wendy. *Undoing the Demos: Neoliberalism's Stealth Revolution*. New York: Zone Books, 2015.

Bruya, Bryan. "Appearance and Reality in *The Philosophical Gourmet Report*: Why the Discrepancy Matters to the Profession of Philosophy." *Metaphilosophy* 46, nos. 4–5 (October 2015): 657–690.

Buchanan, Larry, Quoctrung Bui, and Jugal K. Patel. "Black Lives Matter May Be the Largest Movement in U.S. History." *The New York Times*, July 3, 2020. https://www.nytimes.com/interactive/2020/07/03/us/george-floyd-protests-crowd-size.html.

Burbules, Nicholas. "Postmodernism and Education." In *The Oxford Handbook of Philosophy of Education*, 524–534. Edited by Harvey Siegel. New York: Oxford University Press, 2009.

Bush, Vannevar. "Science: The Endless Frontier." *Transactions of the Kansas Academy of Science* 48, no. 3 (December 1945): 231–264.

Carnap, Rudoph. "Überwindung der Metaphysik durch logische Analyse der Sprache." *Erkenntnis* 2 (1931): 219–241.

Castells, Manuel. *Communication Power*. New York: Oxford University Press, 2009.

Chiwaya, Nigel. "The Five Charts Show How Bad the Student Loan Debt Situation Is." *NBC News*, April 24, 2019. https://www.nbcnews.com/news/us-news/student-loan-statistics-2019-n997836.

Chomsky, Noam. "On Academic Labor." *Counterpunch*, February 28, 2014. https://www.counterpunch.org/2014/02/28/on-academic-labor.

Cohen, Patricia. "In Tough Times, the Humanities Must Justify Their Worth." *The New York Times*, February 25, 2009. https://www.nytimes.com/2009/02/25/books/25human.html.

Committee on the Status and Future of the Profession. "Department Advocacy Toolkit." Newark, DE: American Philosophical Association, 2019. https://www.apaonline.org/page/role_of_phil.

Craig, Russell, Joel Amernic, and Dennis Tourish. "Perverse Audit Culture and Accountability of the Modern Public University." *Financial Accountability & Management* 30, no. 1 (February 2014): 1–24.

Darder, Antonia. "Neoliberalism in the Academic Borderlands: An On-Going Struggle for Equality and Human Rights." *Educational Studies* 48, no. 5 (2012): 412–426.

"Data Feed." PhilJobs: Jobs for Philosophers. Accessed September 28, 2020. https://philjobs.org/appointments/dataFeed.

"Data Snapshot: Contingent Faculty in US Higher Ed." American Association of University Professors (AAUP). https://www.aaup.org/sites/default/files/10112018%20Data%20Snapshot%20Tenure.pdf.

Davidson, Donald. "Knowing One's Own Mind." *Proceedings and Addresses of the American Philosophical Association* 60, no 3 (January 1987): 441–458.

Davis, Angela. *Abolition Democracy: Beyond Prison, Torture, and Empire*. New York: Seven Stories Press, 2005.

Dean, Jodi. *Democracy and Other Neoliberal Fantasies: Communicative Capitalism and Left Politics*. Durham, NC: Duke University Press, 2009.

De Beauvoir, Simone. *The Ethics of Ambiguity*. Translated by Bernard Frechtman. New York: Citadel Press, 1976.

Delanty, Gerard. *Challenging Knowledge: The University in the Knowledge Society*. Philadelphia, PA: Open University Press, 2001.

Deleuze, Gilles and Felix Guattari. *A Thousand Plateaus: Capitalism and Schizophrenia*. Translated by Brian Massumi. Minneapolis, MN: University of Minnesota Press, 1987.

"Demographic Statistics on the APA Membership, FY 2016 to FY 2018." American Philosophical Association. https://cdn.ymaws.com/www.apaonline.org/resource/resmgr/data_on_profession/fy2018-demographic_statistic.pdf.

"Department Advocacy Toolkit." American Philosophical Association. Accessed September 2, 2020. https://www.apaonline.org/page/deptadvocacytoolkit.

Dotson, Kristie. "How Is This Paper Philosophy?" *Comparative Philosophy* 3, no. 1 (2012): 3–29.

———. "On Intellectual Diversity and Differences That May Not Make a Difference." *Ethics and Education* 13, no. 1 (2018): 123–140.

Duster, Chandelis. "Obama Cautions Activists Against Using 'Defund the Police' Slogan." *CNN*, December 2, 2020. https://www.cnn.com/2020/12/02/politics/barack-obama-defund-the-police/index.html.

Edwards, Richard. "All Quiet on the Postmodern Front?" *Studies in Philosophy and Education* 25, no. 4 (July 2006): 273–278.

"Essential Learning Outcomes." Association of American Colleges and Universities (AAC&U). Accessed September 4, 2020. https://www.aacu.org/essential-learning-outcomes.

Etzkowitz, Henry, and Loet Leydesdorff. "The Dynamics of Innovation: From National Systems and 'Mode 2' to a Triple Helix of University–Industry–Government Relations." *Research Policy* 29, no. 2 (2000): 109–123.

Fabricant, Michael and Stephen Brier. *Austerity Blues: Fighting for the Soul of Public Higher Education*. Baltimore, MD: Johns Hopkins University Press, 2016.

"Faculty." Department of Philosophy, New York University. Accessed September 28, 2020. https://as.nyu.edu/content/nyu-as/as/departments/philosophy/directory/faculty.htm.

"Faculty." Department of Philosophy, Rutgers University. Accessed September 28, 2020. https://philosophy.rutgers.edu/people/faculty.

Fesmire, Steven. "Democracy and the Industrial Imagination in American Education." *Education and Culture* 32, no. 1 (2016): 53–61.

Feyerabend, Paul. *Against Method, Third Edition*. London: Verso Books, 1993.

Fisher, Mark. *Capitalist Realism: Is There No Alternative?* Winchester, UK: O Books, 2009.

Fisk, Milton. "Multiculturalism and Neoliberalism." *Praxis Filosófica* 21 (2005): 21–28.

Forman, Michael. "One-Dimensional Man and the Crisis of Neoliberal Capitalism: Revisiting Marcuse in the Occupation." *Radical Philosophy Review* 16, no 2. (2013): 507–528.

Foucault, Michel. "The Confession of the Flesh." In *Power/Knowledge: Selected Interviews & Other Writings 1972–1977*, 194–228. Edited by Colin Gordon. Translated by Colin Gordon, Leo Marshall, John Mepham, and Kate Soper. New York: Pantheon Books, 1980.

———. *History of Sexuality, Volume 1: An Introduction*. Translated by Robert Hurley. New York: Vintage Books, 1990.

———. *The Birth of Biopolitics: Lectures at the Collège de France, 1978–1979*. Edited by François Ewald, Alessandro Fontana, and Michel Senellart. Translated by Graham Burchell New York: Palgrave Macmillan, 2010.

Freire, Paolo. *Pedagogy of the Oppressed, 50th Anniversary Ed.* Translated by Myra Bergman Ramos. New York: Bloomsbury Academic, 2018.

Freud, Sigmund. "Formulations on the Two Principles of Mental Functioning." In *The Standard Edition of the Complete Psychological Works of Sigmund Freud, Volume XII (1911–1913): The Case of Schreber, Papers on Technique and Other Works*, 213–226. Translated and edited by James Strachey. London, Hogarth Press, 1958.

———. *Beyond the Pleasure Principle*. Translated by James Strachey. New York: W.W. Norton, 1961.

———. *Civilization and Its Discontents*. Translated and edited by James Strachey. New York: W.W. Norton, 1961.

Friedman, Thomas. *The World Is Flat: A Brief History of the Twenty-First Century*. New York: Farrar, Straus, and Giroux, 2005.

Frodeman, Robert, and Adam Briggle. *Socrates Tenured: The Institutions of 21st-Century Philosophy*. New York: Rowman & Littlefield, 2016.

Frodeman, Robert, Adam Briggle, and J. Britt Holbrook. "Philosophy in the Age of Neoliberalism." *Social Epistemology: A Journal of Knowledge, Culture, and Policy* 26, nos. 3–4 (2012): 1–20.

Gakis, Dimitris. "Philosophy as Paradigms: An Account of a Contextual Metaphilosophical Perspective." *Philosophical Papers* 45, nos. 1 and 2 (March and July 2016): 209–239.

Gardiner, Michael. "An Autonomist Marcuse?" *Rethinking Marxism: A Journal of Economics, Culture, and Society* 30, no. 2 (2018): 232–255.

Garfield, Jay L. Foreword to *Taking Back Philosophy: A Multicultural Manifesto* by Bryan W. Van Norden. New York: Columbia University Press, 2017.

Garfield, Jay L., and Bryan W. Van Norden, "If Philosophy Won't Diversify, Let's Call It What It Really Is." *The Stone, New York Times*, May 11, 2016. https://www.nytimes.com/2016/05/11/opinion/if-philosophy-wont-diversify-lets-call-it-what-it-really-is.html.

Garrison, Mark. "Resurgent Behaviorism and the Rise of Neoliberal Schooling." In *The Wiley Handbook of Global Educational Reform*. Edited by Kenneth J. Saltman and Alexander J. Means. Hoboken, NJ: Wiley Blackwell, 2019.

Gibbons, Michael, Camille Limoges, Helga Nowotny, Simon Schwartzman, Peter Scott, and Martin Trow. *The New Knowledge Production: The Dynamics of Science and Research in Contemporary Societies*. Los Angeles: Sage, 1994.

Gilmore, Ruth Wilson. *Golden Gulag: Prisons, Surplus, Crisis, and Opposition in Globalizing California*. Berkeley, CA: University of California Press, 2007.

Ginsberg, Benjamin. *The Fall of the Faculty*. New York: Oxford University Press, 2011.

Giroux, Henry. *Neoliberalism's War on Higher Education*. Chicago, IL: Haymarket Books, 2014.

The Global Human Capital Report: Preparing People for the Future of Work. World Economic Forum (WEF). Geneva, Switzerland: World Economic Forum, 2017. http://www3.weforum.org/docs/WEF_Global_Human_Capital_Report_2017.pdf.

Gordon, Lewis. *Disciplinary Decadence: Living Thought in Trying Times*. New York: Routledge, 2016.

———. "Decolonizing Philosophy." *The Southern Journal of Philosophy* 57, Spindel Supplement (2019): 16–36.

Govindarajan, Vijay, and Anup Srivastava. "A Post-Pandemic Strategy for U.S. Higher Ed." *The Harvard Business Review*, June 2, 2020. https://hbr.org/2020/06/a-post-pandemic-strategy-for-u-s-higher-ed.

Gurría, Angel. Foreword to *Human Capital: How What You Know Shapes Your Life*. By Brian Keely. Paris: OECD Publishing, 2007.

Habermas, Jürgen. *The Theory of Communicative Action, Volume 1: Reason and the Rationalization of Society*. Boston, MA: Beacon Press, 1984.

Harraway, Donna J. *Modest_Witness@Second_Millenium.FemaleMan_Meets_OncoMouse™: Feminism and Technoscience*. New York: Routledge, 1997.

Harris, Adam. "Alaska Still Hasn't Saved Its Universities." *The Atlantic*, September 3, 2019. https://www.theatlantic.com/education/archive/2019/08/alaskas-higher-education-system-still-trouble/596191.

Hart Research Associates. "Fulfilling the American Dream: Liberal Education and the Future of Work: Selected Findings from Online Surveys of Business Executives and Hiring Managers." Washington, DC: Association of American Colleges and Universities, 2018. https://www.aacu.org/sites/default/files/files/LEAP/2018EmployerResearchReport.pdf.

Harvey, David. *A Brief History of Neoliberalism*. Oxford: Oxford University Press, 2005.

Haslanger, Sally. "Changing the Culture and Ideology of Philosophy: Not by Reason (Alone)." *Hypatia* 23, no. 2 (2008): 210–223.

Havis, Devonya. "'Now, How You Sound': Considering a Different Philosophical Praxis." *Hypatia* 29, no. 1 (Winter 2014): 237–252.

Hegel, G.W.F. *The Phenomenology of Spirit*. Translated by A.V. Miller. New York: Oxford University Press, 1977.

Heidegger, Martin. "The Question Concerning Technology." In *The Question Concerning Technology and Other Essays*, 3–35. Translated by William Lovitt. New York: Harper & Row Publishers, 1977.

Herritt, Robert. "Google's Philosopher." *Pacific Standard*, December 30, 2014. Updated: June 14, 2017. https://psmag.com/environment/googles-philosopher-technology-nature-identity-court-legal-policy-95456.

"Higher Education." Unkoch My Campus. Accessed November 30, 2020. http://www.unkochmycampus.org/highereducation.

"Human Capital Project." World Bank Group. Accessed August 15, 2020. https://www.worldbank.org/en/publication/human-capital.

Husserl, Edmund. *Ideas Pertaining to a Pure Phenomenology and to a Phenomenological Philosophy, First Book*. Translated by F. Kersten. Boston, MA: Kluwer Academic Publishers, 1998.

Ihde, Don. *Postphenomenology and Technoscience: The Peking University Lectures*. Albany, NY: SUNY Press, 2009.

"Improving Human Capital in a Competitive World—Education Reform in the U.S." March 3, 2011. U.S. Department of Education. https://www.ed.gov/news/speeches/improving-human-capital-competitive-world-education-reform-us.

"Interview with Former Philosophy Graduate Student and Investor Bill Miller." *Blog of the APA*. American Philosophical Association. Accessed September 2, 2020. https://blog.apaonline.org/2018/03/02/interview-with-former-philosophy-graduate-student-and-investor-bill-miller.

Johnson, Steven. "Colleges Lose a 'Stunning' 651 Foreign-Language Programs in 3 Years." *The Chronicle of Higher Education*, January 22, 2019. https://www.chronicle.com/article/Colleges-Lose-a-Stunning-/245526.

Jones, Daniel Stedman. *Masters of the Universe: Hayek, Friedman, and the Birth of Neoliberal Politics*. Princeton, NJ: Princeton University Press, 2012.

Kara, Siddhartha. "Is Your Phone Tainted by the Misery of the 35,000 Children in Congo's Mines?" Modern Day Slavery in Focus, *The Guardian*, October

12, 2018. https://www.theguardian.com/global-development/2018/oct/12/phone-misery-children-congo-cobalt-mines-drc.

Katzav, Joel, and Krist Vaesen. "On the Emergence of American Analytic Philosophy." *British Journal for the History of Philosophy* 25, no. 4 (July 2017): 772–798.

———. "Pluralism and Peer Review in Philosophy." *Philosophers' Imprint* 17, no. 9 (September 2017): 1–20.

King, Martin Luther, Jr. "An Experiment in Love." In *A Testament of Hope: The Essential Writings and Speeches*, 16–20. New York: Harper One, 1986.

———. "The Power of Nonviolence." In *A Testament of Hope: The Essential Writings and Speeches*, 12–15. New York: Harper One, 1986.

———. "The Role of the Behavioral Scientist in the Civil Rights Movement." *Journal of Social Issues: A Journal of the Society for the Psychological Study of Social Issues* 74, no. 2 (1968): 214–223.

Klein, Naomi. *The Shock Doctrine: The Rise of Disaster Capitalism*. New York: Metropolitan Books, 2007.

Knighton, Andrew Lyndon. "Beyond 'Education in Sickness': A Biopolitical Marcuse and Some Prospects for University Self-Administration." *Theory & Event* 20, no. 2 (2017): 769–787.

Kornbluh, Anna. "Academe's Coronavirus Shock Doctrine." *The Chronicle of Higher Education*, March 12, 2020. https://www.chronicle.com/article/academes-coronavirus-shock-doctrine.

Kotsko, Adam. "Not Persuasion, but Power: Against Making the Case." *Boston Review*, May 6, 2020. https://bostonreview.net/forum/higher-education-age-coronavirus/adam-kotsko-not-persuasion-power-against-"making-case."

Kuhn, Thomas. *The Structure of Scientific Revolutions, Fiftieth Anniversary Edition*. Chicago: University of Chicago Press, 2012.

Kuklick, Bruce. *A History of Philosophy in America, 1720–2000*. New York: Oxford University Press, 2001.

Lea, David. "The Future of the Humanities in Today's Financial Markets." *Educational Theory* 64, no. 3 (June 2014): 261–283.

Lewis, Tyson. "Biopower, Play, and Experience in Education." In *Marcuse's Challenge to Education*, 45–57. Edited by Douglass Kellner, Tyson Lewis, Clayton Pierce, and K. Daniel Cho. Lanham, MD: Rowman & Littlefield, 2009.

Locke, Kirsten. "Performativity, Performance, and Education." *Educational Philosophy and Theory* 47, no. 3 (2015): 247–259.

Lossin, R.H. "Why CUNY Faculty and Staff May Go on Strike." *The Nation*, December 21, 2020. https://www.thenation.com/article/activism/cuny-union-strike-remote.

Loughead, Tanya. *Critical University: Moving Higher Education Forward*. Lanham, MD: Lexington Books, 2015.

Lyotard, Jean-François. *The Postmodern Condition*. Translated by Geoff Bennington and Brian Massumi. Minneapolis: University of Minnesota Press, 1984.

Ma, Jennifer, Sandy Baum, Matea Pender, and Meredith Welch. "Trends in College Pricing 2017." College Board, October 2017. https://research.collegeboard.org/pdf/trends-college-pricing-2017-full-report.pdf.

Macias, Amanda. "Trump Signs $738 Billion Defense Bill. Here's What the Pentagon Is Poised to Get." *CNBC*, December 20, 2019. https://www.cnbc.com/2019/12/21/trump-signs-738-billion-defense-bill.html.

Manian, Maya. "Immigration Detention and Coerced Sterilization: History Tragically Repeats Itself." *News and Commentary*. American Civil Liberties Union, September 29, 2020. https://www.aclu.org/news/immigrants-rights/immigration-detention-and-coerced-sterilization-history-tragically-repeats-itself.

Mann, Bonnie. "Three White Men Walk into a Bar: Philosophy's Pluralism." *Radical Philosophy Review* 16, no. 3 (2013): 733–746.

Marcuse, Herbert. *One-Dimensional Man: Studies in the Ideology of Advanced Industrial Society*. Boston: Beacon Press, 1964.

———. *Eros and Civilization: A Philosophical Inquiry into Freud*. Boston, MA: Beacon Press, 1966.

———. *An Essay on Liberation*. Boston, MA: Beacon Press, 1969.

———. *Counterrevolution and Revolt*. Boston, MA: Beacon Press, 1972.

———. *The Aesthetic Dimension: Toward a Critique of Marxist Aesthetics*. Boston, MA: Beacon Press, 1978.

———. "Lecture on Education, Brooklyn College, 1968." In *Marcuse's Challenge to Education*, 33–38. Edited by Douglass Kellner, Tyson Lewis, Clayton Pierce, and K. Daniel Cho. Lanham, MD: Rowman & Littlefield, 2009.

Marginson, Simon. "Limitations of Human Capital Theory." *Studies in Higher Education* 44, no. 2 (2019): 287–301.

Marmadoro, Anna, and Erasmus Mayr. *Metaphysics: An Introduction to Contemporary Debates and Their History*. New York: Oxford University Press, 2019.

Marx, Karl. *Capital*. In *Karl Marx: Selected Writings, Second Edition*, 452–546. Edited by David McLellan. New York: Oxford University Press, 2000.

———. *Economic and Philosophical Manuscripts*. In *Karl Marx: Selected Writings, Second Edition*, 83–121. Edited by David McLellan. New York: Oxford University Press, 2000.

———. *The Eighteenth Brumaire of Louis Bonaparte*. In *Karl Marx: Selected Writings, Second Edition*, 329–355. Edited by David McLellan. New York: Oxford University Press, 2000.

———. "Theses on Feuerbach." In *Karl Marx: Selected Writings, Second Edition*, 171–174. Edited by David McLellan. New York: Oxford University Press, 2000.

Marx, Karl, and Friedrich Engels. *The Communist Manifesto*. In *Karl Marx: Selected Writings, Second Edition*, 245–272. Edited by David McLellan. New York: Oxford University Press, 2000.

McCann, Leo, Edward Granter, Paula Hyde, and Jeremy Aroles. "'Upon the Gears and Upon the Wheels': Terror Convergence and Total Administration in the Neoliberal University." *Management Learning* 51, no. 4 (2020): 431–451.

McClaren, Peter. "Chapter III: White Terror and Oppositional Agency: Towards a Critical Multiculturalism." *Counterpoints* 4 (1995): 87–124.

McCumber, John. *Time in the Ditch: American Philosophy and McCarthy Era*. Chicago: Northwestern University Press, 2001.

———. *The Philosophy Scare: The Politics of Reason in the Early Cold War*. Chicago: Chicago University Press, 2016.

McIntyre, Lee. *Post-Truth*. Cambridge, MA: MIT Press, 2018.

McMillan, Chris. "'I've Learned to Question Everything': Critical Thinking, or, the Pedagogical Logic of Late Capitalism." *Journal of Critical Education Policy Studies* 16, no 1 (April 2018): 1–29.

McWhorter, Ladelle. "The Abolition of Philosophy." In *Active Intolerance: Michel Foucault, The Prisons Information Group, and the Future of Abolition*, 23–40. Edited by Perry Zurn and Andrew Dilts. New York: Palgrave Macmillan, 2016.

Melamed, Jodi. *Represent and Destroy: Rationalizing Violence in the New Racial Capitalism*. Minneapolis: Minnesota University Press, 2011.

Mills, Charles. *The Racial Contract*. Ithaca, NY: Cornell University Press, 1997.

Mitchell, Michael, Michael Leachman, and Kathleen Masterson. "A Lost Decade in Higher Education Funding: States Cuts Have Driven Up Tuition and Reduced Quality." Center on Budget and Policy Priorities, August 23, 2017. https://www.cbpp.org/sites/default/files/atoms/files/2017_higher_ed_8-22-17_final.pdf.

Moore, Tim. "Critical Thinking: Seven Definitions in Search of a Concept." *Studies in Higher Education* 38, no. 4 (2013): 506–522.

Museus, Samuel D., María C. Ledesma, and Tara L. Parker. "Introduction." In "Racism and Racial Equity in Higher Education." Special Issue. *ASHE Higher Education Report*, 42, no. 1 (2015): 1–15.

Myrdal, Gunnar. "The Negro Problem: A Prognosis." *The New Republic* 147, July 9, 1962.

New Vision for Education: Unlocking the Potential of Technology. World Economic Forum (WEF). Geneva, Switzerland: World Economic Forum, 2015. http://www3.weforum.org/docs/WEFUSA_NewVisionforEducation_Report2015.pdf.

Newfield, Christopher. *Unmaking the Public University: The Forty Year Assault on the Middle Class*. Cambridge, MA: Harvard University Press, 2008.

Nietzsche, Friedrich. *Twilight of the Idols*. Translated by Richard Polt. Indianapolis, IN: Hackett Publishing, 1997.

Noble, David. *Digital Diploma Mills: The Automation of Higher Education*. New York: Monthly Review Press, 2002.

Nussbaum, Martha. *Not for Profit: Why Democracy Needs the Humanities*. Princeton, NJ: Princeton University Press, 2010.

Ong, Aihwa. *Neoliberalism as Exception: Mutations in Citizenship and Sovereignty*. Durham, NC: Duke University Press, 2006.

Pack, Justin. *How the Neoliberalization of Academia Leads to Thoughtlessness: Arendt and the Modern University*. Lanham, MD: Lexington Books, 2018.

Papastephanou, Marianna, and Charoula Angeli. "Critical Thinking Beyond Skill." *Educational Philosophy and Theory* 39, no. 6 (2007): 604–621.

Peters, Michael. "The New Prudentialism in Education: Actuarial Rationality and the Entrepreneurial Self." *Educational Theory* 55, no. 2 (2005): 123–137.

"Philosophy and Popular Culture Series." Open Court Publishing Company. Accessed September 28, 2020. http://www.opencourtbooks.com/categories/pcp.htm.

Piketty, Thomas. *Capital in the Twenty-First Century*. Translated by Arthur Goldhammer. Cambridge, MA: Harvard University Press, 2017.

Pierce, Clayton. "Education for Life and Death: Marcuse's Critical Theory of Education in the Neoliberal Era." *Radical Philosophy Review* 16, no. 2 (2013): 603–624.

Piggliuci, Massimo. "Neil deGrasse Tyson and the Value of Philosophy." *The Huffington Post*, May 16, 2014 (Updated: July 16, 2014). https://www.huffpost.com/entry/neil-degrasse-tyson-and-the-value-of-philosophy_b_5330216.

Pilaar, Jeremy. "Starving the Statehouse: The Hidden Tax Policies Behind States' Long-Run Fiscal Crises." *Yale Law and Policy Review* 37 (2018): 345–383.

Plato. *Apology*. In *Complete Works*, 17–36. Translated by G.M.A. Grube and edited by John M. Cooper. Indianapolis, IN: Hackett Publishing, 1997.

———. *Gorgias*. In *Complete* Works, 791–869. Translated by Donald J. Zeyl and edited by John M. Cooper. Indianapolis, IN: Hackett Publishing, 1997.

"President Barack Obama's Inaugural Address." Accessed December 20, 2020. https://obamawhitehouse.archives.gov/blog/2009/01/21/president-barack-obamas-inaugural-address.

"President Bush Addresses the Nation." *The Washington Post*, September 20, 2001. Accessed December 20, 2020. https://www.washingtonpost.com/wp-srv/nation/specials/attacked/transcripts/bushaddress_092001.html.

"President Obama to Announce Launch of Skills for America's Future." National Archives and Records Administration, October 4, 2010. https://obamawhitehouse.archives.gov/the-press-office/2010/10/04/president-obama-announce-launch-skills-america-s-future.

Pullen, John. *The Marginal Productivity Theory of Distribution: A Critical History*. New York: Routledge, 2010.

Quine, W.V.O. *From a Logical Point of View*. New York: Harper & Row Publishers, 1961.

Quintana, Chris. "Meet the Philosophers Who Give 'The Good Place' Its Scholarly Bona Fides." *The Chronicle of Higher Education*, February 6, 2018. https://www.chronicle.com/article/Meet-the-Philosophers-Who-Give/242462.

Rappaport, Alan. "Philosophers (and Welders) React to Marco Rubio's Debate Comments." *The New York Times*, November 11, 2015. https://www.nytimes.com/politics/first-draft/2015/11/11/philosophers-and-welders-react-to-marco-rubios-debate-comments.

Reichenbach, Hans. *The Rise of Scientific Philosophy*. Berkeley, CA: University of California Press, 1951.

Reitz, Charles. *Art, Alienation, and the Humanities: A Critical Engagement with Herbert Marcuse*. Albany, NY: SUNY Press, 2000.

"Remarks by the President in the State of the Union Address." National Archives and Records Administration, February 12, 2013. https://obamawhitehouse.archives.gov/the-press-office/2013/02/12/remarks-president-state-union-address.

"Resources for Undergraduates." American Philosophical Association. Accessed September 2, 2020. https://www.apaonline.org/page/undergrad_resources.

Rhodes, Terrel. *Assessing Outcomes and Improving Achievement: Tips and Tools for Using Rubrics*. Washington, DC: Association of American Colleges and Universities, 2010.

Rorty, Richard. "Philosophy in America Today." In *The Consequences of Pragmatism*, 211–232. Minneapolis, MN: University of Minnesota Press, 1982.

Russell, Bertrand. *The Problems of Philosophy, Second Ed.* New York: Oxford University Press, 1998.

Scarritt, Arthur. "Selling Diversity, Promoting Racism: How Universities Pushing a Form of Diversity Empowers Oppression." *Journal for Critical Education Policy Studies* 17, no. 1 (2019): 188–228.

Schram, Sanford F. "The Knight's Move: Social Policy Change in an Age of Consolidated Power." In *Rethinking Neoliberalism: Resisting the Disciplinary Regime*, 215–235. Edited by Sanford F. Schram and Marianna Pavlovskaya. New York: Routledge, 2017.

Schrecker, Ellen. *The Lost Soul of Higher Education: Corporatization, the Assault on Academic Freedom, and the End of the American University*. New York: The New Press, 2010.

Schultz, Theodore W. "Investment in Human Capital." *The American Economic Review* 51, no. 1 (March 1961): 1–17.

———. "Reflections on Investment in Man." *The Journal of Political Economy* 70, no. 5, part 2 (1962): 1–8.

Sennett, Richard. *The Culture of the New Capitalism*. New Haven, CT: Yale University Press, 2006.

Shore, Cris, and Susan Wright. "Audit Culture and Anthropology: Neo-Liberalism in British Higher Education." *The Journal of the Royal Anthropological Institute* 5, no. 4 (1999): 557–575.

———. "Audit Culture Revisited: Rankings, Ratings, and the Reassembling of Society." *Current Anthropology* 56, no. 3 (June 2015): 421–444.

Slaughter, Sheila, and Gary Rhoades. *Academic Capitalism and the New Economy: Markets, State, and Higher Education*. Baltimore: Johns Hopkins University Press, 2010.

Snyder, Jeffrey Aaron. "Higher Education in the Age of Coronavirus." *Boston Review*, April 30, 2020. http://bostonreview.net/forum/jeffrey-aaron-snyder-higher-education-age-coronavirus.

Spellings, Margaret. *A Test of Leadership: Charting the Future of US Higher Education*. U.S. Department of Education, 2006.

Spera, Rebekah, and David M. Peña-Guzmán. "The Anatomy of a Philosophical Hoax: The Politics of Delegitimation in Contemporary Philosophy." *Metaphilosophy* 50, nos. 1–2 (2019): 156–174.

St. Amour, Madeline. "Who's Up, Who's Down, and Why." *Inside Higher Ed*, November 19, 2020. https://www.insidehighered.com/news/2020/11/19/community-college-enrollments-down-nationally-not-everywhere.

"Statement on Rankings of Departments." American Philosophical Association. Accessed September 28, 2020. https://www.apaonline.org/page/rankings.

"Statement on the Role of Philosophy in Higher Education." American Philosophical Association. Accessed September 2, 2020. https://www.apaonline.org/page/role_of_phil.

Stich, Amy E., and Carrie Freie. "Introduction: The Working Classes and Higher Education: An Introduction to a Complicated Relationship." In *The Working Classes and Higher Education: Inequality of Access, Opportunity and Outcome*, 1–12. Edited by Amy E. Stich and Carrie Freie. New York: Routledge, 2016.

"The Stone." Opinion. *The New York Times*. Accessed September 28, 2020. https://www.nytimes.com/column/the-stone.

"Studying Philosophy at NYU." Department of Philosophy, New York University. Accessed September 2, 2020. https://as.nyu.edu/philosophy/undergraduate/studying-philosophy-at-nyu.html.

Taylor, Astra. "The End of the University: The Pandemic Should Force America to Remake Higher Education." *The New Republic*, September 8, 2020. https://newrepublic.com/article/159233/coronavirus-pandemic-collapse-college-universities.

"TED Speakers." TED: Ideas Worth Spreading. Accessed September 28, 2020. https://www.ted.com/speakers.

Terranova, Tiziana. "Free Labor: Producing Culture for the Digital Economy." *Social Text* 18, no. 2 (2000): 33–58.

Thelin, John R. *A History of American Higher Education, Second Ed.* Baltimore, MD: Johns Hopkins University Press, 2011.

Tokumitsu, Miya. "In the Name of Love." *Jacobin*, January 12, 2014. https://www.jacobinmag.com/2014/01/in-the-name-of-love.

———. *Do What You Love: And Other Lies about Success and Happiness*. New York: Regan Arts, 2015.

Trilling, Bernie, and Charles Fadel. *21st Century Skills: Learning for Life in Our Times*. San Francisco, CA: Jossey-Bass, 2009.

Urciuoli, Bonnie. "Excellence, Leadership, Skills, Diversity: Marketing Liberal Arts Education." *Language & Communication* 23 (2003): 385–408.

———. "Skills and Selves in the New Workplace." *American Ethnologist* 35, no. 2 (May 2008): 211–228.

Usher, Robin. "Lyotard's Performance." *Studies in Philosophy in Education* 25, no. 4 (July 2006): 279–288.

Van Norden, Bryan W. *Taking Back Philosophy: A Multicultural Manifesto*. New York: Columbia University Press, 2017.

Vieta, Marcelo. "Marcuse's 'Transcendent Project' at 50: 'Post-Technological Rationality' for Our Times." *Radical Philosophy Review* 19, no. 1 (2016): 143–172.

Ward, Steven C. *Neoliberalism and the Global Restructuring of Knowledge and Education*. New York: Routledge, 2012.

Weinberg, Justin. "Bowling Green Receives $1.6 Million to Expand Philosophy, Politics, Economics, and Law Program." *DailyNous*, August 5, 2019. https://dailynous.com/2019/08/05/bowling-green-receives-1-6-million-philosophy-politics-economics-law.

What Is the World Bank's Human Capital Index? World Bank Group, October 10, 2018. Video. Runtime 2:59. https://www.youtube.com/watch?v=iCUIAQkOwKw.

"Who Studies Philosophy?" American Philosophical Association. Accessed December 5, 2020. https://www.apaonline.org/page/whostudiesphilosophy.

"Who Studies Philosophy?" American Philosophical Association. https://cdn.ymaws.com/www.apaonline.org/resource/resmgr/diversity/Who_Studies_Philosophy_Poste.pdf.

"Why Major in Philosophy?" Philosophy Department, University of North Carolina at Chapel Hill. Accessed September 2, 2020. https://philosophy.unc.edu/undergraduate/the-major/why-major-in-philosophy.

"Why Study Philosophy?" Andrew W. Mellon Foundation, February 2019. https://mellon.org/shared-experiences-blog/why-study-philosophy.

Wieczner, Jen. "Most Millennials Think They'll Be Worse Off Than Their Parents." *Fortune Magazine*, March 1, 2016. http://fortune.com/2016/03/01/millennials-worse-parents-retirement.

Wilshire, Bruce. *Fashionable Nihilism: A Critique of Analytic Philosophy*. Albany, NY: State University of New York Press, 2002.

Winant, Howard. *The New Politics of Race: Globalism, Difference, Justice*. Minneapolis, MN: University of Minnesota Press, 2004.

Wittgenstein, Ludwig. *Philosophical Investigations, Revised Fourth Edition*. Edited by P.M.S. Hacker and Joachim Schulte and translated by G.E.M. Anscombe, P.M.S. Hacker, and Joachim Schulte. Malden, MA: Blackwell Publishing, 2009.

Young, Iris Marion. *Justice and the Politics of Difference*. Princeton, NJ: Princeton University Press, 2011.

Index

9/11 attacks, 49, 103–4
"21st Century Skills," 55, 110

AAC&U. *See* Association of American Colleges and Universities
AAUP. *See* American Association of University Professors
abolition democracy, 156–57
"The Abolition of Philosophy" (McWhorter), 158
academic capitalist knowledge/learning regime, 1
Academy for Mayan Languages, 108
accountability, 143–44; bottom line in regimes of, 28; of educational institutions, 21
activism: antiracist, 100–101; within philosophy, 120; in university programs, 101
Adorno, Theodor, 69
Aeon (online magazine), 89
affirmative action, 106
affluent society, 71, 72, 74, 83, 85
Agamben, Giorgio, 17n37
agape, 140
Ahmed, Sara, 111, 112, 113–14, 148n28
Alcoff, Linda Martín, 117–18, 121
alienation, 66
Althusser, Louis, 30

American Association of University Professors (AAUP), 24, 54
American Creed, 102–3
An American Dilemma (Myrdal), 100
American Dream, 72
American Exceptionalism, 100, 104
American Philosophical Association (APA), 87, 91, 121; "Department Advocacy Toolkit" of, 52–53, 115–16; performativity in, 54–55; race and, 119–20
American Psychological Association, 139
Amernic, Joel, 27
analytic philosophy, 3, 5, 84, 85–86
Ananke (reality principle), 67
"The Anatomy of a Philosophical Hoax" (Spera and Peña-Guzmán), 17n34
Ancestral Black Vernacular Discourses, 144
Andrew W. Mellon Foundation, 54
Angeli, Charoula, 56–58, 92n13
antiracism, 141–42; American nationalism and, 100–102; capitalism and, 98–101; neoliberal multiculturalism and, 107
APA. *See* American Philosophical Association

apparatus: Agamben on, 17n37; Althusser on ideological state, 30; Foucault on, 13; Marcuse on technological rationality and, 69
applied philosophy, 87–88
Archard, David, 88
Archibald, Robert A., 24
Arendt, Hannah, 146n8
Aristotle, 38
Association for the Study of Higher Education (ASHE), 113
Association of American Colleges and Universities (AAC&U), 55, 110
At the Existentialist Cafe, 89
Augustine (Saint), 82
austerity, in higher education, 20, 130–31
automation, 39, 154

Bachelard, Gaston, 38–39
Baldwin, James, 123n3, 141
basic repression, 68
Beauvoir, Simone de, 57, 120
Becker, Gary, 45–48, 75, 93n28
behaviorism, 62n55
Bennett, Janet M., 110–11
Berardi, Franco "Bifo," 94n45
Berger, Óscar, 107–8
Biden, Joseph, 151
bigotry, 84
Bilge, Sirma, 114–15
bin Laden, Osama, 104
Birth of Biopolitics (Foucault), 22
Black Lives Matter (BLM), 156
Boggs, Grace Lee, 120, 127n79, 145
Bonilla-Silva, Eduardo, 106, 107
Bourget, David, 4–5
A Brief History of Neoliberalism (Harvey), 21
Brier, Stephen, 24, 30
Briggle, Adam, 59n1, 88, 89–90, 143
Brown, Wendy, 22, 31–32, 144; on gender, 50–51, 109; on *homo economicus*, 48–49; on stealth revolution, 135

Bruya, Brian, 118–19
Burbules, Nicholas C., 38
bureaucratization, 27–29
Bush, George W., 21, 49

canon wars, 101, 102; Melamed on, 122; pluralism and, 103
capital, 47–48. *See also* human capital
capitalism, 150–51; academic, 75–81; antiracism and, 98–101; cultural, 112; disaster, 153; Forman on golden age of, 71–72; global, 99–101; late, 30–31, 58–59, 65, 156; neoliberalism connection to, 9, 144; social, 28; Thatcher on, 10–11; White supremacy and, 108
capitalist realism, 10–11, 16n29
Capitalist Realism (Fisher), 150–51
Carnap, Rudolph, 2, 3–4
Cave Allegory, of Plato, 82
Chalmers, David J., 4–5, 90
Chang, Ruth, 90
Chile, 104
Chomsky, Noam, 24
citizenship, 108; global, 107
City University of New York (CUNY), 155
civil rights movement, 99–100, 101
class politics, 29–32
cognitariat, 87
Cohen, Daniel, 90
Cold War, 1–2; stealth in, 43; U.S. in, 99–100
Cold War Philosophy, 1, 72, 86, 90; American university system and, 3; McCumber on, 85, 145; naturalism in, 6; Neoliberal Philosophy shift from, 2–7, 129–30, 137; segregation in, 145
commodification, 56; of art-object, 73–74; of knowledge, 26–27; of labor, 68; Marcuse on, 72–73
The Communist Manifesto (Marx), 69
competition, 49, 97–98
consciousness, 82

consumerism, 66
corporatization, 21, 33n20
cosmopolitanism, 112
COVID-19, 20, 151–54, 155–56
Craig, Russell, 27
creative maladjustment, 10, 139, 158. *See also* maladjustment
critical race theory, 99–100
critical thinking, 131; Beauvoir on, 57; as human capital, 52–59, 129; philosophy marketed as, 58; rationalist versus technicist, 56–57; Uriciuoli on, 135
Critical University (Loughead), 20
cultural heritages, 116–17
culture of legitimation, 120
CUNY. *See* City University of New York

DACA. *See* Deferred Action for Childhood Arrivals
dailynous.com, 89
Darder, Antonia, 114
Davidson, Donald, 4
Davis, Angela, 120, 156–57
Dawkins, Richard, 84
decadence, 131–35
Deferred Action for Childhood Arrivals (DACA), 107
Deleuze, Gilles, 86
"Department Advocacy Toolkit," 52–53, 115–16
depressive hedonia, 11, 151
Descartes, René, 38, 56
desegregation, 144
desire, philosophical, 81–85, 136
desublimation: of libido, 73–74; repressive, 85, 137
Dewey, John, 2
disciplinary decadence, 132, 134–35
discipline policing, 12, 17n34
discourse, 83
discrimination, 106
diversity: Bilge on the neoliberal diversity regime, 114–15; Dotson on, 117; human capital and, 111; of ideology, 133; Melamed on, 110, 113; Neoliberal Philosophy and, 97–123; in Neoliberal University, 109–15; perceptions of Whiteness and, 123; performativity of, 112–13; pluralism and, 9, 130; as racializing technology in higher education, 113; workers, 111
Dotson, Kristie, 13; on culture of legitimation, 120; on diversity, 117
Duncan, Anne, 44
Dunleavy, Mike, 20

economy: knowledge, 39, 41, 75–81, 91, 97, 129; libidinal, 66–67
EDI. *See* equity, diversity, and inclusion
education: automation of, 154; in era of neoliberalism, 41, 62n55; human capital versus, 44; performativity in, 40–41; training versus, 25
educational institutions, 21. *See also* higher education
ego-ideal, 138
The Eighteenth Brumaire of Louis Bonaparte (Marx), 150
Eleventh Thesis, of Marx, 91
"The Elimination of Metaphysics Through Logical Analysis of Language" (Carnap), 3–4
emancipation, 82
empiricism, 83, 84
employability, 9
employment, 68–69
Engels, Friedrich, 69
Enlightenment, 121
entrepreneurial self, 58, 71–75, 109
entrepreneurship, 21, 31, 45–46, 51
equity, diversity, and inclusion (EDI), 113–14, 115–16, 122, 142
Eros, 66–67, 139
Eros and Civilization (Marcuse), 66, 71, 137
erotics, philosophical, 136–41

Fabricant, Michael, 24, 30
Fadel, Charles, 55, 110
fascism, 150
Feldman, David H., 24
femina domestica, 50
Fesmire, Steven, 25, 41–42
Fisher, Mark, 10–11, 16n29, 29, 150–53, 155–56
Fisk, Milton, 107–8
Floridi, Luciano, 88
Fordism, 24, 28
Forman, Michael, 71–72
Foucault, Michel, 22, 66, 109; on apparatus, 13; on gender, 50; on *homo economicus*, 45–46; on *homo politicus* versus *homo economicus*, 49–50; on performativity, 48; on power, 11
freedom-workers, 143, 157–58
free markets, 103
Freie, Carrie, 30
Freire, Paulo, 140–41
Freud, Sigmund, 138; on economics of the libido and psychology, 66–67, 91n1
Friedan, Betty, 112
Friedman, Milton, 153
Friedman, Thomas, 102
Frodeman, Robert, 59n1, 88, 89–90, 143
From a Logical Point of View (Quine), 5

Gakis, Dimitris, 16n30
Galbraith, Kenneth, 71
Garfield, Jay L., 121
Garrison, Mark, 51, 62n55
gender: Brown on, 50–51, 109; Foucault and Brown on, 50
Gibbons, Michael, 76, 87, 96n78, 143
Gilmore, Ruth Wilson, 105
Ginsberg, Benjamin, 28
Giroux, Henry, 28
globalization, 102–3
Goldstein, Rebecca Newberger, 90
The Good Place (television series), 89
Gordon, Lewis, 132–33, 135

Govindarajan, Vijay, 153–54
Great Recession, 23–24, 32
Green New Deal, 151
Guatemala, 107–8
Guattari, Felix, 86
Gurría, Angel, 44

Habermas, Jürgen, 56
Happy Consciousness, 108, 129; of affluent society, 83; Marcuse on, 66, 74, 137, 152; one-dimensionality of, 74–75
Harris, Sam, 84
Harvey, David, 21–22, 29–30, 33n15
Havis, Devonya, 144, 145
Hegel, Georg Wilhelm Friedrich, 4, 66, 150; on Unhappy Consciousness, 74
Heidegger, Martin, 69; Carnap critique of, 3–4
Hieronymi, Pamela, 89
higher education: austerity in, 20, 130–31; changes to, 37; corporatization of, 21, 33n20; cultural heritages and, 116–17; defunding of, 1, 23–25; diversity as racializing technology in, 113; industrial model of, 25–26, 41–42; inequality in, 30; Lyotard on, 40–42; Marcuse on, 60n18; models for post-pandemic, 153–54; neoliberalism linked to behaviorism in, 62n55; privatization of, 23–25; tuition of, 24; in U.S., 130, 153–54; White versus Black students with degrees in, 113
Hiking with Nietzsche, 89
A History of Philosophy in America (Kuklick), 5
Holocaust, 98, 123n2
homo economicus, 58; Brown on, 48–49; Foucault on, 45–46, 49–50; in neoliberalism, 132; performativity within, 108–9
homo politicus, 143–44; Foucault on, 49–50

human capital, 7, 30–32; citizenship and, 108; critical thinking as, 52–59, 129; definition of, 44; diversity and, 111; education versus, 44; Lyotard theory of, 51; Marginson theory of, 47; productivity and, 107; Schultz theory of, 47–48; subjectivity versus, 81; technologies of optimization and, 44–51; theory of, 44–45, 46–47, 69–70
humanities, 20–21
Hurricane Katrina, 153
Husserl, Edmund, 136

ICE. *See* Immigration and Customs Enforcement
idealism, realism versus, 10
identity, labor and, 50–51
ideology: diversity of, 133; of empiricism, 84
Immigration and Customs Enforcement (ICE), 150
imperialism, 99; liberal multiculturalism and, 103
inclusion, Ahmed on, 113–14
industrial model, of higher education, 25–26, 41–42
inequality, in higher education, 30
intellectual diversity, as methodological pluralism, 9
intellectual heritage, philosophy and, 116–17
Investment Age, 23–24
"Investment in Human Capital" (Schultz), 44–45
investments, of students, 52

Jameson, Frederic, 58
Jobs, Steve, 138
justice, 106, 131, 135; in knowledge production, 102

Kafka, Franz, 29, 152
Kant, Immanuel, 84
Katzav, Joel, 2–3

King, Martin Luther, Jr., 139–40; on creative maladjustment, 10, 139, 158
Klein, Naomi, 153
"Knowing One's Own Mind" (Davidson), 4
knowledge: commodification of, 26–27; performativity in, 133
knowledge economy, 39, 41, 81, 97; academic capitalism in, 75–81; neoliberalism and, 91; Neoliberal Philosophy in, 129
knowledge production, 87, 143; justice in, 102
Kornbluh, Anna, 153
Kotsko, Adam, 157
Kuhn, Thomas, 2
Kuklick, Bruce, 5–6

labor: capital relation to, 47–48; commodification of, 68; identity and, 50–51; manual versus intellectual, 133
Lacan, Jacques, 152
language, discourse versus, 83
LCTPs. *See* Less Commonly Taught Philosophies
Lectures on the Philosophy of History (Hegel), 4
Leiter, Brian, 117
Lenin, Vladimir, 11
Less Commonly Taught Philosophies (LCTPs), 142–43
liberal arts, 20–21, 157
liberal multiculturalism, 99, 122; imperialism and, 103; Melamed on, 101
libido: desublimation of, 73–74; Freud on economics of, 66–67, 91n1
Locke, Kirsten, 40
The Lost Soul of Higher Education (Schrecker), 31
Loughead, Tanya, 20, 57; on freedom-workers, 143, 157
love, 139–41
Lynch, Michael, 90

Lyotard, Jean-François, 7, 37, 38–40; on higher education, 40–42; on human capital theory, 51; on performativity, 43; on terror, 134–35; Wittgenstein influencing, 59n6

maladjustment, 139–40, 143, 158
managerialism, 28–29
Manian, Maya, 158n2
Manifest Destiny, 100
Mann, Bonnie, 117–18, 144
Marcuse, Herbert, 1, 94n49, 139; on apparatus and technological rationality, 69; on commodification, 72–73; on Happy Consciousness, 66, 74, 137, 152; on higher education, 60n18; on metaphysics, 81–82; on Neoliberal Philosophy, 8; on performance principle, 67, 69, 70–71; on rationalized domination, 68
marginalization, 122
Marginal Productivity Theory of Distribution, 44
Marginson, Simon, 47
marketing, 137–38; pedagogy shaped by, 43; philosophy and, 53, 58, 149
market logics, 1
market reforms, neoliberal, 103
market Stalinism, 29, 152
Marmodoro, Anna, 86
Marx, Karl, 39, 66, 69, 136, 150; Eleventh Thesis of, 91; on surplus value, 68
May, Todd, 89
Mayr, Erasmus, 86
McCarthyism, 1, 6, 43, 85
McCumber, John, 1, 13–14, 17n34, 19, 37, 43, 60n26, 72, 129; on Cold War Philosophy, 85, 145; on red hunting, 3, 145; on stealth, 6
McGinn, Colin, 121, 122
McMillan, Chris, 58–59, 64n80, 131
McWhorter, Ladelle, 158

Melamed, Jodi, 9, 98, 106, 114; on canon wars, 122; on diversity, 110, 113; on liberal multiculturalism, 101; on neoliberal multiculturalism, 99, 103, 104–5, 108, 141–42; on pluralism, 101–2, 121; on racial break, 98–99; on UPS slogan, 111–12
Meletus, 133
Menchu, Rigoberta, 108
meritocracy, 98–99, 106, 108; in neoliberal multiculturalism, 9; Newfield on, 124n27
metanoia, 136
metaphysical philosophy, 7
metaphysics, 81–82, 86
Metaphysics (Marmodoro and Mayr), 86
methodological pluralism, 9, 14n5
Mill, J.S., 38
Miller, Bill, 54
Mills, Charles, 124n24
Mind (journal), 2–3
multiculturalism. *See* liberal multiculturalism; neoliberal multiculturalism
Murdoch, Iris, 120
Myrdal, Gunnar, 100

nationalism, American, 100–102, 103
naturalism, 6
neocolonialism, 99
neoliberalism, 1; behaviorism linked to, 62n55; Bilge on the diversity regime of, 114–15; capitalism connection to, 9, 144; in Chile, 104; conceiving, 21–23; COVID-19 and, 155–56; definition of, 7–8; education in era of, 41, 62n55; entrepreneurial self of, 75; entrepreneurship in, 51; *homo economicus* in, 132; identity and labor in, 50–51; knowledge economy and, 91; market reforms and, 103; self-sacrifice and, 49; stealth revolution of, 22; value of

philosophy determined by, 52–53, 65–66, 135
neoliberal multiculturalism, 110; antiracism and, 107; Darder on, 114; genealogy of, 99–105; Melamed on, 99, 103, 104–5, 108, 141–42; meritocracy in, 9; as racializing technology, 105–9
Neoliberal Philosophy, 1; Cold War Philosophy shift to, 2–7, 129–30, 137; critique of, 7; diversity and, 97–123; in knowledge economy, 129; Marcuse on, 8; within Neoliberal University, 22–32; one-dimensionality of, 65–91, 131; performativity of, 37–59; philosophical desire and, 81–85; productivity in, 136; social networks in, 122; Whiteness of, 115–23
neoliberal sovereignty, 33n15
Neoliberal University, 1, 6, 7; as class politics, 29–32; diversity in, 109–15; education versus training in, 25; Kotsko on, 157; Melamed on diversity in, 113; models for post-pandemic, 153–54; Neoliberal Philosophy within, 22–32; paradigm shift in, 129–46, 149; philosophy in, 19–36; racialization in, 142; the Real of, 155; self-actualization in, 112; trends shaping, 37, 65, 97
Newfield, Christopher, 106, 113, 124n27, 146n1
New Left, 71, 138
New Public Management, 27
New Racism, 107
New Republic, 100
New Vision for Education, 51
New York Times, 89
New York University (NYU), 54, 85–86, 119
Noble, David, 25, 30
the Nothing, 3–4
Nussbaum, Martha, 20, 30
NYU. *See* New York University

Obama, Barack, 21, 25, 103–4, 156
OECD. *See* Organisation of Economic Co-operation and Development
one-dimensionality, 69, 81, 152; of entrepreneurial self, 71–75; of Happy Consciousness, 74–75; of Neoliberal Philosophy, 65–91, 131; of thinking, 82, 83
One-Dimensional Man (Marcuse), 66, 71
one-dimensional society, 8
Ong, Aihwa, 107
Open Court, 89
oppression, systems of, 10, 140–41
Organisation of Economic Co-operation and Development (OECD), 44, 48
Oxford ordinary language school, 84

Pacific Standard (magazine), 88
Papastephanou, Marianna, 56–58, 92n13
paradigm shift, 1; Kuhnian, 2; in Neoliberal University, 129–46, 149
Pedagogy of the Oppressed (Freire), 140
Peña-Guzmán, David M., 17n34
performance principle, 108; Marcuse on, 67, 69, 70–71; performativity and, 66–71
performativity, 129, 142; in APA, 54–55; of diversity, 112–13; in education, 40–41; Foucault on, 48; generalized spirit of, 39–40; within *homo economicus*, 108–9; in knowledge, 133; Lyotard on, 43; of Neoliberal Philosophy, 37–59; performance principle and, 66–71; in philosophy, 38–43, 54–55, 138; of social actors, 69–70; Usher on, 41
Peters, Michael, 70
phenomenology, 59n1
Philosophical Gourmet Report (PGR), 54, 85–86, 87, 118–19, 122, 126n71
Philosophical Investigations (Wittgenstein), 3
The Philosophical Review (journal), 2

philosophy: activism within, 120; applied versus public, 87–88; in Cold War era, 90; in crisis, 19–21; democratizing, 141–46; as discursive social practice, 11–14; intellectual heritage and, 116–17; job appointments in, 88–89; marketed as critical thinking, 58; marketing and, 53, 58, 149; in Neoliberal University, 19–32; performativity in, 38–43, 54–55, 138; pluralism in, 121, 145; pure versus applied, 87; return on investment in, 42, 53–54; science versus, 37–38, 42–43, 131; skills and, 62n61; technologies of optimization and, 52, 97; of twentieth century, 83; value of, 52–53, 65–66, 135. *See also specific topics*
Philosophy for Children, 90
The Philosophy Scare (McCumber), 1, 15n9, 17n34
Pierce, Clayton, 71, 74, 92n15
Piketty, Thomas, 92n16
Pilaar, Jeremy, 23
Plato, 133–34; Cave Allegory of, 82; philosophical erotics of, 136–37
Plato at the Googleplex, 89
pleasure principle, 66–67, 151–52
pluralism, 117–18; canon wars and, 103; diversity and, 130; Melamed on, 101–2, 121; in philosophy, 121, 145; of U.S., 104
The Pluralist's Guide, 117–18
positivism, 4
The Postmodern Condition (Lyotard), 37, 134
postmodernity, 38–40, 121–22, 131
post-truth, 32n3
power, 11, 122
precariat, academic, 24
prejudice, White, 100–101
presidential election (2016), 19–20
presidential election (2020), 156
prima philosophia, 86
privatization, 23–25

Problems of Philosophy (Russell), 5
production, 39, 47
productivity, 39–40, 53; competition and, 97–98; human capital and, 107; in Neoliberal Philosophy, 136; of worker, 45
profit, 40, 44, 45
psychic income, 46
psychoanalysis, Freudian, 66
psychology: Freud on economics of the libido and, 66–67, 91n1; of U.S., 8
public philosophy, 87–88
pure philosophy, 87

queer studies, 114
Quine, W.V.O., 5

race, 119–20
race liberalism, 99–101; American nationalism and, 100–102; discrimination and, 106; post-war racial break and, 105
racial break: Melamed on, 98–99; race liberalism and post-war, 105; three periods of, 99–100
racial contract, 124n24
racialization, 9, 98; diversity as technology of, 113; neoliberal multiculturalism as technology of, 105–9; in Neoliberal University, 142
racism, 98–99, 106, 111
rationalist, 56–58
rationalized domination, 68
the Real, 152–53, 155
realism, 10
reality principle (*Ananke*), 67
Reason, 81–82
reasoning, scientific, 38–39
rectification of names, 121
red hunting, 3
"red scare," 72
reflexive impotence, 11, 151
reflexivity, 96n78
regional ontology, 59n1
Reichenbach, Hans, 2, 4, 84–85, 86, 137

Represent and Destroy (Melamed), 98
repression, 67, 68, 85
Retrenchment Age, 23–24
return on investment, 39, 42, 53–54, 108
Rhoades, Gary, 1, 3, 26
The Rise of Scientific Philosophy (Reichenbach), 84–85
Rorty, Richard, 2, 5
Rubio, Marco, 19–20, 133
Russell, Bertrand, 5
Rutgers University, 54, 85–86

Sanders, Bernie, 151
scarcity, 67
Scarritt, Arthur, 112
schooling: Becker on, 46–47; employment after, 68–69
Schram, Sanford, 22
Schrecker, Ellen, 31
Schultz, T.W., 44–45, 47–48
science: philosophy versus, 37–38, 42–43, 131; in postmodernity, 38–40; profit versus, 40
science, technology, engineering, and mathematics. *See* STEM education
scientific philosophy, 84–85
segregation, 140–41, 145
self-actualization, 81, 112, 137
self-sacrifice, 49
semiotics, 41, 43, 52
Sennet, Richard, 28
Silicon Valley, 90
Singer, Peter, 90
Slaughter, Sheila, 1, 3, 26
social actors, 11–12, 41, 47, 51–52, 77; performativity of, 69–70
Social Darwinism, 137–38
socialist realism, 16n29
social networks, 122
Society for Applied Philosophy, 87–88
Socrates, 133–34, 135, 158
Socrates Café, 90
solidarity, 140–41
"Spellings Report," 21
Spera, Rebekah, 17n34

Srivastava, Anup, 153–54
stealth: Brown on, 135; in Cold War era, 43; McCumber, 6; revolution of neoliberalism, 22
STEM education, 42
Stich, Amy E., 30
The Stone (blog), 89
student loan, 24, 31
subjectivity, 49–50, 81
sublimation, 67, 81
surplus repression, 68, 73–74
surplus value, 68
surveillance, 28
Symposium (Plato), 82

Tarski, Alfred, 2
Tax Revolt, 1970s, 23–24
Taylor, Paul, 117
technicist, in critical thinking, 56–58
technological rationality, 69
technologies of optimization, 6–7, 39, 40–41; human capital and, 44–51; philosophy and, 52, 97; skills as, 70
technoscience, 39, 40, 42. *See also* science
TED Talks, 90, 131, 138
terror, 134–35
Thatcher, Margaret, 10–11, 150, 153
Thelin, John R., 3
thinking, 133; one-dimensionality of, 82–83
Third World, 101
Thünen, J.H. von, 44
Tokumitsu, Miya, 138
totalitarianism, market, 133
Tourish, Dennis, 27
training, 45–46; as aim of university, 25–26, 31; education versus, 25
tribalism, 124n21
Trilling, Bernie, 55, 110
Trump, Donald, 19, 32n3, 107, 149–50, 153
Truth, 82
tuition, 24, 30
Tyson, Neil deGrasse, 90

Undoing the Demos (Brown), 22
unemployment, 83–84
Unhappy Consciousness, 74
United States: in Cold War, 99–100; consumerism in, 66; higher education in, 37, 130, 153–54; imperialism and neocolonialism of, 99; philosophy in, 6; pluralism of, 104; postwar culture of, 1, 99–100; psychology of, 8
university: activism in programs of, 101; training as aim of, 25–26, 31
University of Wisconsin, 25
UPS slogan, 111–12
Uriciuoli, Bonnie, 111, 125n36, 135
Usher, Robin, 41

Vaesen, Krist, 2–3
Valid Assessment of Learning for Undergraduate Education (VALUE), 55, 110
value, of philosophy, 52–53, 65–66, 135
Van Norden, Bryan W., 121, 142–43
Vieta, Marcelo, 69

Walker, Scott, 25
Walsh, Rachel, 123n2
Ward, Steven C., 21, 27
Weber, Max, 69
"What Do Philosopher's Believe?" (Bourget and Chalmers), 4–5
What Is an Apparatus and Other Essays (Agamben), 17n37
Whitehead, Alfred North, 2

Whiteness, 113–14; diversity changing perceptions of, 123; of Neoliberal Philosophy, 115–23
White supremacy, 98, 105, 108, 144, 156–57
"Why Study Philosophy?" (WSP), 53–54, 119, 138
Wilkerson, William, 117
Williams, Raymond, 64n80
Winant, Howard, 98
"Wisconsin Idea," 25
Wittgenstein, Ludwig, 3, 12; criticisms of Oxford ordinary language school, 84; Lyotard influenced by, 59n6
word processing, 45
workers: diversity, 111; as economic agent, 46; foundational literacies of, 51; freedom-workers, 143, 157–58; productivity of, 45
work ethic, 71, 138
World Bank, 48
World Economic Forum, 48, 51
WSP. *See* "Why Study Philosophy?"

Young, Iris Marion, 106
Young Men's Christian Association (YMCA), 139
Young Women's Christian Association (YWCA), 139

Žižek, Slavoj, 58, 112, 152
Zoom, 155

About the Author

Brandon Absher is associate professor of philosophy in the Department of Humanities and director of the Honors Program at D'Youville College. He is also the co-coordinator of the Radical Philosophy Association and has served as a co-editor for the *Radical Philosophy Review*. His work has appeared in the *Radical Philosophy Review*, *New Political Science*, the *Journal of Speculative Philosophy*, and elsewhere.